Anywhere Away From Here

The story of a woman's
fight-or-flight escape
via eight marriages

Anywhere Away From Here

The story of a woman's
fight-or-flight escape
via eight marriages

Janey Hadley

Memory Lane

First published in Great Britain by Memory Lane
ISBN 978-0-9567697-9-4
Printed and bound by Good News Books, Ongar, Essex, England.

Without the help of my very special friend Jo, and Martin Noble I would not have been able to write this book.

CONTENTS

Part One

Ripples

Chapter One

Ripples in a Pond

Like ripples in a pond after a stone sinks into its still waters, the actions of our parents and our parents' parents have deep, powerful and unforeseen consequences, the repercussions of which will affect the lives of their children and their children's children.

My grandmother was born Ellen (Nell) Brown in a coalmining village near Swansea, South Wales in 1894. She was the sole survivor of three sets of twins in a large family; her father frequently told her how he wished her brother had lived as they could have sent him out to work. At fourteen, Nell went into service, as was expected of her, but in her twenties, her life was shattered when her sister died at forty, leaving three children in need of care. Nell felt it was her duty to care for the children, but that it would be impossible for her to move in unless there was a marriage between herself and her sister's husband, Bert.

So in her early twenties, Nell suddenly found herself with a home and children to take care of, and a violent and obsessively jealous husband with a great liking for alcohol. Bert, my grandfather, dictated Nell's every move in life, with no love or affection to ease the burden she had taken on.

In the two black and white photographs I have of Bert, he is smiling, looking kindly and benevolent. It just shows, as I was to learn throughout my life to my terrible cost, that you can't trust appearances. In one picture, Bert sat looking dapper in a smart suit and felt cap in the centre of his surrogate family, hands on knees. In another he was at the helm of a big motorbike, goggles strapped to his forehead, with Nell sitting meekly behind. He probably made sure that she sat behind him on that bike whenever they went anywhere.

Bert ruled Nell's life from morning to night. He watched her all the time, and even if she just went into town, he counted every minute she was gone. His meals (breakfast, lunch and dinner) had to be placed in front of him, cooked exactly as he expected them, on the hour. If she was late, or the meals were not cooked properly, or anything was missing, Nell was in for a beating. Nell was short and plump with long black hair, which she plaited. One of Bert's favourite punishments was to tie the plait around her neck and pull until it almost strangled her.

In 1921, when Nell was twenty-seven, she gave birth to my mother Iris. By the time she was old enough, Bert would get his daughter, Iris to keep an eye on Nell, almost as though my grandmother were a prisoner and Iris had been co-opted as a junior prison guard to report back anything suspicious to the prison governor. When Nell undressed at night, Bert would smell her knickers and accuse her of going with other men; there would be more beatings. I think that Iris, my mother, was terrified of all this and simply kept quiet.

Nell's misery was to last another seventeen years or so, until my grandfather's suicide in 1939. It happened like this.

One of Bert's favourite games was to time everything that my grandmother did to the second, even if it was something for which he had given his permission. He had agreed one evening to allow Nell and Iris to go to the pictures. Off they went to see the wizard, the wonderful Wizard of Oz, showing at the picture house in Merthyr Tydfil.

Bert had worked out exactly what time they should have arrived home. Nell always made him a cup of cocoa every night in bed, at ten o'clock precisely, so the outing had to fit in with this routine. There was a gas fire in the bedroom and he had blocked up all possible ventilation: the windows and air vents, and turned on the gas. This was one of his occasional tricks to frighten Nell. However, the pictures were running slightly late and by the time Dorothy had reached the end of the rainbow, visited Munchkinland, was finally back in Kansas, and the Wicked Witch of the West was dead – so was Granddad.

We never found out whether the trick with the gas fire was intentional or just one of his sick jokes.

Naturally, Nell and Iris were shocked, but their main reaction was of huge relief: they didn't have to put up with him anymore.

*****

Life for Nell and the children was very difficult financially after his death, and although Iris was very bright – she came fifth in the county in matriculation at school – she was unable to continue in further education and got a job in a shoe shop. The year was 1939 and in September, as war broke out, Iris joined the army. In the photo I have from this time she looked very smart and proud in her WAAF uniform, brass buttons shining, as she sat between her two half brothers, my uncles. One of them, in military uniform, looks very dashing – just like Noël Coward playing the Captain in that movie about a WW2 destroyer, *In Which We Serve*. That was my Uncle Bill who chopped my hair off when I was twelve.

Relationships during the war were, by necessity, short-lived and people lived each day as it came. Iris was involved with an army officer 17 years her senior who was already married with two sons. At twenty-four, she became pregnant and was discharged from the Army, returning home to Merthyr Tydfil, where Nell still lived in her rented house with the eldest of her stepchildren and his family. Both Iris and Nell had felt that it would be impossible to stay in their home with an illegitimate baby on the way, so Nell's eldest son took over renting the house in Merthyr Tydfil, Nell and Iris moved to London to stay with the eldest daughter of the family, Audrey, who was living with her husband Fred in Isledon Road, Holloway in London.

It was there that I was born at the end of the war, in July 1945.

Chapter Two

Headless Chickens

My earliest memory of living in my aunt and uncle's house was at the age of three and a half. Uncle Fred stood me on a wooden chair and told me to watch out of the kitchen window. He had gone down the garden to where the chickens were kept and the next moment I screamed as I saw two chickens running around the garden headless.

'God, Fred, what did you do that for?' shouted Auntie Audrey.

It had been difficult enough for us cooped up together like headless chickens in their two up two down – this was the last straw for Mum. I was in a state of shock and she tried to comfort me, tucking my head in her lap to shield me from that horrible vision.

A few days later, we moved across the road into two attic rooms and a landing. One room was used as a living room, the other as a bedroom for the three of us. I slept in a cot until I was five.

The cooker was on the landing and there was a white enamel bucket for straining things. All the water had to be carried up from downstairs. The lavatory was also downstairs and I was terrified to go down there; the gas geyser over the bath frightened me so much that Mum had to get in the bath with me. But that luxury only lasted for a week: Nan – my grandmother – was the one who really brought me up and looked after me, as Mum had to go out to work. She worked as a sales assistant in Jones Brothers store while we were in London and sometimes modelled for them. On her half day off, she cleaned so she could buy extras for me because things were still hard after the war.

The house we lived in always frightened me, and some nights I was physically sick because I couldn't settle down to sleep. I always wanted my Teddy Bear plumped into just the right position, cuddling into my back, as it made me feel safer. Many nights I woke up and called out, but no one came – I was all on my own up in that attic.

After a year of being left alone at nights in the attic, when Iris and Nell went to the pub with Audrey and Fred, they started taking me out with them. They sat me on a step outside and gave me lemonade and crisps, while they went into the pub. So I was still left on my own and terrified.

*****

One night there was a big fuss about getting me to go to bed really early. I had to promise to be very good and keep really quiet because Mum was bringing a friend home. When I woke up and called out, I was given a good walloping. I never tried to get out of the cot because I knew that it would really cause trouble if I wandered into the other room.

Not long after the night of the visitor, I was told I was to meet this person. I was all dressed up and warned about being on my best behaviour. Then this man arrived for tea. He was introduced to me as my father who had been away in the war and had now returned. This all seemed very strange to me as he had never been mentioned before, and of course he didn't live with us. Later I learned that he was a salesman in Jones Brothers and that was where Mum met him.

I started school in London when I was five years old, but I was not there very long. One day I was taken to a wedding by my Nan. Mum and George Hicks, the man who had been coming to our home, who I had been told to call Daddy, were getting married.

Soon after the wedding, George went off to work in Bath, where he had been living in digs while he found somewhere for us to live. I was taken to visit the place – a dark room in a house in some back street. It smelled of horrible cooking. They made me eat baked beans – which I hated. Soon somewhere was found for us to live and a lorry that had delivered furniture to London brought us back to Bath on the night return journey. Everything was loaded and Nan, Mum and me all sat at the front with the removal men. I had never been on anything other than a London tram or bus before, and I was always sick on those, so it was a dreadful journey for me.

The house was on a road that ran into town – you go under railway arches and over a river bridge. It was run down but not a slum – although it was very close to buildings which were bombed during the war. I don't know what I expected of our new home, which we would live in for the next five years, but it turned out to be a very creepy place, especially at night. It was a three-storey house and we were renting the bottom floor, which consisted of a front room, which was only used as a front room on special occasions. The rest of the time, Mum and Dad (as I had come to call him) slept in there on a bed settee. The middle room was used for eating, sitting, and the weekly bath (in a tin bath), and listening to the radio.

Through a hallway and up some steps was the scullery where Nan did all the cooking and hot water was heated in a copper boiler. On the side of the scullery was a lavatory – although this was indoors you still needed to take an umbrella when it rained. There was gas lighting in the house with a meter that took pennies. Those lights hissed all the time but when the mantels have a hole in them they terrified me as flames shot out of them. Upstairs on a small landing there was a bathroom, but it was unusable for one reason or another. The landlady Bessie – an old lady who was almost totally bedridden and expected help when needed from my family – wouldn't repair it and you could even see down through the floorboards and plaster into the house next door. On the top floor, we had one bedroom. We had to go up these stairs by candlelight and Nan and I shared this room.

So there we were, the three big people in my life and me: Nan, Mum and Dad.

Sometimes I thought Nan was like a Welsh version of Queen Elizabeth, King George's wife. She was quite short but she looked huge to me, like a big tank. She seemed to control Mum all the time and they both controlled Dad and I was at the bottom of the heap. Also I did not think that the Queen swore and Nan swore a lot (apart from snoring) and hated all men, who she called 'bleeders'. I wondered if that was why Dad had a razor. I thought maybe men had to make themselves bleed to live with women, because they all seemed unhappy most of the time, at least Mum, Nan and Dad were.

Mum must be like Princess Elizabeth as she was slim with light brown hair and very pretty. She always did just what Nan told her, just as I supposed Nan did what Bert told her, so I thought maybe Nan was getting her revenge. Mum worked very hard to feed and clothe me but she often didn't seem to notice me or think about the way she treated me.

Dad was tall and wore horn-rimmed glasses and sleeveless jumpers and his grey hair was plastered back on his head. I didn't think he was anything like the dashing Duke of Edinburgh. Dad was more like a tall shadow. He was not really a person at all. He didn't seem to have a personality, and hardly ever said anything, although he was always well dressed. There was no conversation at home but I supposed he must have chatted at work as he was a salesman and that's what they do. He must have had some character at work. Why else would they have paid him?

Nan just said it was the man's job to go out to work and the woman's to put the meal on the table when he comes home and do all the other wifely chores, which she herself does as Mum works.

*****

Being put to bed in this house was even more frightening than being in bed in London because of scary Bessie on the next floor down; Mum was even further down.

Mum always sent me to get change from Bessie so we could have pennies for the gas meter. I think I found her creepy not only because she was old and bedridden but because she was very, very large and seemed to hang over the small bed like a great big crumpled eiderdown. The room was always badly lit and she would ask me to come closer so that she could see me. I imagined I was Red Riding Hood and she was the Big Bad Wolf – and she always smelled funny.

Many nights, when I was too scared to go to sleep and called downstairs, I got a beating. The railway line also ran just across the road from the bedroom. It was high up over the arches and shook my bed every time a steam train went past. Sometimes, later on in the evening, Mum would come up and lay on the bed with me and we would both cry, because she was sorry she beat me. I was sorry I had made her cry.

I lived on Wells Road and started at a school just up the hill, St Mark's Church of England School. I enjoyed my infants school – we spent most of the time playing and there was a climbing frame in the playground and I liked it when we lay down for a rest in the afternoon. But life at home was quite strained. We had moved to Bath because my parents thought the cost of living would be cheaper and Mum wouldn't need to work, but they had soon found that this wasn't the case: Mum had to go back to work at the Ministry of Works in Great Pulteney Street and once again Nan was my sole carer.

The atmosphere at home had become very strange: Mum and Dad spoke very little and Nan was the one in charge, and both women didn't seem to even like Dad.

Chapter Three

Bruises

My move to junior school was very difficult for me; I didn't fit in very well. By the age of six or seven I had put on weight and the children called me 'fatty'. Because I didn't speak the same as the others – they all had Somerset accents – they would take the mickey out of me, and either bully and hit me, or didn't speak to me. When Mum asked where the bruises had come from, and realised that children had been knocking me about, her only response was that I should hit them back harder. If I came home with the same story, and more bruises, she would give me another hiding to go with them.

Junior school had an assembly every morning and the vicar came once a week and said things like 'Jesus said, 'Suffer the little children to come unto me'' but if we did anything wrong, the teacher hit us really hard across the knuckles with a ruler. I was not sure whose side Jesus was on, or if he would make my bruises go away and stop them from bullying me. But I didn't dare ask the vicar. I often fainted in assembly, as I hated standing with a lot of people. I was also starting to get terrible migraines, and when that would happen, I didn't know what was up or down or left or right and I had to lie down until they went away. Sometimes Mum had to get the doctor out.

School dinners were horrible and after a while I walked home from school for mine because at school we were made to eat them, however long we sat. There was no normal home life as I always thought there would be—with a mother and a father—as nobody ever seemed to talk or have a conversation. I suppose I had got this idea from the books I had started to read: Enid Blyton's *Famous Five* seemed to have a normal home with a mum and dad who talked to each other, and they talked to each other in *The Archers* and *Mrs Dale's Diary* on the radio. When I went round to my friend Susan's house, which was close to the school, they talked too, so why didn't mine? Susan's Mum and my Nan were friends and we all watched their television on Coronation Day – all apart from Dad who said we couldn't afford TV.

There was one good thing about Dad though. He liked music and we listened to his records and he talked to me about them. He liked all types of classical music (his favourites were Beethoven and Haydn) and took me to concerts to see people like Myra Hess, a concert pianist. It was very highbrow. Dad played the piano as a child and although we didn't have much money, my dream was to learn to play the piano and be a concert pianist. I was thrilled one day when he bought a second-hand piano. I started to play when I was eight and from then on, my piano playing helped me bury my pain and forget that the love that I craved from a father was constantly denied from me. I soon realised that the only interest Dad had in me was with regard to my piano playing: it was as if he wanted to, through me, do what he had been unable to do himself. Later he even put me off playing – the only thing he ever said to me was that I needed to practise in order to play for other people. Even so, in the early years I practised for hours.

Dad also had lots of records of all the big dance bands, and sometimes on Sundays we would roll up the lounge carpet and he taught me to dance. I loved dancing and after trying out ballet and tap, I decided I preferred modern dancing and started lessons. Apart from ballroom, there was Latin American (cha-cha, samba) and jive, and I loved them all. Playing the piano and dancing were like best friends and parents to me all rolled into one.

*****

When I was ten years old, Bessie, our landlady died, and Mum and Dad found out that she never even owned the house – she rented it and wasn't legally allowed to sublet it. After a court hearing, my parents were issued an eviction notice.

We were eventually given a council house in Combe Down, three and a half miles out of Bath. In contrast to our old home, this was absolute luxury for me – a house with three bedrooms, electric light, and a garden. At last I could have a room of my own, no trains to scare me and keep me awake, and no sharing with Nan.

But instead, new sounds that I had not heard before because of the size of our old house, brought different problems. Despite being in desperate need of repair, the previous house was in fact very large with thick walls and it was on three floors. But in a normal-sized house like our new one, everything could be heard between walls, and often at night I could hear my dad screaming from nightmares. Apparently his ship had been torpedoed in the war and he was in the water for many hours. I also started hearing rows between my parents, because the sixteen-year difference between them affected the way they wanted things in life to be. I longed for a brother or sister but this wasn't to be: Mum told me later that Dad was totally disinterested in sex and she eventually moved in to sleep with Nan.

*****

I had grown up quickly: I lived with adults and adult conversation and unfortunately started my periods at ten and a half – just before starting secondary modern school.

'You want to keep away from boys, a girl your age,' Nan said, sitting arms folded in her old armchair that we had brought from the last house. It was green with a faded floral pattern on it; Nan and her chair started to look like each other a long time before. If she wasn't sitting with her arms folded, she would be sewing or mending, but it wouldn't really make any difference as the expression on her face, like a sour milk pudding, was just the same.

'She's right, Janey,' said Mum, coming in from the kitchen and picking up the *Daily Express* from the coffee table to carry on with her crossword. She was always working on a crossword or knitting, and looking across to Nan as though checking in with her. 'None of them are any good. Don't you ever let any of them touch you.'

'Why should they all be bad?' I asked.

Nan just snorted disapprovingly and Mum gave me a grim, tight-lipped look. There were never any straight answers.

'Why did you never marry again?' I asked Nan. 'You were still young when Granddad died.'

'I wouldn't have another one,' she sneered, 'even if his arse was studded in diamonds.'

This all left me very bewildered about the role of men.

Chapter Four

Leslie

By age twelve I was very plump, so once again there was more bullying at school – although it was more mental than physical (they still called me a snob and stuck up and I had no idea why). In any case, physical abuse no longer bothered me because I was able to defend myself – even if my parents raised a hand to me. If they would hit me, I would hit them back. I was starting to rebel against my earlier childhood beatings. Also, Mum and Nan had become so concerned that I have nothing to do with the opposite sex that I was hardly allowed to move without either of them wanting to be with me.

By the time I went to secondary school, I had a good friend named Janet who was slim with long blonde hair that she wore in plaits – which I really envied. I thought the fact that she only had a mother, as her father died, brought us together. I felt somehow that I only had one parent at home too. I sometimes stayed at her house on weekends, and she stayed at ours on others, but it was very embarrassing taking anyone home because of the atmosphere of silences and the slamming of doors when my parents were having rows.

There was another problem too. When I first went to my secondary school, I needed my birth certificate but my parents wouldn't let me take it myself or see it. This preyed on my mind because I knew things weren't quite right. I had brought up the fact several times when I had thought back to Mum and Dad's wedding when I was five, but both Mum and Nan just said that must have been something I have imagined. But I was only five years old and wondered how on earth I could have imagined it and why they wouldn't talk to me about it.

And then one day I found the evidence in a box of photos inside a drawer: a black and white photo of their wedding day and there I was, aged five, standing on my own in front of the grownups with a ribbon in my hair. All the family were there – Mum's stepbrothers and their wives and Nan and Win, and in the centre there was Mum and Dad dressed up to the nines. She had her arm in his and he had a carnation in his jacket buttonhole. There was no question that they must be the happy couple tying the knot. But I kept this discovery to myself, mainly because I would have had a hard time explaining how I found the photo: I wasn't supposed to be looking in their drawers.

*****

I spent some school holidays in Merthyr Tydfil in Wales (where my Nan and Mum lived) with my Mum's half brother Bill and his family – his wife Gertrude and my two cousins who were a lot older than me. Uncle Bill was the oldest of the three children that Nan took on. I was always frightened of him: he was very strict and his word was *law*. There were also a lot of rows between him and my aunt. One evening, when he was angry about something or other, he chopped all my hair off. Everywhere I went, everyone seemed to be living the same sort of miserable life and I had begun to assume that, as Nan had said, all men are bastards.

Around that time, when Nan was ill, I was sent to live in Wales with the family because Mum worked and there was no one to look after me. So I went to school there for a while, which was a horrible experience as they all seem to be speaking Welsh, which was alien to me.

One weekend I met a distant cousin by marriage. John was my aunt's sister's son and a little older than me, but we spent quite a lot of time together. It was my first taste of affection from the opposite sex. I was with John in his room and although we were only larking about and kissing and cuddling, I was suddenly yanked out of there and not allowed to go again. Later I was to hear whispered conversations about John sleeping with his mother and how awful it had been.

Not understanding about this until I was much older only added more confusion to my mind, which was already cluttered with things I didn't understand. On my father's side there was a brother and his wife, which of course meant they were not my blood relations, because by the age of twelve, I was convinced that the man I called Dad was not my real father. However Uncle Harry, unlike his brother George, was a very affectionate man and I was very fond of him and his wife, my Auntie Win.

Harry was tall and slim but didn't look much like Dad as he had a hooknose. Also, unlike Dad, he was chatty and friendly with everyone. Also unlike Dad, he was not always dressed smoothly in a suit, and often wore casual clothes. Auntie Win was always telling him to tidy himself up. She was a small woman with long fair hair that she wore in a bun with shorter hair on top, rolled into big curls like they did in the 1940s. She was very bossy and had a frightful temper when she was roused.

They were unable to have children of their own, and had always made a great fuss of me. By this time they had their own shop – a ladies and gents' outfitters selling everything from haberdashery to suits – and a large house in Martock, Somerset, and I loved to go and visit them. Life always seemed so calm and peaceful there.

*****

Soon after we moved into our house in Combe Down in Bath, Nan, Mum and I made friends with the family next door. They were very friendly and welcoming and there was a husband and wife, three sons (one about my age) and a grandmother. We spent time with one another in each other's houses, but I was mostly the one who did so, because it all seemed so much more normal than my home – and also I was getting a lot of attention and even affection from the boys' father Leslie.

I thought he was very good looking. He was quite stocky with black, curly hair and had a short, snub nose, which, for me doesn't detract from his looks, and as time went on, I developed a schoolgirl crush on him. He was the best looking man I had ever seen and I had started to make any excuse possible to be in his company. He was a painter and decorator and worked from home. I watched from my bedroom window to see him going out in the morning and coming back in the evening and then I would rush around to his house after tea. If he went out in the evening I would lie awake in bed until I heard him pull up outside and then would rush to the window to watch him.

Within months I was totally besotted with him. I seemed to think of very little else and daydreamed about what it would be like if he cared for me. At thirteen I was much less plump than I had been – my love of dancing had also helped me lose weight – and I was already starting to look like a woman.

Then Mum arranged for him to come and decorate our sitting room. After this arrangement had been made, Nan was not too well and decided to go and stay in Merthyr Tydfil for a break. Mum now worked for the Admiralty on Combe Down just up the road from where we lived and it was agreed that I would be able to go home from school as Leslie would be working in our house, and of course I could always go next door if necessary until Mum came home.

The first day after Nan's departure I could think of nothing else all day except that I would get to be alone with Leslie when I came home from school. He let me in and seemed extra friendly, almost excited to see me. I took my coat off and went into the kitchen to put the kettle on to make him tea, but when I turn around he was standing right behind me.

The next moment I was completely taken by surprise when he put his arms around me and kissed me. After my initial shock, I realised I was thrilled – pleased and excited – it was what I had been dreaming would happen and my dreams had come true!

As the week passed, this progressed to him putting his hand inside my shirt on my breast. I hadn't realised the implications of what was happening. I just felt as if I was in heaven because he kept saying how much he loved me, and of course I loved him too.

20

The week soon ended and I was heartbroken because I could not see him on my own any more. Most Sundays I went to church. I occasionally went with Mum and Nan to the Church of the Nazareen or, more often, the Baptist church. I always found it quite comforting, although religion didn't mean that much to me. One Sunday morning while I was waiting at the bus stop to go to church, Leslie pulled up in his car and offered me a lift, which I of course accepted.

'Do you really have to go to church,' he said, 'or will you come somewhere with me?'

'I'd love to come somewhere with you,' I said, feeling excited though slightly nervous.

He drove off a road on the Bear Flat in Bath to a workshop that he owned. As soon as we were inside, he started kissing me again and I could feel his hands all over me. But then I became frightened as he had taken out his penis and put it into my hand, whispering to me, 'Do you think you can take me darling?' as he tried to push me on to my back.

I had never been with a boy or a man without clothes on, and although he kept saying, 'I love you darling,' and 'I won't hurt you,' I was still scared and I pulled away.

'You must take me home now,' I said hurriedly. 'I'll be expected back from church on the bus.'

He was fine about this – he didn't seem to be in a particular hurry, though I was not sure why – and took me home. After that day, we meet for short periods of time after school. He would pick me up in his car and also on Sunday morning. I loved seeing him: I thought about him all the time and couldn't wait between our meetings. I truly thought I was in heaven. I believed – as maybe you do when you're young and have never had a father figure who will give you love and affection – that I really loved Leslie so much that I couldn't live without him.

Chapter Five

Secrets

My first mistake was to get my best friend Janet to lie for me so that in the summer, I could meet Leslie in the evenings. I knew she was the first person Mum would see to find out where I was. One evening he took me to a house that he said belonged to his mother who was away on holiday. He took me to a bedroom and we lay on the bed and I really thought we would have made love as I was no longer afraid. But it just so happened that I had had my period and although he said it didn't matter, having a period was something else that Mum and Nan made sound so awful that you were not even supposed to talk about it. (While Nan was prepared to say that all men are bleeders, she wouldn't go into any kind of detail about how women are also bleeders and what exactly that involves.) I was still mostly ignorant about sex, apart from a few things I had been told by a girl called Gwen who lived on our estate.

Leslie and I continued to meet in secret, best friend telling lies for me, but of course other people saw him pick me up from school and I was nearly always home late. It all seemed very complicated and desperate to me because I just wanted to be with him all the time. I looked much older than thirteen and felt older, having spent almost all of my life with adults. Admittedly, the adults I had spent most of that time with were Nan, Mum and Dad – hardly the most scintillating conversationalists – but I suppose by default I had entered the adult world because there had been nothing much to hang on to as a child.

Then during the Easter holidays in 1959, I spent a week in Martock with my uncle and aunt. Although I liked Auntie Win, I got on much better with Uncle Harry. While I was there, I helped Uncle Harry with deliveries for the shop. My head was in turmoil during the holiday, as I hadn't wanted to stop seeing Leslie. It felt like I was being wrenched away from the person I loved and whom I believe loved me.

One day, with all of this going on in my head and needing to talk, I decided to confide in my uncle.

'If if I tell you a secret, will you promise not to tell Auntie Win or Mum?' I said, after he had pulled up the van in a side street.

'Well, that really depends on what it is ...' he said a little doubtfully.

But having brought it up, I felt that I really needed to talk, so I poured out my heart: everything that had happened and everything that I felt.

'What can you possibly expect to come of this situation?' he said, and it was obvious he was quite shocked: disapproval was written all over his face – but there was also a trace of something else in his expression, though I couldn't place it.

'I don't know. I only know that I can't live without him.'

Not surprisingly, even though I had asked him to promise, (although admittedly he didn't say he would) Uncle Harry immediately told Auntie Win my story after I had gone to bed. I got the third degree from my aunt the next day.

'Who is this Leslie?' she said. 'What can you expect to come of this relationship? Even if he were to leave his wife, and family, think of the age difference. He's thirty-six! Twenty years older than you. He's old enough to be your father! And you're still just a child! It's not just indecent – it's criminal! And anyway, how could it possibly work? He'll be an old man when you're still young.'

'I don't care,' I replied. 'I just want to be with him.'

The holiday was nearly over and although I had come by train, my aunt and uncle drove me home to see the family. The journey was fortunately not too long and I had managed to say almost nothing. My aunt continued her lecture of how dreadful this all was and that they would be talking about it with my parents. A quick cup of tea on arrival at home was all that Auntie Win managed before she launched into the subject of Leslie and our relationship.

It then transpired that my parents had received a visit from Leslie's wife while I was away – not the usual friendly neighbourly stop-in – but a visit to say that she knew what was going on between her husband and me, because she had been told. She had informed Mum that this wasn't the first time for him: there had been other girls in places they had lived and they had left the last town after a young girl there had got pregnant with his child. She had warned Mum that she had been to see a solicitor and that if it didn't stop between Leslie and me, she would drag it through the courts so she could get a divorce – although divorce wasn't really what she wanted – she still wants him. Mum had made a promise that I would be watched at all times and it would stop and hopefully we would move.

Then the questions began from my Mum, Nan and aunt and uncle (although I had already told Win and Harry, they still kept firing questions at me) as to what had happened between the two of us and whether there had been any sexual contact. As usual Dad said little or nothing. I denied that there has been intercourse (which was true) although we came very close. But they didn't believe me and then left me out of it altogether to talk amongst themselves as to what should be done.

We didn't have a telephone – that was still a luxury we couldn't afford in the late 1950s, so Mum and Win and Harry went to the telephone box. On their return I was told that a private appointment with Dr Hargreaves, the lady doctor we had at our surgery, had been made at her house that afternoon and that I was being taken for an examination. My uncle would pay for this, as my parents didn't have much money.

My humiliation was complete, and would stay with me for the rest of my life: at the age of thirteen to be taken to a room by this doctor and told to remove your pants and lie on the bed.

'Draw up your knees and open your legs,' she said. She seemed like a cold woman with no compassion for how I must have been feeling.

After this degrading examination was over, I never felt the same towards Mum again. To have put me through that because she didn't believe me – that their entire preoccupation was over what people might have been saying or thinking. Nobody seemed to care at all about how I was feeling. The ground rules were then laid down: basically I would be kept in all the time except for going to school, and my comings and goings to school would be monitored by the times of the buses. I was not allowed to go to Janet's house as of course they now knew that she had lied to cover up for me.

In the meantime, Dad would look for a job elsewhere. He was a buyer/salesman in Colmers department store in Bath.

Life was suddenly hell. I felt like I was in prison. Presumably Leslie had been told by his wife of the conditions, which she had laid down, so all I could do was still watch him from my bedroom window.

One day after a couple of months, I came out of school and could see his car up the road so I left the girls and ran and got in. I told him how dreadful things had been at home for me.

'Don't worry, pet,' he replied reassuringly. 'I'll try to see if I can do anything for you.'

True to his word, he spoke with Mum about how I was being penalised. This of course was interpreted as 'You've gone behind our backs again going to see this man.' My aunt and uncle were telephoned and arrive once again to discuss what should happen to me. As they were the ones with the money, it was suggested that I go to boarding school, which I flatly refused to do.

'Well,' said Aunt Win, 'if you don't want that then you'd better come and live with us in Martock.'

So with no other options available, I moved in with my uncle and aunt.

During all these months of upheaval at home, I mentioned once again the wedding I was taken to at the age of five and finally I got a truthful answer– that my father had adopted me.

'Least said about that bastard the better,' said Nan when I asked about my natural father.

Win and Harry's house, my new home, was very big. It was attached to their shop and had sixteen rooms, though only the main ones were used for their living accommodation, but it was pure luxury compared to our three-bedroom council house.

After moving to Martock, I started at Stoke-sub-Hamdon Comprehensive, a co-ed school, which came as a shock to me as I had been used to a girls school. The school I had gone to in Bath was run by a very prim headmistress and we were expected to act like young ladies at all times while in uniform and discouraged from having anything to do with the boys in the next school. Apart from hating being wrenched away from my friend and my piano and dancing lessons, I initially found it difficult to adjust to a mixed school with not much regard for uniform. The children were all bussed in from the villages, some of them are quite rough-looking and life again was miserable for me as everyone in my class thought I was stuck up because I was related to the Hickses of Martock – they had a shop and money.

Chapter Six

Uncle Harry

I was now thirteen and a half and of course, my contact with Leslie before I left Bath had awakened my dormant sexuality, although as I was still only a child. I had been told that this was actually abuse on his part, as he was a grown man. I still thought about him though and wished all the time I was back there with him.

Then one day Uncle Harry called me into the office in the shop, which was in a hidden corner and started putting his hand up my skirt and into my panties.

'What do you think you're doing?' I said. 'You're my uncle.'

'Well, I'm not really am I, because George, my brother, isn't really your father.'

I was horrified and couldn't believe this was happening. I had always trusted Harry, and after having been sent away from Leslie who I really felt I loved (even if it was puppy love) and for whom I cried every night this felt like the ultimate betrayal. But I didn't know what to do or who to turn to as I didn't feel anyone would believe me. Harry was liked by everyone and was a pillar of the community – and I was also afraid of where I might be sent next.

The only way I could deal with it was to somehow to disassociate myself from what was going on. Although at no time did Harry force himself on me or force me to touch him, I was very, very unhappy. I found myself being drawn into another relationship which included very heavy petting, when Win was not around, or Harry and I were out doing deliveries. It was almost like Harry had taken over where Leslie left off, although I didn't have the same feelings for him – only the sexual ones.

I was very confused to start with, as to why he ever told my family about Leslie, but as I grew older, I felt that he might have been preparing the ground for himself and waiting for his chance.

His and my aunt's relationship seemed to be a very business-like affair. Auntie Win was very much like a schoolmistress. She treated Harry most of the time like a naughty schoolboy, and talked of men as something to be 'put up with' rather than people with whom you could share feelings. They were both, of course, in their fifties, which to me was quite old and it probably wasn't always like that between them. Uncle Harry said that Auntie Win wanted nothing to do with sex. Fortunately I always managed to avoid actual intercourse with him and although my relationship with him was sexual and without any passion, he was actually affectionate to me most of the time.

In school I had managed to make one good friend, named Sarah, whose older sister once worked for my aunt and uncle; she was a tall girl with a blonde bob and the one person in the school who took the time to make friends with me and help me. I had also joined the school orchestra and choir. Uncle Harry played the violin and had taught me and as I was a quick learner I was soon allowed to play in the orchestra. There were a lot of extra music lessons, which involved contact with many of the boys as they played many of the larger instruments.

By that time I had begun to like the mixed school environment and realised that generally I got on better with the boys than the girls. I became involved with Des who played double bass. There was a lot of kissing and cuddling but nothing else and I felt that perhaps the younger people of the opposite sex were much nicer than the few men I had met. We had school dances and outings where the orchestra and choir went to perform, so that relationship was quite a change for me, as I was still trying to deal with my uncle at home. Aunt Win brought up the subject one day.

'If you have a boyfriend at school,' she said, 'I would rather you brought him home to tea than do things behind my back.'

'OK,' I said. 'There is this boy Des in the orchestra and as we're playing for the school play at the end of term you can meet him then.'

A week or so after Aunt Win met Des at the play I asked her, 'When can I bring Des home to tea?'

I was totally surprised at her reply. 'I've been doing some checking up on his family and his mother is divorced. They're not really our sort, you know.'

A flaming row followed. I was furious that he should not be judged on his own merit.

'What does it matter if his mother's divorced? Your brother-in-law married my mother with an illegitimate child.'

But this of course was still the 1950s, and people were still judged, and judging others, on the basis of Victorian moral values.

'I don't want you to see this boy any more,' she said.

My uncle never had any say in any decisions in the household either, so once again I was confused and once again I rebelled against this attitude towards my life, and started to spend more time with Eddie, the trumpet player in the orchestra, who was known as the school rogue, because I knew it was what would be disliked the most.

Eddie was the biggest boy in my class and he was always in trouble, not taking kindly to discipline. The only thing he seemed to like was the trumpet, which suited me, together with the fact that he never tried to touch me: a kiss and a cuddle are just that and nothing else was expected of me.

I'm sorry to say that once again I used my best friend – this time Sarah – to create an alibi to get out to see Eddie. Although she didn't really like the idea, she was prepared to say that I had been with her.

*****

I arrived home from school one day to find Aunt Win with a face like thunder.

'I want to talk to you,' she said.

My mind immediately flew to all the things that had gone on with Uncle Harry and me. Somehow she's found out, I thought, in panic.

'Where have you been going?' she said. 'And who have you been seeing when you go out?'

Of course I realised there's no need for her to ask, because when you have a shop you find out everything in time. In no uncertain terms Aunt Win declared what a dreadful family Eddie came from and how awful I had been in becoming involved with him after everything that had been done for me. I was really tempted to tell her about her own husband, but I resisted the urge and kept quiet.

Imagine my surprise at her next words: 'Well there's nothing else for it,' she said briskly, 'you'll have to go back home again. Go and get your things packed.'

'What now?'

'Yes, as this is Thursday and the shop is closed for half a day we might as well do the trip to Bath now.'

So I was dragged away again, with not a word of goodbye to anyone and taken back to my parents and Nan. Dad by that time had actually found himself a better job in Devizes, still in the same line of work as a buyer/salesman in a gents and boys' outfitters and the family are supposed to be trying to move house, but this is something that never happened because of Mum's job and Nan's poor health.

I only had a very short while left at school. Every school I had been to I had hated, either because I had been bullied, or through lack of friends – at Martock this was because I was considered stuck up because I was related to, and lived with, 'The Hickses of Martock'.

Now that I was older I had started to realise that the reason why I was bullied and the children found me 'different' is because, maybe by nature or perhaps as a way of adapting to the pervasive atmosphere of silence in which I was brought up, I had developed a slightly detached, remote exterior. Other kids may have found me acting 'superior' because I had learned to be self-protective. In a way, that forced me to behave in a more adult way; I felt more at ease with people who were older than me.

There was still no way I could stay home for the next six weeks so I was put into yet another school in Combe Down in Bath, not too far from where we lived. At this time, it's the only mixed comprehensive in Bath, as schools were still single sexed in those days. The last few weeks of my schooling drag, by and there were rows at home because I wouldn't stay on at school or go to Bath Technical College to learn secretarial skills, which my family thought would be a fitting employment for me in due course. I, on the other hand, was determined to work in a fashion shop and had several interviews lined up.

*****

I left school in July 1960, two weeks before my fifteenth birthday, and had an interview for a job as a junior sales assistant at Richard Shops at the top of Milsom Street. I was successful and was offered the job but could not start until I was fifteen.

The week before my birthday, my Auntie Gertrude came from Merthyr Tydfil to stay. This was the aunt I was sent to stay with when I was young. Although as a child – and was still – scared of my Uncle Bill, who I found very intimidating, I was very fond of her.

Apart from music my other great love has always been dancing and I had lessons until I went to live in Martock. We had a large dance hall in Bath and I had wanted to go. Mum and Nan, who were once again in my life, were watching every move I made – and I don't just mean dance moves. I wanted to go with a friend but this wasn't allowed, so Auntie Gertrude make a suggestion:

'Why don't you and me go with her, Iris? It would make a change and then you wouldn't worry.'

We set out for the dance hall on Friday evening, and I felt absolutely ridiculous, sitting there with my mum and aunt. It was not very crowded in 1960, as it had been converted from a theatre and hadn't really taken off yet. We had a drink and then just seemed to sit there for ages. Finally both Mum and my aunt were asked to dance, as most of the clientele were older men.

Then a young man came up and asked me to dance. As we waltzed, I had no idea that he was soon to be the first of my roller coaster of eight marriages.

Chapter Seven

George

His name was George, like my father. He was small like me, five-foot-four, with black hair as he was half-English and half-Mexican. My first impression, which proved to be the case, was that he was a very pleasant, laid back, placid person with very good manners and practically no temper at all.

He was in the Merchant Navy and home on leave, staying with his sister who lived in Great Poulteney Street. He was born in La Paz in Bolivia to an English father and Mexican mother; his mother had died soon after giving birth due to the altitude and his father had been in Bolivia working for the railway. The sister he was staying with was from that marriage. His father was married in England and he had a half-brother there. A nanny whom his father later married had brought him up. As far as I could gather it had not been a happy life. Both he and his sister came to live in England upon the death of his father, and George subsequently joined the Merchant Navy at fifteen.

He was nineteen years old on the night that we met and we spent the rest of the evening dancing and talking. I didn't talk much about my life, except to say that my mother seemed to go everywhere that I did, but he made it plain enough that he liked me.

'May I see you again?' George said at the end of the evening. 'Tomorrow night, yes? I am here for two weeks, and then have to go away.'

I agreed and we made the arrangement. I was not sure how it would work out but I'd worry about that later.

'Can I go out with George this evening?' I asked Mum.

'Where?'

'Oh probably to the dance hall again.'

'No, I don't think so, not on your own.'

'Whatever is the matter with you, Iris?' my aunt came to the rescue. 'You've got to let the girl go out some time.'

So started my first relationship. We went on normal dates, but during my first week of knowing him he took me to his sister's flat while they were out and the usual kissing and petting starts, then he wanted more. I refused to start with, because I had been hoping for a relationship where someone would just love me for myself.

I thought I loved George, but had no real way of knowing, apart from the feelings I had for Leslie, which were probably just puppy love. But at fifteen there were a lot of hormones racing around my body.

George, of course, had said that he loved me but when I refused he didn't seem too upset.

'No problem, Janey,' he said, 'if you do not love me, I will find someone else.'

I had gathered by then that he had been to quite a few foreign countries with the Navy and had been able to get what he wanted whenever he wanted it.

I tried to explain how I felt – that I was only fifteen, and frightened of getting pregnant.

'Don't worry,' he said. 'I'll treat you good and not hurt you.'

I left it to him – and that night I lost my virginity. It was good for me – not like I know it had been for other girls – because George was experienced and wasn't only interested in his own pleasure. I was really happy for a short while, but of course he was quickly offered work on a ship, which he took because they were short, monthly trips on a Fyffes banana boat, which meant that he would be home on leave quite soon.

*****

A month is a long time when you're only fifteen. Work took up the day and I just moped about the rest of the time. I was a junior sales assistant at Richard Shops, working on commission, with very low basic pay. The system was geared so that the first sales girl Valerie always took the customer; if she was busy, the second sales girl Jackie took the next. As junior, I could only sell if they were also serving. Jackie was okay, but Valerie was a bitch to me, often taking customers away from me when she was finished with her previous one. She was also very bossy and would make me clear up all her mess that she had made deliberately. But I enjoyed the job and I was good at it – a fact that Valerie hated. Finally, she went too far one day, and when she swore at me, I got her sacked.

My working hours were the normal ones for shop work, nine to five, Monday to Saturday, with a half-day on Thursday. That left Sunday when I still went to church. It had started to mean a lot more to me and I liked our minister. I was also playing the piano quite a lot now that I was back in Bath and able to go to my old teacher, Mrs. Isaacs. She was a small, elderly lady, a wonderful teacher – and also very considerate: she always had drinks and cakes ready for pupils in the dining room if we were waiting for an earlier lesson to finish.

When George was home on leave, we had a lot of sex, although Mum and Nan were inevitably suspicious, insisting that we should not be left in the house on our own together.

'What's the difference in us being here together rather than anywhere else?' I asked her.

'You wouldn't be safe,' she replied dryly. 'You know what men are like.'

'Well, do you think these things can only happen when you're left in a house on your own? Have you never heard about what goes on behind the bike sheds?'

This all made me feel dreadful after what she put me through over my relationship with Leslie. Mum and Nan's other gripe was that I could surely do much better than George – just because he was a foreigner. They couldn't understand what he was saying and he spoke very quickly and sometimes got some of the words in the wrong places; I had no trouble understanding him.

It was soon clear that this relationship was having its ups and downs. For one thing, maybe due to George's Latin American roots, time was of very little consequence to him. It was nothing to be kept waiting for a couple of hours and then he would try to make up for it with a bunch of red roses and a box of Cadbury's Milk Tray. He seemed to spend most of his time in the pub with his mates – there were a lot of Italians in Bath around that time. Their first languages were similar; they all seemed to understand each other and of course shared a Latin temperament and outlook.

On one occasion when he was home on leave in the first nine months of our relationship, he brought Marco, a friend from the ship, home with him and asked me if my friend Christine, the window-dresser from work, would make up a foursome one night. So the next day I asked her.

'How about coming out, Chris?'

She was a little taller than me, five-foot-five with a slim figure and shoulder-length blonde hair, and we had started seeing more of each other outside work. But she looked a little doubtful.

'Well, as I've never met this Marco and have no idea what he's like I'm not sure.'

'Come on, it's a blind date – it will be fun,' I say. 'Anyway I've never met him either, but it can't really matter for a meal and a couple of drinks at his sisters', can it?'

She finally agreed and it was arranged. What we had not realised was that his sister and brother-in-law were going to be out that evening.

It was pleasant enough to start with, until after we had eaten and then the two men automatically wanted to get on with the kissing and cuddling. So George put the lights out and we were lying on the settees for a while – and then he thought it would be a good idea if we changed partners. Christine didn't object, so I go along with it, rather than be called a spoilsport. At first it was okay, until this unknown man started groping me and tried to put his hand inside my knickers. As 'liberated' as I had been up until then (Mum had started to despair of me as I seemed to be out all hours of the night drinking and by day, when I wasn't working, running around Bath shoeless and with small cowbells on my knickers) this was too much for me and I flipped. At that stage in my life, after the way things had been, I had come to believe in an exclusive relationship between one girl and one boy, and I hadn't banked on other people's ideas.

Then George and I had a row and after that I heard very little from him on his next trip away. But when he returned he said he was sorry and I forgave him and we carried on as before. I didn't like the relationship as he was often at sea, so he said that because he wanted to marry me when I was old enough – if my parents gave their consent – he would leave the Navy and get an ordinary job.

He did just that and the job just happened to be in a greengrocers in town, so he was not too far away from where I worked. But it soon became obvious that George was hopeless with money. Having been used to periods at sea, then being paid and spending it all at once, he had no idea how to manage. So at the age of fifteen, I would meet him on a Friday to take his wages, so that I could look after things for him. For a start, we needed to save up for our marriage, as he wanted to get engaged on my sixteenth birthday in July 1961.

The next big eye-opener for me was when I went for a weekend to Martock to visit my aunt and uncle. Aunt Win started having a go at me about how much better I could do than George.

'If you were to marry someone suitable later on,' she meant of their choosing, 'we would pay for you to have a big wedding in Bath Abbey and of course as we have no children of our own, our money would eventually come to you.'

This felt like bribery and it was obvious that there had been discussions with my family in Bath.

I never visited them in Martock again, and only saw them when they came to Bath (at that point, he acted as if our 'fling' never happened) and of course the more they all nagged at me, the more determined I was to marry George. Going back to work after my weekend away was not as happy as it was before I had left, as Christine, who was by then my best friend, had gone to work for another fashion shop. I missed her being around and went to see her during my lunch hour.

We arranged to meet up later in a café in the centre of Bath. I was sitting across the table from her and I noticed an odd look on her face.

'Had a good weekend then?' I said.

'Yes, I did as a matter of fact,' she said quickly. 'I saw George.'

I stared at her. 'What do you mean, you saw George? Did you go out with him?'

She glanced away, sipped her coffee, and then looked me straight in the eye.

'Yes.'

At least she had the grace to look guilty as she added with a nervous laugh. 'Actually we ended up in bed together.'

I couldn't believe what she had just told me, and of course, I was devastated. How could she do that to me? And how could he? But somehow I blamed her more than him. After all, I already knew what he was like, but I never thought Christine would do such a thing! Her treachery caused a rift between us, which was to last a long time.

When I met George I gave him a piece of my mind.

'You went out with Christine and jumped into bed with her while I was only away for a weekend!' I shouted at him.

Of course he denied it instantly. 'I didn't. She's no good. She just winds you up.'

I lost my temper and we had a flaming row.

'What does it matter anyway?' he said, changing his tack. 'It meant nothing.'

'So you're telling me now that you did sleep with her?'

'Yes,' he shrugged, 'but it's no big deal.'

'How could you do that!' I screamed. 'That's it! I never want to see you again, ever!'

And so we split up – for a while. It was just one of many splits in our relationship.

Chapter Eight

Bob

George kept pestering me, and even though I had told him I never wanted to see him again, I found myself going back on my word and started seeing him again: our breakups never lasted long.

I resigned from Richard Shops in March 1961 – not because I didn't like the job but because working as an office clerk with the Gas Board I could earn three times as much money and the hours were more civilised: 8.30–5.30 p.m., Monday to Friday. I hated office work though: the same people with the same conversations, every day. I was not particularly good at the work, but didn't need to be, as most of it was repetitive and boring.

On my first day at the Gas Board I sat opposite the woman who was training me, Mrs. Franks, a nice enough lady in her fifties with short, curly greying hair. A man came into her office with a ledger. I noticed the peculiar way he had of throwing one foot forward when he walked. He was about six-feet tall, slim, with brown curly hair, a mischievous face and he reminded me a little of Georgie Fame. He put the ledger down on our table and as he was talking to someone else in the office, we happened to look at one another and our eyes lock.

A frisson of excitement ran through my body. I couldn't help it.

'It's no good looking at Bob,' said Mrs. Franks as he walked away. 'He's married.'

I suppose you could say I had become 'man-mad' and I have to admit I was starting to become promiscuous. But I don't think I was any more promiscuous than most girls I knew at that time. 'Free love' wasn't something I believed in, or wanted my life to be like, but I did have an intense need for love and sex seemed to be the only way to get it. The intensity of the feelings I was about to have for Bob would even make me ill – that intensity and the illness that seemed to go with it seemed to follow me throughout my life.

*****

It was about a month before my sixteenth birthday. The offices were very close to the beautiful Sidney Gardens and quite often if the weather was nice, some of the staff would go there on the lunch hour.

By that time, I had come to know Bob and one day in June we went out to Sidney Gardens together during lunch. I have to admit, I was infatuated with him and the fact that he showed any interest in me at all was fantastic.

'You wouldn't be interested in me if you knew how old I am,' he said.

'Age doesn't matter,' I replied. 'How old are you anyway?'

'I'm 27, and married, although…'

'Although what?'

There was a pause. 'Well, let's just say…we haven't been happy together for some time. There are problems…and I'm ill.'

I could see he was embarrassed.

'Tell me about it,' I encouraged him.

He hesitated again and then took the plunge. 'I'd been going out with my wife for six years before we married and it was something that really just followed on. I really love her but she said she doesn't love me and we live with her mother, who hates me and neither of them understand about my illness…'

He hesitated again.

'What is the illness?'

He showed me his hands, which were absolutely red-raw.

'I have Obsessive Compulsive Neurosis.[1] I have to keep washing my

---

[1]*Later called Obsessive Compulsive Disorder (OCD).*

hands and many other things because my brain thinks everything is contaminated.'

I took his hands and kissed them. Somehow I was aware that this was the start of something that would be massive in my life. He gazed at me and then seemed to make up his mind.

'Meet me here, tonight, after work.' He stopped and looked at me again. 'How old are you?'

'I'm sixteen,' I lied.

*****

I met Bob in the park a few hours later and he put his arms around me and kissed me. After a while, we walked to one of the shelters that line the gardens and we were soon making love. He was fastidious about using a condom, and afterwards very concerned that I was not under age. I still said I was sixteen and by then I was madly in love with him.

'This can only ever be for sex,' he said. 'I still love my wife, even though I'm seeing a solicitor about a divorce, because life between us is intolerable. But I always hope we can move out of her mother's, and that things will be different. We don't have sex any more, because it feels as if her mother can hear everything we do.'

My heart sank. I felt in that instant that he only wanted to use me, but as I was not even sixteen, I still felt that with time I would be able to make him love me.

We met several times a week in Sidney Gardens after work, and from this time on, Mum and Nan were always questioning me about why I was so late home from work. So my lies began again: 'The queues for the buses are very long' or 'I was late leaving work and missed a bus.'

I went out most nights of the week to see George, and some nights when Bob could get out, we arranged to meet in some fields in Prior Park, halfway between where we both lived. I would run for about two miles to meet him, we would make love and then I would run another two miles to meet George. It doesn't matter, I would think. After all, he often kept me waiting. But it was starting to happen so often that he was beginning to wonder what I was doing and started asking me, but I always managed to lie my way out of it.

'You know I long to marry you so much,' he said, 'so we can make a family together. That is my dream. We can get engaged just before your sixteenth birthday, OK?'

I agreed to the engagement and we went off to look at rings. George put a deposit down on an oval sapphire surrounded with diamonds and then paid it off over the coming weeks.

Mum and Nan were not pleased at the news (my father was never consulted about anything) but both say, 'Well, there's probably nothing we can do to stop you so we'd best make the most of it.'

*****

During the weeks before my birthday, I still carried on with both relationships. I couldn't even contemplate not seeing Bob. My birthday fell on a Saturday and we were engaged. All of my family and George's sister gave us cards and presents and we went out for a special meal at a restaurant in Bath where you selected your own fish out of the tank. It was a lovely day and I thought, perhaps it would work out.

My main reason for wanting to get married young was to get away from home. Home was a place I hated being in: the feeling of living with these two women who would really love to totally control me, and the very peculiar way everything was with my father. He ate with Mum, Nan and me, but otherwise he almost seemed to be in another world, another planet. We didn't have a television until I was fifteen but once we got one, he just seemed to sit and watch it.

In the early days there had been the semblance of conversation – well, at least they had rows – but by this time, there was just a blanket of silence between them. Mum still put Nan first all the time – maybe because she felt that she sacrificed her life to go to London with her – and Mum still shared Nan's room and bed. They still had to put up with Dad's terrible screaming during his nightmares and Mum still resented the fact that Harry and Win hadn't warned her about them.

The other bone of contention Mum had every night was that she said he never had a bath.

'Only dirty people bathe,' he would say if she confronted him with it. 'I wash my hands, face and neck every morning and my feet sometimes when you're out,' which was of course very rarely.

It somehow gave me a kick to go to work on the Monday morning after our engagement to flash my ring at Bob at our lunch hour, thinking it might make him jealous, and to say that it had been on my sixteenth birthday. He was absolutely horrified to think he had been making love to me while I was under age.

Why was I such a bitch?

Chapter Nine

Johnny

I continued my double life, sleeping with George and having sex wherever we could manage it, in shop doorways, parks – and the one that seemed to get the adrenalin going most was on the front doorstep of our house, when saying goodnight, with Mum shouting, 'When are you coming in, Janey, you've been out there long enough!'

Bob and I continued to meet in the Gas Board Social Club and made love mainly out of doors, except for one night after he and his wife Audrey had moved into a flat of their own. His wife and landlady were both out and he snuck me into one of the rooms. There was another occasion when Nan had gone off on one of her holidays to Wales and Mum was at work at the Admiralty on a Saturday morning. I let Bob into my bedroom in our house and had sex with him in my bed.

Although Dad had found a job in Devizes, we never moved there because once Leslie and his family had moved from next door, there was no need for our family to move. But he only got that job so that we could move away on my account; he now had to travel by bus from Bath to Devizes every day. I did feel guilty that he had to do so much travelling.

I may have been engaged to George, but my thoughts revolved around Bob most of the time and by that time, he was starting to talk about the possibility of us being together if he could get a divorce. Although, he still said that he loved his wife. George and I always had rows and split-ups. The latest was because during one of our separations, I had arranged to go for a week's holiday to a Butlin's holiday camp in Bognor Regis with Mum and a work friend of hers and my friend Christine (by then I had forgiven her and George for their one night stand). There was nothing much he could do about it anyway, so he eventually said, 'Well, you book it and have a good time, and don't go looking at other men.'

Needless to say, George had the classic Latin double-standard when it came to what he, as a man, could get up to and what I, as a woman – which at the age of sixteen I officially was – was allowed to do.

We set off by coach but when we arrived we were disappointed because the camp wasn't properly finished – the chalets were pretty basic. But we were determined to have a good time and take advantage of everything that was going on.

At one of the dances I met a good-looking young man named Johnny. Like my 'puppy love' Leslie, he had a snub nose and a fashionable Billy Fury coiffe to his dark brown hair. We got on well straight away and spent the whole week together, going out early in the morning on to the beach to swim, then spending the days in the bars and dance halls, and in the evenings at shows, dancing. There were competitions as well and I came third in the Miss Butlin's competition for that week, which consisted of many girls parading up and down a catwalk in swimsuits. Of course Johnny was sharing a chalet with some other boy he didn't know, because you could double up with other people if there were no other vacancies.

Johnny was twenty-two and had been living with a divorced woman with children who, not long before that holiday, had committed suicide after he split up with her because life was too difficult. He was an understanding sort of person, and being six years older than me with a responsible job in Southall in London, I told him all my problems – about home, my engagement and how I felt about Bob. He finally persuaded me to stop seeing Bob and end my engagement with George, as he obviously wasn't right for me – why else were we always splitting up and why would I have felt the need for another relationship?

Inevitably, this innocent holiday romance was starting to become sexual – and halfway through the week Johnny arranged for the other person in his chalet to be out and we went to bed together. I was becoming increasingly aware of the lack of love or affection in my childhood, and I thought it was because of this that I craved love from anyone who was kind or caring towards me. I had quickly become very close to Johnny –

maybe because just in those few days he had given me a tenderness and understanding I had never felt before.

At the end of the holiday we exchanged addresses, although he promised not to write unless I did and he said that when I got home, I needed to sort myself out. I cried when the coach left, as I watch him standing there, waving goodbye.

*****

George was waiting when I arrived, but I couldn't really be bothered with him, as I was thinking more about what to do about Johnny and Bob.

'You've *changed*,' George said after a few days. 'Why do you act different? You met someone else?'

'Yes,' I said and told him about Johnny. I said I thought it would be better if we made a final split because this was never really going to work. He had also had suspicions about Bob and me for a while, having been to the Gas Board social club and seen how we looked at each other.

But in spite of my fears of George's Latin jealousy, he accepted the situation and we agreed to call it a day, even though he didn't really want to. This meant cancelling the house we were planning to buy (including the grant to put in a bathroom), and going to Colmers department store where we had furniture stored in their warehouse for which we had been making payments for our wedding in two years' time in March 1964.

I had told Bob about Johnny, as my relationship with Bob didn't seem to be going anywhere – and he still hadn't got a divorce. His illness was very bad at that time. Even in that short period, Johnny had been unable to resist sending me a card, which made me feel that it was probably the right road to take, although I still found myself unable to stop seeing Bob: if I didn't see, him I felt as if my heart would break.

I wrote to Johnny and told him that Mum has agreed that he could come down for the weekend when he was ready. He came the next weekend, and the following two after that. Then wanted me to go to

Southall to meet his mother. He had asked me to marry him and explained that if he got married, we would probably get a house straight away because, although he was only twenty-two, he worked as a building inspector for the council.

It was all arranged for me to go by train in a fortnight's time when during a conversation he said,

'My mother's very possessive as I'm her only son. When we're married you'll have to ignore her because she'll probably come around saying, 'Johnny doesn't like things like this or that."

After I watched him drive away in the evening, I started to think about what he had told me and the more I thought about it, the more I realised that I just couldn't marry him and simply replace Mum and Nan with his mother, someone who would be watching my every move just like Mum and Nan did, like malignant prison guards.

I wrote to Johnny to tell him that it was over and ask him not to write back, because I didn't want to be put into the horrible state of indecision that I had found myself in with George.

A few days later he replied to my letter, saying how upset he was, but that he would respect my wishes and would not contact me again.

And that, as they say, was the end of that. I may have liked Johnny, but I certainly didn't want his mother to come too.

Chapter Ten

Just One Night

'I won't be seeing you for a while,' said Bob as we sat in the park during lunch hour.

'What?' I stared at him. Was he ditching me, like I had just dumped Johnny?

'I'm going to be off work for a long time, six months at the very least. I'm going into hospital.'

'But why?'

'They're going to operate on me. It's a fairly new form of surgery, they say it's experimental and there's a risk, but I want to go ahead with it.'

'Risk? What risk?'

'Well, it involves drilling holes into my brain over the next few months and then they'll insert electrodes into the brain which they hope will eventually stop the OCD. Of course, there's a chance of brain damage and I could even die—'

'Please don't do it!' I begged him.

'I have to give this a chance. I've tried everything else, I've taken every drug they've got on the market, I've spent time in all the psychiatric hospitals, I've had ECT which is quite barbaric and taken chunks of my memory away, and nothing has ever worked. You just can't imagine what this is like to live with—'

'So tell me then. Explain it to me!'

'OK, well, one day after washing myself all over several times and managing to get dressed I needed to go to a shop to buy cigarettes, and I knew from previous experience, the day before actually, that the shops were contaminated – in my mind, that is – so I thought I'd go to Bristol. I went to the bus station and got a bus. I tried to keep away from people.'

'Difficult on a bus.'

'Exactly, and I had been on the bus hardly any time at all when someone touched me. So although I tried hard not to, I had to get off the bus and then I had to walk all the way to Bristol and back for cigarettes...'

We talked a long time about the illness. By then his wife was back living with her mother and Bob was on his own. The more he told me about it, the more the sound of the operation terrified me. He said that these electrodes would be inserted in his brain over quite a long period of time and it was just a *hope* that they got the right nerves severed.

'Please don't do this!' I pleaded with him again. 'I could be with you instead and we could try to work through the illness together. I'll do everything to try and get you well and able to live normally, but don't take risks with your life.'

'I have to! I'm being given this one last chance and I must take it.'

*****

After Bob had gone into Frenchay Hospital in Bristol, I continued going to dances in big dance halls in Bath, Bristol and Weston-super-Mare. In the early days it was all live bands but later they had records – Elvis, Cliff, Adam Faith and Billy Fury – and later the Beatles, Stones, Gerry & the Pacemakers and Dave Clark Five. I loved all the fashions, ever since working with Win and Harry and then in the clothes store when I left school. I wore all of the fashions, the big skirts with all the petticoats and hoops, then minis when Mary Quant took over. I loved it all, the music, the fast cars – even though I sometimes got travel sick – and I just couldn't wait to learn to drive.

There was always sex with some man or another – one or two I worked with, or someone from one of the clubs we drank in, and a few from naval dances. I didn't set out with the intention of picking them, it just happened. 'You've got come-to-bed eyes,' I was told more than once. Usually I would see them again but sometimes I would have a hard job getting rid of them. I felt as if I was looking for something, when what I really wanted was Bob. I wasn't on the birth control pill – I left all of that up to the man.

It seemed to be the thing that so many of the girls I knew were doing: it was the Sixties. Auntie Gertrude in Wales had this saying, 'Women give sex to get love' and I think this is probably how I felt. I didn't even particularly enjoy the sex because I had to be with someone who really knows me before I enjoy it. I desperately needed love and I suppose at least the closeness and intimacy of sex made it feel like love at the time, although of course that feeling didn't last. And all the time the only person I thought about was Bob. And it all seemed to keep my mind off the things that hurt. I kept away from home as much as possible.

On the day of the Grand National at the end of March 1963, I bumped into George in town.

'I have just won money on the National,' he said. 'You must come to dinner with me for old times' sake'

I had nothing much in particular to do that evening, so I said, OK. He arranged to pick me up in the evening and I went home to get ready. The evening was excellent with a great meal and of course I drank a little too much champagne. We left the restaurant so that George could take me home, but instead he drove to some secluded place and parked.

'Come on, we'll go in the back,' he said.

So we both got into the back of the car. I didn't worry because George had always been careful and a very good lover, although he had never used condoms and depended on withdrawal. In any case, it was still quite difficult for me to get the pill because we were not engaged or married.

That particular night, I realised that he hadn't bothered with protection. I gave it a brief thought but when you're young you think, well, one night won't matter.

He asked to see me again and I said I would think about it. I was seeing a man named Barry who was quite a bit older than me. Our relationship was more like that of brother and sister, but I was really only interested in the fact that he had a car, so he could teach me to drive (as I was now seventeen) and that he was a good dancer – we went all over the place to dance halls.

*****

'You're seeing a married man,' said Mum when I got home from work one night.

My mind immediately flashed to Bob.

'We've been told by someone,' she added ominously.

'Of course I haven't,' I said.

The man turned out to be Barry – someone thought he was married, which he wasn't, but it reminded me that I was still being watched all the time at home.

*****

A month after the Grand National, my period failed to arrive and several days later I had a day of light bleeding but I convinced myself that it was OK.

Next month – still no period.

I got in touch with George and told him. He had a friend who was a chemist, and who gave him some great big tablets for me to take which were supposed to do something about it. I had already of course tried the usual old wives' remedy: sitting in a hot bath with a bottle of gin.

I took the tablets as directed, and spent several days in absolute agony sitting on the loo with the runs and feeling sick, but still no period. I was home from work for a couple of days and worry about what Mum and Nan are thinking. When I felt better and was back at work, I went to see

George. He was now working for Fry's Chocolate Factory and was on the nightshift.

'You go and see doctor,' he said.

'I can't go to mine,' I replied. 'He's been our family doctor ever since we've been in Bath.'

'I'll go make you an appointment with mine. He can see you before I go to work.'

Sure enough, George's doctor was able to fit me in at the end of his surgery. George took me over there, as it was on Great Poulteney Street, across the road from where he lived.

'You stay in the waiting room,' I said to George. 'I'll go in on my own.'

The doctor chatted with me and then examined me and said that I was two months pregnant.

'Is there anything I can do?' I asked.

'No,' he replied. 'Abortion is illegal and even if you could get one, I know at least one young girl who did get an abortion and was never able to have any more children and she regretted it all her life. Take my advice and go home and tell your parents tonight. Don't brood about it – you can always have the child adopted as you're still very young.'

I couldn't believe it, but in my heart I knew it was true, and that I had only had myself to blame – and George, of course, for being so careless.

I told him when I came out of the surgery, expecting him to be as upset as I was. Far from it!

'Great,' he said with a joyful look in his eyes. 'I always wanted to marry you. Now we marry and have many, many babies.'

'I wouldn't marry you if you were the last man on earth!'

Chapter Eleven

Mike…and Other Mistakes

It was time for George to go to work and I didn't want to go home, so he took me back to his house. He lived in the top flat but he took me down to the basement flat where we had friends.

Mike was at home, looking after the children.

'You take care of Janey until she's ready to go home,' George said.

Mike and I looked at each other.

*****

He was one of those blond, good-looking lady-killers. We knew him well because we all drank at the same clubs and partied with the same people. The whole time I had known him, his wife had either been pregnant, or at home looking after the babies. He had even had an affair with some girl while his wife was in the hospital having their second baby. I thought he chatted up every good-looking girl in Bath, and I'm sorry to say that that evening he did the same thing with me – successfully. The last thing on my mind had been to have sex with Mike, but I was tearful and distressed and really didn't know what the hell I was going to do. There was one thing certain: he couldn't get me pregnant, I was already in that mess. I eventually went home and drank coffee around the kitchen table with Mum and Nan, chatting as if everything in the garden was rosy.

I couldn't sleep with everything that was going around in my head, and at two in the morning I couldn't stand it any more. I woke up Mum.

She sat silent while I told her. She said nothing afterwards. We then went to her bedroom so we could tell Nan whose reaction was slightly different.

'Was that the only bloody way he could get you?'

'It does take two,' I said defensively. 'I wasn't forced into it.'

We spent the rest of the night drinking tea and discussing the options. I could have the baby adopted, but I really didn't think I could carry the baby and then give it away, even though I knew other girls who had done just that. But I had always wanted children, having longed for a sister or brother of my own.

The alternative was to get married – this of course was what George wanted.

'Where would we live?' I said. 'When we'd planned to get married we were buying a house to do up. Now we have no money and I won't be able to work for much longer.'

'You'd have to live here while you saved some money again,' said Mum. 'Of course, you could always live here with the baby – you don't have to marry him, you know. We'll take care of you and you can look after your baby.'

Alarm bells rang at the thought of this. My life had been bad enough and I had longed for the day when I could get away.

'No,' I said hastily, 'I want to marry George and we'll soon get some money together and get a place of our own.'

The die was cast.

*****

After I had informed George the next day that I would marry him, everything seemed to happen like grease lightning. Mum took over, because she was determined that I should be married before anyone could tell that I was pregnant. Even so, she still kept asking me if I was sure.

Now that I was engaged, I was able to get the pill from Family Planning because I had a wedding date set. However, they didn't really agree with me and made me feel sick – and, what was just as bad, I put on a stone in weight in about five or six weeks.

We took off for Swansea for a week away – Nan's youngest brother Bob lived there with his wife Hettie – because we had to tell the family. My dresses, and two dresses for my bridesmaids, were bought while we were away. The bridesmaids were going to be my best friend Stella from the Gas Board, a very large girl with a lovely personality (as she's an Irish Catholic she had to get permission from her priest) and the other was five-year-old Judith, my youngest cousin who is Uncle Bill and Auntie Gertrude's daughter. She came as rather a surprise to Auntie who had her when she was forty-four.

Mum wouldn't hear of me getting married in white, even though she wanted me married before people could tell I was in the family way. Of course I thought that not wearing white would be the biggest giveaway. But there was no mistaking the fact that we were now in the Swinging Sixties and nobody was supposed to really care about those things any more. So I would wear pale blue, my friend would wear peach, and my young cousin would be the only one in white. The wedding was arranged for three weeks away. We were to marry at my parish church, as I was a Baptist and George a Catholic.

Even though the pill had already made me start to put on weight, on the big day the dresses looked fantastic – shame all the photos were in black and white. The pill had been quite a long while before and I was less than size 10 and 7st 10lbs by then.

*****

The buffet reception, paid for by Mum and Dad, was held at the Angel Hotel in Bath. There were about fifty family and friends (minus Harry and Win who don't approve of George, as Win was such a snob). It was all going well until the dancing started. George was in his usual place at the bar, so I was dancing with my arms around Mike, who was George's best man, when someone shouted out, 'Well we know who the best man is at this wedding!'

My thoughts went back to a couple of weeks before when I was at work and Bob phoned me from Frenchay in Bristol.

'How are you?' he said. 'I'm missing you terribly.'

'Don't call me any more,' I said. 'I'm pregnant and getting married next week.'

This may sound harsh but for one thing I couldn't have a proper conversation with him as he had called me at work. I had wanted Bob for two years and made myself ill over him to the point where the Gas Board had sent me to see their doctor who had advised me, 'Just go and live somewhere with him,' which I would gladly have done. But instead Bob chose to go for the operation. I was devastated and quite desperate, so once I knew I was to have a baby, I felt I had made my bed and would have to lie on it.

There had been a long silence.

'I take it it's George's baby?' he said. 'Please don't marry him – wait until I come home. I'll get a divorce and marry you. I'll bring the baby up as my own.'

'I can't,' I said. 'I don't trust you, I've waited nearly two years for you to do something and you never have up to now.'

Bob had always told me that he still loved his wife and that out relationship was just sex. Then he would say that he was going to leave her because she said she didn't love him. He would go and see a solicitor, but nothing ever happened. He had never given me any reason to believe that he would do what he was then saying, and with his illness I didn't think that he could possibly cope with another man's child. I had to put him out of my mind and somehow make my marriage to George work.

Soon the wedding was over and we were off to catch a train. We couldn't use the car, because George had had an accident a few weeks before and it was still in the garage. Neither could we have a proper honeymoon as we had no money (Mum had lent George the money for his suit) so we were just going to a flat that belonged to Nan's brother Bob, and his wife Hettie for a week while they were on holiday.

We were married on 29 June 1963, exactly one month before my eighteenth birthday. It had rained all day and continued to rain for the whole of the next week.

It felt as though the honeymoon was over before it had begun.

Chapter Twelve

Married for the First Time

'This is not the way I expect the honeymoon,' George said as I got out of bed, having refused him sex, yet again.

'I just don't feel like it,' I replied.

'Well, you always wanted it before.'

'Perhaps it's because I'm pregnant. It may make you go off that sort of thing.'

All I could think about was Bob and how things were going for him at Bristol. At least he had come through the main operation and there was some sort of thing in his head. There were four holes where wires were put in every few days to pass a current through, which were supposed to destroy the parts of the brain that cause the abnormal thoughts.

The other thing that was bothering me was that we were going to have to live at home with my family, as there was no money for us to do anything else.

We arrived back home after our week's honeymoon and settled back into the usual pattern – we were both going to work as before – except that George was now living with me at home with Mum and Nan. I supposed we had to be grateful that Nan cooked our meals for us. But I found it so difficult. Between them, Nan and Mum were suffocating me. Auntie Gertrude once said to me that she was surprised how well I had coped with them.

'If you stay for about two years you should be able to save for a deposit on a house,' said Mum.

'I don't really want to stay that long,' I replied. 'I think we need to be on our own if this marriage has any chance of working.'

The irony is that I had opted for marriage because I couldn't bear the thought of still being controlled at home. But inevitably life for George and me was uncomfortable at home and we could only be on our own in the bedroom. That was a problem in itself. We were sleeping in the biggest room that until then, Nan and Mum shared. I could see Nan in it everywhere. It had her huge great walnut bedroom suite in it, with the very high bed and walnut head and footboards.

Lying in that bed with George was almost like Nan was in there with us. It felt awful sharing a bed with him. I had the sensation of being suffocated with someone's arms around me and by then there was even more tension between George and me because I was even less interested in the sexual side of our relationship than when we were on our honeymoon. This wasn't just because I was pregnant and stuck with Mum, Dad and Nan, but because I felt trapped in a marriage I didn't want.

*****

'I've got to get out of here,' I said to George one night after we had gone to our room.

'How do we do that?' he asked.

'I'm going to put an advert in the paper saying, 'Young couple looking for one bedroom flat to rent'.'

'We have no money, even if we get replies,' he said, which wasn't very helpful.

'And what about the baby?' he added. 'Landlords don't like children.'

'I don't intend to say anything about the baby; it won't matter once we've found somewhere.'

I duly placed the ad in *Bath Evening Chronicle* and receive four replies. We looked at them all and there was only one we can afford. The house, which was obviously quite old, was in a small crescent and divided into self-contained flats, with ours on the ground floor. The rent was £2,15 a week. The landlord, who didn't live there, accepted us and we agreed everything and fixed a date to take over the keys. The only thing left to do was tell the family.

'Why are you doing this,' said Mum, 'when you could stay here and save your money?'

'Because it's what we want,' I replied.

When they had finally accepted that we were going, Mum helped us clean the place, stain floorboards, put lino on the bedroom floor. Jane, the wife of George's best man Mike, made curtains for us and the essentials, we were able to buy with wedding present money. I had collected 'bottom drawer things' from the time we first got engaged and had managed to acquire other items – for instance, I was able to buy a gas cooker for next to nothing as I worked for the Gas Board. And although Harry and Win didn't come to the wedding, they sent a cheque for £30.

The house in which our flat was situated in, was in Widcombe Crescent on Widcombe Hill, quite a steep hill, in Bath. There were a lot of back lanes and fields and it was quite well known, as just behind us was a beautiful eighteenth-century mansion owned by the inventor/engineer Jeremy Fry. Princess Margaret spent a lot of time there, and there always seemed to be wild parties going on. We often saw Princess Margaret driving around in her Land Rover.

*****

George was very good as a husband. He was better at cooking than I was and helped out with all the household chores, as we were both working.

Soon after we were married, when I was six months pregnant, I received a phone call from Bob.

'Please meet me. I need to talk to you.'

'OK,' I agreed, 'but it will only be this once.'

We fixed a day and time when George was at work (he still worked a lot of nightshifts). I met up with him in Sidney Gardens as usual. He had warned me that he would be wearing a woolly hat because his head was shaved. We walked and talked.

'I would really have sorted things out and married you.'

'I've got myself into this,' I replied, 'and now I must try to stick with it because of the baby. I can't see you again after this.'

*****

I had really intended to try to live a normal married life, but any sexual feelings I had had for my husband seemed to have gone because I felt as if I had been forced into a marriage that I didn't really want. Yet the alternative of staying at home with Mum and Nan seemed even worse, and I knew that I wouldn't ever be able to give up the baby even if it wasn't what I wanted at eighteen.

Things were not too bad while I was at work, but on leaving work at the end of September 1963, seven months pregnant, I suddenly found myself very bored. While George worked a dayshift, I seemed to just hang around in bed a lot. We still went out dancing sometimes, although money was a problem: there were some maternity benefits but there was no option to go back to work later.

We still had arguments but not very often – George was basically very placid – and they were only over our lack of a sexual relationship.

Chapter Thirteen

Paula

The winter of 1963–64 was very cold and as we lived on an icy, steep hill, I didn't get out too much, especially as I had become larger with my pregnancy. My baby was due on 1 January 1964.

'You'll have to come and spend Christmas with us,' said Mum, 'and stay until after the baby arrives.'

'Alright.' It seemed the most sensible thing to do.

George had finished work early on Christmas Eve and came home early so we could go. I waited and waited for hours. He finally arrived late in the evening, having been out drinking with his mates. There had been other instances of this in our marriage and they only served to remind me how unreliable men are.

Christmas passed uncomfortably. It didn't help when Mum said, 'Of course you'll come back here and stay for a while after the baby is born.'

'No, I won't,' I replied. 'I want to go back to my own home and get on with life my own way.'

'You'll need help for a while,' chipped in Nan.

'I'll be absolutely fine,' I replied. 'I'll be in hospital for ten days – and anyway, how hard can one small baby be?'

There were several dreadful rows during the period before I went into hospital. George and I had had rows throughout my pregnancy because he wanted to attend the birth. But they had only just started letting fathers into the maternity ward to be there for the births – and even then you had to be really pushy about it.

'I don't want you anywhere near me,' I said. 'The whole thing is bad enough without you being there.'

Because George was so placid, most of our arguments are fairly one-sided, I was very quick tempered at this period and once I had left work, I hated the endless time on my own.

I finally gave birth to a baby girl, Paula, at 7:30 in the evening of 3 January 1964. The labour was very long – about fourteen hours or more – with only gas and air. Fortunately it was a normal birth and she weighed 7 lbs 2 oz. As soon as I saw her I fell in love with her and thought she was the most beautiful thing in the world and she was all mine.

After ten days in St Martin's Hospital, Bath, I returned to our flat as planned. Life resumed, but with a different pattern. I found looking after my baby very easy, but it was still the boredom that really drove me mad. And I was still having arguments with Mum and Nan, these times because when they visited they kept trying to tell me how I should do things.

*****

Maybe out of boredom, I had started a relationship with Mike – the best man at our wedding – and when George was working nights he would come round to see me. I didn't seem to care whether we were found out, even though I was friendly with his wife. There was no one in the first part of my marriage to George, because at that time I really hoped I could make it work. Although I used to feel that it was important to be faithful and monogamous – one boy for one girl, as I used to say – time and experience had changed me, especially after the period in which I became promiscuous. And now that I was married, it was almost as if I felt that 'having a bit on the side' was the norm.

I had this sexual need, but no desire to have any sort of relationship with my husband. From the night my pregnancy was confirmed and I spent time with Mike and had sex with him (which in itself was really irrelevant to me). I didn't want to have sex with George ever again. I had always felt that he got me pregnant on purpose so that I would marry him. I did love him in a way, but of course I still hadn't got over Bob, and wouldn't for many years.

It wasn't just sex with Mike though. I really felt something for him, probably because, as I later found out, he was a womaniser and knew how to make me feel as if I was the only woman alive. As usual, I got very little pleasure out of intercourse itself, and as always it was the closeness of it and the feeling of love that I wanted.

One Friday night when Paula was six months old and George was at work, Mike visited me. We slept together and, for once, I knew he had not been careful, as he usually was, about not getting me pregnant. It was really worrying me.

On Sunday we were invited out to some friends' place, Clive and Yvonne, for the day. Men unfortunately talked to each other about the lack of sex in their lives and they then talked to their wives.

'Go and make yourselves comfortable in the lounge while we clear up,' said Yvonne after tea.

This had obviously been pre-arranged because immediately George started making advances at me. I was thinking about my session with Mike and my brain was ticking over fast. If, by any chance he had made me pregnant, I would need to convince George that the baby must have been his. I knew that what I was doing might be judged as cynical and exploitative, but I was anxious and desperate, and by now I had learned how to hide my feelings. This wasn't a lovemaking session or anything close, just a grope and fumble and a coupling, but I felt it would not only keep him quiet, but it would cover up my tracks.

Nine months after that, I gave birth to my second daughter, Amy.

*****

When George wasn't working and had some spare time, he played golf or went off to one of Bath's drinking clubs that we always frequented.

One night George and Mike came home from the drinking club and George mentioned Amy, his new baby.

'What do you mean, your new baby?' said Mike, who by that time was very drunk. 'She's not your baby, she's mine.'

'What does he mean by that?' George asked me when he arrived home. I could see the suspicious look in his eyes and he was clearly quite shocked.

'I really don't know,' I replied quickly but firmly. 'Take no notice of him. You know what rubbish he can talk when he's been drinking.'

'We could get a blood test,' he suggested.

'What's the point?' I replied. 'They can only tell you who is definitely *not* the father.'

Which, of course was correct in 1965.

After that conversation, he never mentioned it again until Amy was much older. But was I lying to save myself or my marriage – or to protect George's feelings? I don't know, maybe a bit of all three. My guilt was assuaged by the piles of Terry nappies and George's shirts that I regularly had to wash and iron. They somehow made me feel at least a little justified in this act of deceit.

This was to crop up now and again throughout our marriage – which only lasted for three years. Unfortunately it was not too long before Amy started to look very much like her father who was obviously Mike. He actually told his wife, and I finally spoke to her about it.

'Well, you're certainly not the first and I don't expect you'll be the last,' she said.

It was then that she told me what a womaniser Mike had been since they were first married, but had thought it was worth tolerating because he had always returned to her.

I apologised for all the hurt and upset and we actually continued to be friends and even sent Christmas cards to each other (she did eventually divorce him many years later).

I told Mum and Nan as I thought it was better for them to know than to find out by chance. Strange as it seems, they didn't seem very surprised and I wondered whether they had already guessed, especially since Amy was the image of Mike.

Chapter Fourteen

Old Flame

One day while walking in town with Amy, now aged six weeks, in my big pram and Paula, sixteen months, on the pram seat, I bumped into Bob.

My heart turned somersaults when I saw him, just as it had always done.

'How are things with you? Did the operation work?'

He looked depressed. 'No, it didn't. I've only recently come out of hospital from the last bout of treatment after I tried to commit suicide. It was really just a cry for help because things just got so bad.'

'Are you working?'

'No,' he shook his head dispiritedly.

Looking at him, all the feelings for him that I had been suppressing until then came flooding back. The last time I had seen him was when I took Paula back to see the girls I had worked with at the Gas Board and he had been back at work. He had quietly asked me to phone him when we had a moment on our own, but I never had and I had really hoped I would be able to make my marriage work.

Meeting him that day in town was unfortunate. I was still only nineteen and looking for love and excitement in my life. I felt desperate seeing him again and instantly found myself longing for him.

'I've got a flat on Lansdown Hill,' Bob said. 'You could come up and visit me.'

I had never been quite sure when Bob and his wife split up, but I had since gathered it was when he went into hospital for the operation.

'What about my children?'

'Bring them with you,' he replied.

During the period when I hadn't been seeing Bob, I had always felt that were it not for the complication of having children, I could have helped him with his illness – and as I had never stopped loving him I hoped it might still be possible.

We arranged that I should go to visit one afternoon.

*****

I couldn't wait for the time to come. It was a three-mile walk from our flat to his – I lived past the railway station at one end of town and he lived at the other end –but I was young and fit and longing to see him and I didn't even notice the walk. When I arrived and rang the bell, I realised it was a top floor flat. When he answered the door, the first thing I said is: 'What am I going to do with the pram?'

'Put it up in the corner of the hall with my bike,' he said, 'and we'll carry the children up.'

It was a long way to his flat, up three flights of stairs, as they were big old Georgian houses. Once upstairs, we put Amy in Bob's bed and Paula was quite happy playing. He made tea and we talked for hours.

'Are you happy?'

'No, not ecstatically, but life ticks on. I have a roof over my head and a husband who works and allows me to do pretty much as I like.'

'Please come and live with me,' he pleads. 'My wife got in touch with me and said we would get back together again. We met for one night in a hotel and then she changed her mind. After that she got in touch to say she was pregnant but didn't want anything to do with me.'

'How do you know it's your baby?' I asked. 'It might be someone else's and she spent the night with you to cover it up.'

I should know all about that, I thought. But I didn't care about her, I cared about him. And he might have wanted and needed me to love him but I knew he didn't love me. Whereas I had tried to understand his illness and love him anyway, both his wife and mother-in-law had ridiculed him because of the illness, but I knew that he still loved her. Even so, I asked him the obvious question:

'Do you still love her? You always told me you loved her and that I was just sex on the side. You didn't care about my feelings.'

'I think I'm over her,' he said, 'and we could give it a go together.'

'I'll have to give it a lot of thought,' I said. 'I have two children to consider. We have a ground-floor flat and my husband has always been in work.' I said it with a smile, but I was deadly serious. I had a lot to consider. I was still not yet twenty and I had two children, from two different fathers, and I had already made a real mess of my life – Bob still couldn't say the three magic words I longed to hear.

'Please don't think about it for too long as I *need* you,' was his reply – not I love you, which was what I had always longed to hear from him.

Even so, I did give it a very great deal of thought and decided that I couldn't put my children into that position – I couldn't break up my marriage because of what it might do to them – but that didn't mean that I didn't want to see Bob for purely selfish reasons, because I had to confess to myself that I still felt a lot towards him.

One evening some weeks later, when I was able to get a babysitter, I set off to see Bob (neither of us had phones) to tell him that I was prepared to keep seeing him but not to leave my husband and move in with the children. When I arrived, someone let me in the door on the street. I climbed the stairs to his door and rang the bell several times. There was no reply, so I knocked on the door hard a couple of times. I was just about to leave and had gone down a couple of stairs when Bob came to the door half-dressed.

'I came to talk to you,' I said.

He had the grace to look embarrassed and apologetic.

'Well, I'm afraid you've left it too long, I thought you weren't coming back. I've got someone here with me that I met at the hospital. I can't live on my own.'

I nearly fell down the stairs in tears because I couldn't get out fast enough.

This was yet another person in my life that I hoped would return my love one day.

Chapter Fifteen

Wild, Wild Life

After that, my life started to go a bit wild.

'You go out and enjoy yourself,' George had told me. 'I've had a lot more fun in my life before we got married than you have. Just don't get involved with anyone seriously.'

Although this was a generous gesture – he said that he felt he had been my first boyfriend and that I had done very little in my life, whereas he had spent five years having fun before he met me. I still couldn't forgive him for deliberately getting me pregnant.

George had a sister Maria – she was small with dark hair and sallow skin like George – with whom I went out to dances, a lot of which seem to involve servicemen on naval camps. I had many one-night stands with men I never saw again and one or two I met a few times. As usual, I didn't really enjoy the sex and I suppose the reason for the adrenalin rush was down to doing something I shouldn't have been doing. I was unhappy, discontented and looking for something more to try and replace what I felt I could never have – Bob.

George had joined the Bath Youth Operatic Society. He was a good singer but only took small parts and was usually in the chorus. A lot of the members were young, but some were quite a lot older and had been with the company for many years. When I first met these people at an end-of-show party for *The Mikado* everyone seemed to be bed-hopping from person to person.

I soon became involved with one of them, a man named Brian, an older member who was an expert lover. He lived with his French wife Suzanne in a very nice flat in the Weston area of Bath. I visited him several times at his home in the evening when she was on night duty.

On one occasion, when we went out, Brian drove his car deep into a field so we couldn't be seen and we got into the back. It was very late and when we were ready to leave, Brian started the car but as he revved up, nothing happened.

'Why aren't we moving?'

'I thought it was bumpy on the way in,' he replied. 'The field must be furrowed and I can't get out.'

It was 1:30 a.m. and he had to go and knock up at a farmer, who came out with a tractor to pull us out. By this time, it was 2:30 and when we got home to our respective partners we were both given the third degree.

At the next operatic get-together, Suzanne suddenly flew at me screaming,

'You've been fucking my husband!'

'Why would I want your husband?' I yelled. 'I've got enough to do with one of my own.'

Someone pulled her off me, and things calmed down but I didn't bother to get involved with the group anymore.

*****

While all these things were happening in my life – and there were far too many of them – I was always searching. I was not happy in my marriage, and still felt that it was something I was forced into.

George and I were still in the same one-bedroom flat and now that we had two children it was clearly not big enough for us to live in. We put our name on the Council housing list as soon as we were married and hoped that we would get a house. The children now had the bedroom and we slept on a put-u-up settee in the sitting room.

A woman from the Council made an appointment to see me and arrived one afternoon.

'You've no hope of getting anything,' she said. 'We've got much worse cases than yours. In any case, everything here is very clean and tidy and both your children are girls.' This may seem like an extraordinarily sexist remark, but what she meant was that at some point a boy and girl would need separate bedrooms, and purely on that criteria, we didn't qualify for a new flat.

I was really upset when George came home from work, so we decided to look around at some larger flats, but soon realised that there wasn't any way that we could afford to pay the rent and that we would have to stay where we were. We had been saving up some money for moving because we were so sure that we would get a house, but now, as we were feeling so let down, we decided to use the money to buy a small second-hand van so that George could get to work and we could get around with the children and carry their pushchairs.

About two weeks after we had bought the car, we received a letter from the Council asking us to go to the office with our rent book: they were going to offer us a house.

When George got home from work I couldn't contain myself.

'We've got a house!' I shouted, waving the letter at him.

But we couldn't understand why we had been given this house. Why then, after they told us we would probably have to wait years. The next day, when I went to the office they explained that new houses had been built in a district called Southdown three miles out of town to replace the old prefabs, which had been pulled down and they need clean, respectable people to live in them. It was a terraced house with a small sitting room, kitchen/diner, two bedrooms and bathroom, and a small enclosed garden with a brick-built shed. After we had looked at the house and had been given the keys, the problem was the same as when we got married: we had no money. Once again I borrowed from Mum so we could hire a van and do things like fitting stair carpet in the house.

On moving day I felt as if this could be a new start and that everything would be OK. I didn't know why I thought that was the case though, because the only thing that would change was the accommodation.

Chapter Sixteen

Roger

My second child was one year old not long after we moved into the house, and because money was in very short supply, I said to George, 'Why don't I get a job in the afternoons?'

He was working a permanent nightshift by then.

'You could go to bed when you get back from your nightshift at 6.30 and get up at lunch time to look after the children,' I added.

He wasn't happy about it but agreed that we could try it. Having worked in fashion when I first left school, I easily found a part-time job as a sales assistant in a high-class shop called Marion's at the bottom of Milsom Street in Bath. Marion's sold very expensive classic dresses, suits and evening wear for well-off clientele. The staff and boss were all very nice and things worked well for several months. I made friends with other people, but especially with a girl named Julie, a dark-haired bubbly, friendly girl with a nice figure (as we all needed to have to work there). We were always laughing together, prompting our boss to say,

'Can we have a little more decorum here girls, please.'

'Yes, if we can find this Dick Oram,' said Julie.

We would go out into town and to the odd dance. George, meanwhile, was working continental shifts at Fry's factories, so he didn't work on a Friday night. One of our luxuries was an automatic washing machine, because there were so many nappies to wash. One Friday night the machine broke down and wouldn't spin out the water.

'I'm going to have to put all the washing into black sacks,' I told him, 'and go down to the phone box to ring Julie,' (who was lucky enough to have her own phone) 'to see if she'll come to the launderette with me.'

'I'm going dancing with a friend of mine, Sue,' she said. 'Why don't you come and then we'll go to the launderette afterwards?'

We made the arrangements to meet and I went home.

'I'm going dancing and then to see to this washing,' I told George. 'Help me get it into the boot of the car will you?'

'OK. Try not be too late home.'

'I won't. I've got to work tomorrow.'

I picked Julie up from her home and her friend Sue was with her. She was the same age as me, twenty, with bleached blonde hair and is slim considering she was pregnant – by a boyfriend who had decided not to marry her. Her mother was a very hard person who had told her that when she got nearer to her time, she would make arrangements for her to go away into a mother and baby home. Then her mother expected her to have the baby adopted and come home and carry on as if nothing had happened.

I had hoped we would have time to see to my washing before we went dancing so I could get home earlier, but after we had listened to Sue's story, we didn't have the time.

'Let's get going to the dance now,' Julie said.

'Well, don't forget I've got this washing to see to afterwards – and I don't want to be too late.'

'OK,' she replied. 'We'll leave fairly early.'

I was the only one with a car – and the only one who could drive, having passed my test a few months before. We drove into town, parked and went into the dance hall. As usual, the girls put their handbags in a little pile on the floor and danced around them, while all the men propped up the bar, and it went on like this for a couple of hours until 9.30. Then we got a drink (mine was a G&T) and sat at a table. In due course, we were all asked to dance by different lads. One of the men who sauntered up and asked me was wearing motorbike leathers. He was six-feet tall, slim, with light brown curly hair and my first impression was that he was a biker trying to show off.

'I'm Roger Mitchell,' he told me while we were dancing. 'I'm home on leave from the Royal Navy.'

'Well, I'm just here for a while with my friends. I'm married with two young children.'

I didn't really know why, but he reminded me of Bob. The only resemblance really was that they were both six-feet tall and had curly hair. We parted and sat down when the music stopped, but as soon as it started again he appeared by my side. By that time both Julie and Sue seem to be with partners, so I danced with Roger for the rest of the evening.

We were still in the dance hall by closing time, and Julie and Sue were being taken home by the guys they had spent the evening with.

'How did you get here?' Roger asked me.

'I came in my car.'

'I don't drive a car. I've got a motorbike outside.'

'I assumed that from your leather.'

'Yes, well, I can't really take you home on it,' he hesitated. 'Can we go for a ride somewhere in your car, so we can sit and talk somewhere?'

By this time it was obvious that the washing would still be all wet in the black sacks when I got home, but somehow I was really strongly attracted to this young man, so I agreed. I knew Bath very well so I drove us to a secluded spot and parked the car.

We talked for ages. He told me that he came from Melksham and went into the Navy at fifteen. He hadn't been back long from a trip abroad and he was based at Portsmouth.

'How old are you?' I asked him, looking at his relatively boyish face.

'I'm nearly nineteen.'

'Oh, that makes me almost two years older than you.'

'Does that make a difference? I really like you and would like to see you again.'

'I told you, I'm married with two small children, and of course it makes a difference.'

He put his arms around me and kissed me, and I forgot all about being married, children and the washing in the boot of the car, and how I might explain to George why I hadn't done it. When I married George, he told me about how he had learnt about sex from prostitutes abroad when he was in the Merchant Navy, which was why I had never had a bad experience with him (even if our sex life had come to an end) – unlike lots of girls with boys who didn't know what they were doing. Roger had the same skill, confirming my hunch about how life was in the Navy and what virtually all the men do when they came ashore.

Roger suggested that we get in the back of the car. This wasn't easy with him being six foot and my very small car, but this didn't stop him from making love to me like a man, not an eighteen-year-old boy.

Even though I tried to explain to him that this could only be a one-time experience because of my marriage, this brief time with Roger had been very different for me: I usually looked for older men who were more like father figures – perhaps because I was still searching for the father I never had: someone who would show me love and affection. Roger wasn't by any stretch of the imagination one of those. And even if I could detect a resemblance to Bob, I also sensed there was something more about Roger, and I wondered whether my resolve not to see him again would hold.

Chapter Seventeen

Comings and Goings

I was late home, so I crept into the house and into bed, fortunately without being detected. The next morning, I managed to make excuses about why I was late – and fortunately George had forgotten about the washing altogether.

The conversation with Roger had been varied, but I made sure I didn't tell him where I lived or give him any information about my family. What I hadn't been so clever about was that I had told him where I worked.

Around lunchtime the next day, Julie looked out of the shop window from upstairs.

'Isn't that boy across the road with the motorbike the one you were with last night?'

It was Roger, of course. He hung around for ages and eventually I took my lunch break.

'What the hell are you doing here?'

'I had to see you again,' he said.

'I told you that last night was just a one-off. I can't get involved with you.'

We walked around the town and by the end of my lunch hour, I assumed I had made things clear.

But obviously not clear enough: each day I was at work, he parked his bike across the road and then started to walk up and down outside the shop. No amount of telling him on my part that I couldn't see him seemed to make any difference.

*****

'My leave's up soon,' he said one lunchtime. 'I've got to be back on board ship next week and after that I'll only be home once a fortnight, so would you at least go out with me on Saturday night?'

I knew I should have said 'no', but I finally agreed to see him. I worked all day Saturday and then we spent a wonderful evening together. I realised I was going to miss him. He gave me his address and the name of his ship and asked me to write to him. He also gave me the phone number so I could phone the ship when he was off duty. I gave him my address, knowing that George had always gone to bed by the time the post arrived.

All this happened very soon after we had moved into our new council house and I was then confined to home for several weeks as my children had a particularly bad dose of chicken pox. Being young, I found this difficult to deal with, although I loved my children very much.

*****

One evening after a long, fretful day with the children, I had finally got them to sleep when there was a knock at my front door. It was David, an old boyfriend.

'Hi, how are you?' he said. 'I was told you'd moved, so I thought I'd call in.'

'Come in, sit down. Let's have a drink.'

We talked for ages and caught up on our lives since we last met. This was another evening that was to end up with sex. It was almost as if I needed sex to make me feel I was not worthless – or maybe it was the other way around: maybe I needed to have sex *because* I felt worthless and it somehow confirmed it – and yet I didn't want anything to do with my husband in that way. I only had sex with George on that one day before my second baby to cover up the mistake I had made.

That was the last time I saw David.

*****

George had obviously been suspicious about what I might have been doing and had managed to get to the post before me on a Saturday and confronted me with a letter from Roger. The letter was very explicit about our sexual relationship and George was understandably very upset – but he was not a person to lose his temper.

'How come you want to make love with other men and not want to make love with me?' he said.

I tried to explain that I had never felt the same about him from the beginning of our marriage because I felt pushed into it. We talked and he said that we should put it all behind us and try again. I said yes, knowing all the while that it wouldn't work. I continued to phone Roger and saw him when I could.

There was a ship's dance in Portsmouth that Roger wanted me to go to, so I arranged for my friend Sue, with whom I had now become quite close since the night of the dance and the washing, to sleep over and look after the children so I could go. I travelled down to Portsmouth, Roger met me and we booked into a B&B and went to the dance. As I worked in a fashion shop, I had bought a beautiful white cocktail dress with Grecian style back and very high-heeled shoes. We had a lovely evening and back at the B&B I set my alarm clock so that I had time to drive back before George came home from work.

But this was not to be: the alarm clock failed to go off, so I woke up later than I wanted to and set off in a hurry. I hadn't taken any other clothes so I had to drive back in my white dress. To add to my woes, I managed to get lost on the drive back, so I arrived home even later.

'Where have you been?' Sue whispered when I got back. 'George is in and I told him ages ago that you'd gone out to buy a paper.'

'So where did you go?' George said. 'Sure you haven't gone out to buy a paper, eh?'

'I went to a friend's twenty-first birthday party,' I lied.

George, placid as ever, allowed this to drop and went to bed after his nightshift.

In the days that followed, it emerged that Clive and Yvonne, the friends we visited on the Sunday I had tried to cover up my mistake over my second baby, had been having marital problems of their own. She came round to me one morning and said her husband was having an affair (which she seemed to find impossible to believe because they had always appeared to have the perfect marriage). She wanted me to drive around with her and follow him when he went out. I agreed to do this, feeling like a private detective.

We followed him to a house where a woman opened the door and he went in. Yvonne was nearly hysterical but I persuaded her to save her emotions for that night. I tried to talk to her and get her to talk to her husband to make an effort to sort it out, but she wanted to confront this woman and have it out with her. I agreed to take her to follow her husband again but felt very bad about the whole thing. I was well aware of what her husband was like, as I had had a short affair with him after my second child was born – around that time it seemed there was no husband I didn't have brief flings with. It was something that had started at a Christmas party while I was expecting my second baby. We had both gone into the kitchen to get a drink and he had grabbed me.

'I'd love to have you,' he had said.

And so he did.

We drove her to this woman's house and Yvonne insisted I go in as a witness. There was one almighty row between them and she threatened this woman.

'Leave my husband alone or I'll have you sorted out!'

I believe Yvonne and Clive split up for a while, but she was another friend I drifted apart from.

Part Two

Out of the Frying Pan

Chapter Eighteen

Anywhere Away from Here

In June 1966, on a Sunday morning, I looked out of my kitchen window to see Roger walking up and down the path that ran between our back gardens. I panicked, wondering what he was going to do. Obviously, it was his weekend leave from the ship. Then he disappeared and I hoped he had just come to see where I lived. A short while later, there was a knock on the front door. I was in a cold sweat and I couldn't move.

George opened the door and as I listened to the conversation, it was like watching a car crash in slow motion.

'Yes, what do you want?'

'I'm Roger, I'm in love with your wife and I want you to divorce her so that I can marry her.'

Roger at this stage hadn't told his parents that I was married. I had visited them with him and he had told me that they thought I was the best girlfriend he had ever had.

In the evening, after Roger had left and the children are in bed, George and I talked for hours. I was very mixed up and didn't really know what I wanted to do. Although I didn't have any great feeling of love for George, and we no longer had sex, I did feel very guilty about the children, and of course divorce wasn't easy even in the so-called liberated Sixties.

The other side of the coin was the great sexual attraction between Roger and me – and of course we could still go out for motorbike rides and dances. I talked to Roger about his parents and how they would be – he was only nineteen and I was married with two children. Finally, I gave him an ultimatum: I would do something about my marriage when he told his parents. Of course, they told him that if he carried on with me, they didn't want anything to do with me – yet, a short while ago I was the best girlfriend he'd ever had. I was very hurt – after all, I was the same person.

'Well, she's done it once,' his mother said, 'how do you know she won't do it again to you?'

*****

On 28 July 1965, the day before my twenty-first birthday, I was at home on my own with the children and George was at work. The car had broken down, and we hadn't had the money to repair it. I was totally depressed about the situation I had got myself into, and my eldest child, Paula had been particularly difficult. I grabbed the children, walked to the phone box and rang Fry's Chocolate Factory, asking to speak to George.

'You'll have to come here,' I said. 'I can't cope with these children any more.'

'OK, I'll come home. I have to get a bus or train from Keynsham and then taxi to the house.'

'Don't let the taxi go when you get home. I need it.'

I bundled a few things into a bag and by the time George arrived I was ready to go.

'Where are you going?' he said in the doorway.

'Anywhere away from here.'

*****

The taxi took me to the station and without really thinking, I got a train to Portsmouth where Roger was stationed. I had no idea whether he would be on duty or even off the ship. When I arrived, I phoned the ship HMS *Belerophon* and gave his name and number. They let me speak to him. I was so relieved when I heard his voice.

'Where are you?' he said. 'Stay there and I'll come as soon as I can.'

It wasn't too long before he arrived. He had been allowed some time off as he was due to go home the following evening on the naval coach.

We found a B&B for me to stay in, and arranged to meet the following evening, when he could arrange for me to go home on the coach with him.

I was in a dreadful state over what to do with my life. I loved Roger and wanted to be with him, but his parents had refused consent for him to marry me, so that couldn't happen until he was twenty-one.

I lay awake most of the night and after breakfast I had to leave the B&B. It was my twenty-first birthday, so I found a phone box and rang Mum at work, because I knew she would be really worried. I promised to phone again when I knew where and when the naval coach would arrive. I spent the day wandering around the shops and went to the hairdressers to kill time. Eventually the day was over and I boarded the coach with Roger. He tried to stop me worrying and told me we'd get it sorted out.

Mum, who had never met Roger before, met us off the coach. I rushed, sobbing, into her arms.

'This isn't how we had hoped to spend your twenty-first,' she said.

As much as I had resented Mum's intrusion throughout my life, I realised then how much I still relied on her emotionally and that I did love her.

But what she was worried about was that George had said he was going to a solicitor to say that I had deserted him and left him with the children, and that he would divorce me and get custody of my children. So although I dreaded it, I had to go home that evening. I arranged to ring Roger, and then went home.

*****

The next week was a horrendous one of talking – some of which was actually helpful but mostly we bickered and hurled recriminations – and dreadful feelings of guilt on my part. George kept trying to persuade me that we could put everything behind us and that he still loved me. He thought we should start all over again, while I was trying to explain that I didn't feel that it could work because I hadn't really wanted to marry him in the first place. In the end, he agreed to find a bedsit and left. Later, he would often say, 'I should never have let you back in after you left me with the children,' and maybe he was right.

Chapter Nineteen

Turmoil, Confusion and G&Ts

On the night George left, my mind was in complete turmoil because at the same time as I wanted him to go, I flung my arms around his neck and cried.

I had no idea how I was going to manage financially. The benefits available were pretty meagre and didn't begin to cover my expenses. So I took on a full-time job at my work and the children had to go to a childminder. Although Roger moved in with me straight away, he didn't earn very much in the Navy at nineteen and things were very tough. He was only home every couple of weeks for the weekend, travelling up on his motorbike on Wednesdays, and then had to leave in the middle of the night to get back Thursday morning, because although he was off duty, he wasn't really supposed to be off the ship.

I had remained close friends with Sue, and when she had to give up work because her mother was going to send her away to the mother and baby home, she moved in with me instead. It saved her having to go away and she was able to look after my children while I worked. I was still in a state of confusion and depression. I had suffered from migraines all my life but at this point they could be so bad that I would bang my head on the wall or floor. On days like those, I thought perhaps there could be more help for me, because they were brought on by stress.

Sue didn't like Roger and kept telling me how awful he was with my children when I wasn't there; she said he bullied and smacked them. I didn't believe her, of course. Mum wouldn't accept that I was actually sleeping with Roger, so if she called round, everything had to be rearranged to make it look as if he was sleeping on the sofa when he was home. Both Mum and

Nan had tried to persuade me to stay with George until the children were grown up, but I had said 'I have only got one life and I'll get what I want out of it; the children will have their whole lives ahead of them. I'm too young to think about what my life may do to them.'

I got very depressed when George picked the girls up on the agreed days, and he looked so sad. He only had one room and of course in winter it was really difficult. One lunchtime when Roger came to meet me, he found me in the pub on a barstool drinking gin and tonics and crying, out of guilt, about what I had done to George and the girls.

*****

Sue made some things easier like childminding, but other things would be more difficult, especially when Roger was at home, and I had taken on extra work after the person in the alteration room at the shop left. I now took home the sewing to do at night so that I could earn a bit of extra money for the sake of the children. Sometimes I worked until 2 or 3 a.m.

Roger and I started to talk about how much better it would be if he was out of the Navy, but with the number of years he had signed up for, it was far too expensive for us to be able to buy him out. He decided to try and 'work his ticket' as he called it, meaning that he was going to try to get himself out on health grounds. He pretended that he was depressed and they sent him to see doctors and psychiatrists, and of course his CO had been told the story about us, and had offered to get him a posting abroad if that's what he wanted. He had definitely decided to get out of the Navy.

*****

After Sue's baby was born, life became unbearable. There was obviously all the normal things with a new baby in the house, but she also had problems because of the baby's father. There was a lot of tension between Sue and myself, mostly over Roger and his temper; of all the things she told me about him, that was what I didn't want to believe.

I came home one day to find that Sue had just left. Life on my own was grim, trying to bring up two children without any help and no adult to be with, even for conversation. Somehow I managed financially with Roger – and Mum and Nan did help with the money side.

Roger finally got a medical discharge from the Navy on mental health grounds. He was paid a small cash sum, which we decided to use so that I could get a divorce. It was difficult to get a divorce because it cost quite a lot and the only easy way was for George to divorce me for adultery. I talked to George and asked him to put in the petition for the divorce and that we would admit it. He didn't really want to divorce me though, as he still hoped we could get back together some time. I assured him this wouldn't happen and also told him that I was aware that it was all my fault (even Mum and Nan acknowledged that he was a good husband), which is why we would admit the adultery and pay the costs. After a lot of persuasion, he agreed.

Of course Rogers' parents weren't going to give consent for him to marry me so we would just have to wait until he was twenty-one.

*****

Roger got a job in the rubber factory in Melksham working shifts, and around this time I started to realise that he was becoming obsessively jealous. Whenever he came home he would question me about where I had been and whom I had spoken to. He wanted to know in detail about every minute of the time he'd been away from me. He was never satisfied with my responses but wanted to go over it again and again.

I also realised that some of the things Sue said about the children were true as well, especially Amy. Roger had shouted at them and bullied them; he always pushed Amy away if she tried to sit on his lap or do anything with him. And this had all happened because I thought it was the decent thing to do to tell him that she was not George's child, although George still paid some maintenance for her as he had accepted her as his.

Soon the rows began, mostly because he was now convinced I was seeing other men while he was at work.

'How would I be able to do that with two children?' I replied.

Of course he didn't have answers or proof.

Chapter Twenty

Nan

Nan was ill in these early stages of my relationship with Roger. She had been seriously unwell before and had recovered from it, but then she had a stroke. I visited her one Sunday morning, although I didn't know if she knew I was there. She was expected to die soon. I went home at lunchtime and in the afternoon Mum sent someone round to let me know that Nan had died, as of course, we didn't have a phone. This was a terrible blow to me: it was really Nan who brought me up and I couldn't get over the fact that I had left without really saying goodbye.

In spite of all my negative feelings towards her over the years, it came back to me in a huge wave of sadness that Nan was always there for me. When I would come home from school she did everything for me – the washing, the cooking. She was really the mother figure in my life; she could stop me saying or doing something with just a disapproving glance or glare.

When someone has been there all your life, there is a need to say goodbye.

*****

Roger seemed to calm down and became different for a while, at least through the funeral. He looked after the children while I went and tried to be understanding. But soon the rows started up again and to my horror, one day his anger turned to violence. It was only a matter of slaps and pushes to start with, and he was always sorry afterwards. But then he would shout at me, 'I know you're a fucking liar and you won't stay faithful to me!'

'Why would I want anyone else?' I asked. 'You're all I want.'

And it was true. We still had a wonderful sex life and I didn't understand why he was like that. The irony is that I had actually made a promise to myself that after the affairs I had in my first marriage, there would be no more of that, and that I would marry Roger and be the perfect wife and that was what I really wanted to do.

'I'd be better with one doggo but faithful,' he yelled, meaning he would be better off with someone ugly who nobody else would want. Apparently it was an old naval saying.

He was now working nights and before long, the violence when he was home grew to the point where he was really hitting and punching me, because whatever answers I gave him didn't satisfy him. It didn't occur to me that he might actually be mentally ill. He didn't drink, so it was purely obsessive jealousy, and all in his head. I was also the sort that fought back – not the passive kind – so with the difference in our size, him a big, strong six-foot man and me an eight stone woman of five-foot four, I would come off even worse.

On one particular day I had really had all I could take.

'Get out of my house now!' I screamed, 'or I'm going down to the phone box to call the police!'

I grabbed the children and managed to get out of the front door and started running down the road. He got on his motorbike and roared off in front of me. By the time I was at the phone box he was nowhere to be seen, but I couldn't use the phone because all the wires had been pulled out. I knew he had done that so I couldn't use it. I went into the local butchers and explained what had happened and he let me use his phone. I also explained everything to the police, but they wouldn't do anything about domestic violence. They were more interested in the criminal damage to the phone box.

I went back to the house, but I was too scared to stay, for the children's sake, so I collected some things and went to stay with Mum and Dad for a while. I didn't hear from Roger and assumed he had also gone home to his mum. The police did nothing about the violence towards me, but they did catch up with him at his parents' house and eventually prosecuted him for damage to the phone box.

*****

Once I had left the house, of course, I didn't really want to go back there, even though I missed Roger terribly, because once again I thought that I was really in love with him and wouldn't be able to live without him.

I decided to stay on with Mum for a while because of course, she was still missing Nan dreadfully. They had been together since Mum had been discharged from the Army. I would be able to do the housework for her while she was at work, and she could babysit for me so I could sometimes go out with Sue and my friends again (I hadn't seen her very much because of Roger.) Mum helped me buy my first car, (George had taken the car we bought between us) and I was able to find a cleaning job where I could take the children with me. To save money, I only used the car when I really needed to, and walked to work most of the time with Amy in a pushchair. This job came to an end when the family moved to Bromley. Although, living on Combe Down in Bath with lots of villages and large homes around, I soon found another job where the lady I worked for was able to pick us up and bring us home. Through a recommendation, I was asked to go to someone else's house to clean. I also did one evening a week when Mum could look after the children. Apart from that, I did all the work for Mum, anything to pass the time and be able to look after the girls.

I started meeting Sue for the occasional drink or outing with the children and we decided to go on holiday in a caravan to Chesil Beach not far from Weymouth. The only thing I knew about my blood father, Jim, was that he lived in Weymouth at one time, so I decided that now Nan was gone, I would ask Mum about him again, as it was Nan who hadn't wanted to talk about him.

Chapter Twenty-One

Oh My Papa

'His name,' Mum said, 'is Cecil, but as a young man he hated it and had always been known as Jim.'

Mum told me the story of meeting him in the Army and of his constant promises to get a divorce, even getting leave to go home to sort it out. She later found out that he had gone home because one of his two sons had died of TB. He had been in Belgium when I was born, but when he came home, she went to live with him and me for six months in Weymouth where he had gone into partnership with another man who had a shop on Weymouth Bridge. My father was an electrical engineer so he had worked very long hours to buy his way into this business. The only person who had been friendly and good to Mum was my father's sister May.

However, living together without being married back in 1945 was frowned upon, and Mum still wanted him to get a divorce. When I was six months old, they had talked about it again and my father said he would go and see his wife – and Mum insisted on going with him. When they all met, of course, my father's wife used every argument she could to keep him from leaving her, like reminding him about the son they had lost, and threatened to kill herself if he divorced her.

'Think about it,' she told him, 'do you really want a divorce?'

Unfortunately, my father hesitated – which was just too much for my mother's pride and she went back to the flat and started packing to leave for London to go back to Nan and Auntie Audrey and Uncle Fred. She then saw a solicitor and took my father to court so she could get maintenance for me, but in the meantime through his solicitor, my father and his wife had tried to persuade my Mum to let them adopt me, arguing that they could give me a better life. This should make me feel that at least my real father had wanted me, but Mum told me that he did this to keep his wife happy because she wanted another child as one of their sons had died. Obviously Mum had refused and she never received a penny maintenance for me because she didn't want to keep going back to the courts – she preferred to work to support me.

Mum also told me something else which resonated in my mind: Jim had been Mum's one true love, and after that, with her disastrous marriage, she never received any love again, which maybe explained the way things had been for me in my childhood.

'Do you knows where he's likely to be now?' I asked Mum. 'Do you think he'd still be in Weymouth?'

She could only tell me that his shop had been called Davis & Hadley. It sold electrical goods and was located just before you went over Weymouth Bridge.

*****

In August 1967, Sue, the children and I left Bath for our week's holiday in Chesil Beach Holiday Park. We were very lucky to have a week of sunshine so we could take the children to the beach to play.

In the middle of the week, with Sue settled on the beach with the three children, she agreed to watch mine while I went to see if I could get any information about my father.

'Try not to be too long,' she said. 'It's not easy with three of them.'

'Don't I know it! I won't. Anyway, it will probably just be a wild goose chase.'

It was twelve noon when I found the shop. Miraculously, it was still there with the same name, so I went in and asked one of the girls if Mr Hadley still owned it.

'Yes he does. He'll be in any minute, would you like to wait?'

The shop looked quite modern and enterprising – there were TVs and radios and record players – but I couldn't really take much in because I was shaking with nerves.

A short while later, a man in his sixties came through from the back of the shop and walked up to me. He had thinning grey hair and spectacles. I don't like this but you could say he was about five feet seven inches and small built. There was something shifty about him, but I couldn't put my finger on it.

'Yes, you wanted to see me?' he said abruptly.

What a horrible man, I thought. He seemed so curt and self-important. But my legs were still shaking and I had butterflies in my stomach.

'Are you Jim Hadley?'

'Yes, why?'

'Do you remember Iris John?'

'Of course I do.'

'Well, I am her daughter.'

I could see his face change colour.

'Come into my office,' he said. 'I thought you were some young woman looking for a flat to rent. I let out some property.'

We talked for a while; he talked about Mum and how he had never wanted it to be as it was, to which I replied that I felt that the least he could have done was pay maintenance for me. He looked put out and tried to tell me how hard it was after the war.

'I'm going out for lunch in a minute. Will you come with me?'

'Yes,' I said, 'I'd like to.'

I was feeling a bit guilty about leaving Sue with the children, but I was sure she would understand when she knew how I'd found him so easily.

*****

'I don't know what to call you.' I was suddenly feeling shy.

'Why not start with Jim and see where we go from there,' he replied with a rueful grin.

'OK, Jim,' I laughed.

He asked someone to get his car and we left the shop. We got into a big Jaguar with personalised number plates and drove into Weymouth along the Esplanade to where there was a very expensive restaurant upstairs overlooking the sea. He was greeted by name and led to a table – he was very well known, it seemed.

I didn't know what I had expected to find, but it was beginning to dawn on me that my father was pretty wealthy. We obviously had many years to catch up on, but I told him I had two children, that I had left them with a friend and I couldn't be too long.

He took out his wallet and extracted from it an old faded grey photo and handed it to me. It was of a six-month-old baby and I recognised it immediately because it was me.

I smiled, 'Mum's got this picture of me on her mantelpiece.'

He smiled too, 'How is she?'

'How do you think?' I said more angrily than I had intended. '... She's ... OK. She doesn't know I came to find you.'

He nodded, apparently content with this minimal information, and after a moment I remembered something. I fiddled around in my handbag, fished out the photo and passed it to him. He was a young man in it, standing at a garden gate in army uniform. Although much younger, you could see it was Jim.

He chuckled, 'So she kept it.'

'Looks like it.'

He looked lost in thought for a moment – maybe thinking about what might have been.

'When are you leaving?' he said.

'In a couple of days.'

'I know someone in the main part of the camp you're staying on and I'll see if I can get you a room for a couple of extra days.'

So we moved into one of the rooms. Later in the week, he bought me clothes and the men from a garage he owned came out to rescue us when we had a flat tire. The tires were almost bald and when Jim saw them, he put four new tires on for me.

The evening before our last, he took me out to dinner. After leaving the restaurant, he drove for what seemed like miles.

'Where are we going?'

He didn't reply, but soon pulled up in a quiet, wooded area.

'I suppose this is the bit where you tell me you've run out of petrol,' I said jokingly as he stopped.

The next moment, he had put his arm around me and was pulling me towards him. I was shocked but that was only the start of it because next he was starting to touch my breasts and tried to get his hand up my panties. I struggled and pushed him, but he seemed very strong for his age. Finally, summoning all my strength, I managed to heave him off me.

'I'm your daughter!' I shouted. 'What the hell are you doing?'

'I've never lived with you and you don't feel like my daughter,' he muttered and didn't even have the grace to look ashamed of himself, nor could he even see why I had objected.

'Well, I am,' I said, 'and you can just start up the car and take me back.'

He did this without a word and we said our goodbyes. I had a phone number for him and I had given him my address.

I was horrified and so shocked that I couldn't even get anywhere near my feelings, as if they were tangled up in that wood he drove me to. All I could think was that he owed me something – and even more, he owed it to Mum.

*****

Back in Bath, Mum wanted to know all about him and I told her, although I didn't tell her what happened that night in the car. She was obviously jealous that I had seen him and she hadn't. She didn't seem at all emotional though, more inquisitive as to what his life was like, so I told her what he told me, although I had no idea whether it was true or not.

'Is he still with his wife?'

'He is, but the marriage is still not a good one and they live their own separate lives. They adopted a little girl after you wouldn't let them have me, because his wife wanted a daughter and it was all arranged very quietly through friends. He's been a counsellor and mayor and is very well known and has a lot of business properties, but he said they haven't been happy and he sleeps on his own in the room over the garage. He drove me past their house. It's one of the big ones on Weymouth front looking over the beach.'

I dropped in at my house every few days to collect mail and see that things were OK. A couple of weeks after my return from holiday, there was a telegram from Jim saying that he was arriving in a couple of days' time to see me.

'He's coming up,' I told Mum in a panic, 'and I'm going to have to cook lunch because I'll have the children, so we won't be able to go out.'

There was no question of taking the children out to eat – it was not something I ever did – and anyway I didn't really think children in a restaurant would be something he'd find suitable.

'Don't worry,' said Mum. 'Just cook something simple, I'm sure he'll be quite happy.'

I still felt slightly odd about calling him Jim and I certainly didn't know what to tell the children to call him because as far as they were concerned, they had a granddad at home – and they already thought of Mum and Dad's as home by now.

*****

When he arrived it was obvious I had no need to worry. Jim seemed a lot more relaxed than before when we had only just met, and he told me to call him Pop like his son, daughter and grandchildren did. The incident in the car was never mentioned again. He was very good with the children and we talked a lot about his time during the war with my mother and he finally got around to asking me if she was happy.

'No, she's never been happy. She's had a miserable life and it's really all down to you.'

He frowned and pursed his lips. 'I should have got the divorce after the war and things would have been quite different.'

'You didn't even send any money for me,' I said. 'I think that was terrible.'

'I know it's no excuse, but things were very hard my end as well, while I was building up the business.'

'But later in life when you had money, you could have looked for us. You knew where the family was in Wales. You could have found us.'

'I'd hoped your mum had found someone else to be happy with and I didn't want to upset things.'

As the afternoon wore on I said, 'Would you like to take me to meet Mum from work and we can come back here for some tea?'

Pop jumps at the chance. 'I'd love to see her again – do you think she would want to see me?'

'I know she would.'

We put the children in the car and went to the Admiralty on Combe Down where Mum still worked as a telephonist. She usually walked home as it wasn't far. Her face was a picture when she saw us waiting for her outside in the Jaguar. Mum and Pop greeted each other with a kiss on the cheek but you could see there was a lot more going on by the way they looked at each other.

'I thought you'd like to come down to my place, Mum, for some tea,' I said.

Mum seemed really pleased, so off we went. Everything went well and Pop left in the early evening, having talked virtually nonstop with Mum for hours.

There were things about my father that I already felt uneasy about, such as the groping session in Weymouth and his attitude towards money: he could see how difficult things were for me, but he had told Mum he wouldn't give me any money.

'If she's really in need of anything, you let me know,' he told her. 'I've worked hard all my life for what I've got and so should everyone else.' And there was the fact that he liked to control people.

But I had no idea that from that meeting that another affair was to begin – between my mother and father.

Chapter Twenty-Two

Leopard and his Spots

I had been back living with Mum and Dad for six months when I received a letter from the Council saying that my neighbours had petitioned for my house to be given to someone else who would use it. I was given two weeks to move back in or I would be evicted. I decided to give up my tenancy – big mistake I know now, but I didn't want to live on my own. The lady I cleaned for, who had a very large house, was good enough to store my furniture.

I was still going out some evenings with Sue, mainly to pubs in Bath that all the young people went to, and one night I met Roger. It had been a while since I had seen him and my stomach did a little flip as I felt the same old feelings.

After we had talked for a while – and he seemed like he was when I first met him – I agreed to see him and soon we were going out together again, when we weren't working and Mum could look after the children. I thought the children should be brought back to him gradually after the last time.

At first, Mum was not pleased with me seeing him – 'Remember the last time: a leopard never changes its spots' – but gradually came around to the idea, once she accepted that I wouldn't change my mind.

Besides, the most bizarre thing had happened, but maybe the most predictable: she had started seeing Pop, and I thought they were even carrying on where they left off over twenty years ago.

*****

Roger and I started talking about marriage, although we knew we would have to wait until after his twenty-first birthday, which wasn't until the summer of 1968. We wanted to get married in church but didn't know if this would be possible as I was divorced. I stopped going to my Baptist church when I married George who was a Catholic, so we had married in my local parish church and the children were christened there. Roger and I went to see a Church of England vicar who told us the reasons why he couldn't marry us, but may consider giving us a blessing after a registry office wedding. This seemed rather hypocritical to me so I went back to see John Mattson, the new minister at Manvers Street Baptist Church where I grew up. He was a lovely man and after many discussions he agreed to marry us as he felt that we loved each other and that I was truly sorry for my adultery in my first marriage. This was all arranged for August 1968.

We started looking for a house. Roger was earning quite good money as he was still in the same job. You couldn't get a mortgage until you were twenty-one, but we were able to reserve one on a new estate that was still being built. The payments were going to be hard, but we would manage somehow. The houses were being left completely bare for the owners to paint, so Roger asked if we could start on ours and they agreed. We bought the paint and one evening we were working there when Roger started up again.

'What did you do while we were apart?'

I told him about the holiday, meeting my father, my jobs and anything else I thought might be relevant.

'How may other men did you go out with?'

'I've had the odd evening out with a couple.'

'I bet you've been out with fucking loads of men since we've been apart.'

'I haven't. Most of the time I've thought about you and surely you've been out with other women?'

'That's different!' he shouted. 'I'm a man. I saw it all when I was overseas with the officers' wives. They were always screwing somebody else. You're all the bloody same.'

By that point he had me pinned up against the wall and just kept on

110

and on, shouting the same thing.

'How many men have you fucked?'

The more I said 'I haven't', the angrier he got, and because I had always had a lot of fight in me, I said, 'Well, if I told you it was six, would that satisfy you more?'

Of course he took that as the literal truth. 'I knew it, you whore!' He started to slap me. Somehow I managed to wriggle out from his grip, slipped out of the house and got myself home.

'I've cancelled the house and the mortgage,' he said next day. 'I don't want to marry a fucking whore like you.'

'Well, I'll have to cancel the church and everything else then,' I replied.

*****

When you're young and you really love someone, you have ideas about how wonderful things will be after you're married and although I knew he had this obsession about not trusting me, I still believed that if we were married and I was the perfect wife he would get over it.

I didn't do anything about cancelling the wedding arrangements. For one thing I didn't actually know how to face John at the church so I just left things as they were. Two weeks later, Roger came round again.

'Can we talk?'

'Yes, if you think it will do any good.'

'You didn't really have all those men did you?'

'No of course I didn't, but it seemed to be what you wanted me to say.'

'I'm sorry, I just can't help it,' he said, taking a hold of my hands. 'I just keep thinking that other men must want you and I don't know why you should want me.'

'Because I love you,' I gave his hand a squeeze, 'and I hoped I could have a second happy marriage with perhaps a child of our own and we could grow up and grow old together.'

'Please would you have another go with me, and carry on with the wedding?' He drew me towards him and kissed me.

Somewhere in the back of my mind, a voice was saying, don't do it, but I said, 'Of course we can, if it's what you want.'

Chapter Twenty-Three

Stitched and Hitched

The only problem was that we had nowhere to live: Roger said that he didn't really want to have a mortgage of that size hanging round his neck at twenty-one: the mortgage would have to be 100%, as we didn't actually have any money. He also said that he didn't really want to live in Bath. He would rather live outside in one of the small villages.

I agreed. I thought it might be a good idea to make a fresh start somewhere else before Paula started school.

'How about if I speak to my father and see if I can get him to give me a private mortgage with payments we can afford?' I said.

'Do you think there's any chance that he will after what you've told me about him?'

'Well, as he's very involved with my mum now, it might make a difference. I'll phone him tomorrow. But don't get jealous about the fact that I will have to go and see him on my own.'

I phoned Pop the next day. His standard answer by now was, 'Well, come on girl, tell me what it's about. Time's money.'

'Can I meet you? I want to talk to you about something.'

We met for dinner the next evening and I explained how things were over the house. He asked a lot of questions about Roger and said he'd want to meet him before he could consider anything.

'Where do you want to live?'

'Well, we've thought about it and decided Trowbridge would be a good area, not too far from Bath because of George seeing the children –

and Roger works in Melksham in Wiltshire and that's where his parents live.'

'I don't keep that sort of money around in cash,' said Pop. (We're talking about £4,000 – which admittedly was a huge amount of money.) 'I'd have to borrow it myself as all my money's tied up.' Then he started on the bit he always loved. 'I'll look for a house for you and buy it and rent it to you after I've seen this young man of yours.'

So that was how it was left and we made a date for him to meet Roger. After he was satisfied he was a decent, hard-working young man, things went ahead quickly as the wedding date was getting closer.

Pop found a house in the Croft, a horseshoe-shaped road, in Trowbridge and sent us to look at it. I fell in love with it immediately and the wheels were set in motion.

Unfortunately, the bank manager phoned Pop when he was out and spoke with his wife, not knowing that she didn't know about the house in Trowbridge. Needless to say, when Pop got home, all hell let loose and she found out about me.

*****

One of the ladies I cleaned for had five Dachshunds and a little girl. She often left them with my children and me, and went out. On a very hot day in July there was a lot of commotion out in the garden.

'Mummy,' said Paula, 'Timmy's bitten Amy.'

Amy appeared at the door, her face deathly white, but I couldn't see anything until she turned her head and I could see that her cheek had been torn open like a banana skin. It looked as if Rory, one of the Dachshunds, had taken a huge chunk out of it. I moved very quickly and found a clean piece of cloth to put over it and called an ambulance. I then called Mum at work. Everyone arrived at once – the ambulance, Mum and the lady whose house it was. Mum went with the children and me in the ambulance. Having done what I had needed to do, I let go.

I was hysterical by the time we reached St Martin's Hospital because I couldn't see what they could do: as I thought the whole of her cheek had gone, and of course I could only think it was my fault. I was absolutely useless in the hospital and when an enormous black doctor with huge hands came to look at Amy, I couldn't imagine how hands that size could deal with my delicate child's face.

He was lovely with her and realised that one of her fingers had also been bitten and needed stitching. When it was time to do it, Mum sent Paula and me into the garden and stayed with Amy – who hadn't even cried until then, but I could hear her screaming when they were stitching it. They put a big plaster over it and told us to come back. Mum got us a taxi home.

Later that day the police come to see me and took a statement. Also, the lady I worked for came to apologise. She brought presents for my daughter and as she knew I'd be leaving just before the wedding. She paid me for the next four weeks and said she didn't expect me to come back. Nothing was done about Rory, because the police decided he was normally quite placid.

As for poor Amy, there was a line of stitches across her cheek and later she developed an infection, which required treatment.

'Try not to take too much notice of how it looks now,' the nurse said to me when the stitches were finally removed. 'It will look better as time passes.'

I cried about her face for days, and it actually took a whole year before the lump went away and it started to look better.

*****

Paperwork for the mortgage seemed to be moving at such a snail's pace that by the time our wedding day arrived there was still no completion on the house. We were going to have to stay with Mum for a while.

I didn't want a big wedding – I was just pleased to be marred in the church. Mum and Dad (George) attended and a few family and friends including Roger's sister Claire and his brother Matthew who was the best man, although his parents Ronald and Dorothy refused to attend. Pop didn't come as Dad still didn't know about the affair between Mum and Pop. I had actually been getting on much better with Dad who seemed to enjoy having grandchildren.

There was a small reception in the Railway Hotel close to the church and for our honeymoon Mum looked after the girls and Roger and I went to the Royal Bath Hotel in Bournemouth for the weekend, and came back home to Mum and Dad's.

Fortunately a couple of weeks later, everything was settled with the mortgage and we had a moving date. I arranged for the removal van to pick up my stored furniture from the other lady I worked for and we moved into our new house in Trowbridge, which was a lovely bay-windowed semi with two reception rooms, three bedrooms, and a glorious 140 foot garden with beautiful borders and trees. It was on the outskirts of town but there was a small parade of shops nearby.

We took out the fireplace from the lounge to make it feel more contemporary, and painted all the walls with Dulux magnolia. Pop had decided we should pay £7 a week rent, as he assured me that didn't even cover his payments to the bank, but I told him it was far more money than we could afford.

'You have to learn to be responsible,' is all he said.

Roger and I went shopping for groceries and worked out what I would need for housekeeping, but he said he couldn't earn enough to give me that much and pay all the bills. I ended up in tears that day; we didn't know what to do. It was already causing friction between us.

'It's all your bloody father's fault,' he said. 'With all the money he's got and he knows we can't afford it.'

By then Mum and Pop were spending most weekends away together so they were obviously very close.

I rang Mum at work. 'Can you come over on the train after work? I need to talk to you.'

When she came round I explained the situation we were in.

'Can you speak to Pop?'

'I already have. He's adamant you have to learn the hard way and I can't change his mind. You send him seven pounds a week for the rent,' she said to Roger, 'and I'll give you two pounds a week back.'

Roger and I discussed what we should do about having a family together and decided we could only afford one child and that we should get on with it as soon as possible so the age gap wasn't too great between my other children.

Dad still didn't seem to know what was going on between Mum and Pop, who we didn't see very often as they were too wrapped up in each other. We only saw Pop now and again, like as when he gave us an electric lawnmower from his shop or when we needed some extra electric sockets.

'You're going to have to put them in for yourself,' he told Roger. 'I'll come over and give you instructions,' which he did.

I think Pop's largest income came from his funeral director's businesses. He told me about it when we first met. A friend of his had persuaded him to put money into one as a sleeping partner and, ironically, he had died suddenly and left the rest to Pop. After realising how much money it made, he bought a few more.

What a strange business, I thought, to be making money out of people dying.

Chapter Twenty-Four

Green-Eyed Monster

Since the wedding, Roger had visited his parents once a month, and of course, without me. Although things weren't too bad between us for the first three months, there were some rows and, as I now knew only too well, Roger had a terrible temper. By then there was no doubt that I was pregnant again.

One evening, Roger's sister Claire and her boyfriend Mark, came over and we told them the news.

'You look after her now,' Claire said to Roger as they were leaving.

He was over the moon, hoping he would have a son, so this of course was what I also set my heart on, hoping it would keep him happy. I didn't bother to book a bed until I felt it was necessary, by which time I discovered that Trowbridge District Hospital didn't have many beds and that I would have to travel to Bradford-on-Avon. Paula had started school in January 1969 and I had become friendly with a woman named Carol, who had two children at the same school, both of whom had disabilities. Sharon was born with brain damage and has slightly twisted feet, while her sister Laura also had some problems with her feet.

Roger started to become suspicious about me taking Paula and Amy to Bath on weekends to see George, and soon he was the same about me going out anywhere. Within a few weeks, we were back to square one.

'What time did the postman come?'

'Oh, about ten o'clock.'

'I didn't ask you *about* what time! I asked you *exactly* what fucking time!'

'I don't know the exact time.'

'Of course you do! I expect you're having it off with him and all the

119

others that call round, the milkman and the coalman.'

'Of course I'm not. Why would I want to? I told you when we were first together I only wanted you.'

'You're a fucking liar and I don't believe a word of it!'

And then he started hitting me, regardless of the fact that I was pregnant. He usually punched me or grabbed me by my clothing and threw me against the wall or into the furniture and I was terrified not only for my life, but for that of my unborn child.

Whenever he had really knocked me about, he would say he was sorry, get down on his knees, put his head in my lap and cry. I was beginning to believe he had serious mental problems.

'I don't even believe that the baby is mine,' he said one day.

'Of course it is. Who the hell else's could it be? I haven't been anywhere.'

'So you say, but I don't believe a word of it! Tell me who's it is!'

I was beginning to be unable to keep arguing with him and just take the beatings, which were never on my face so the bruises didn't show. I started to wonder if my baby would ever be born alive.

*****

I had a friend, June, over the road that I talked to while he was at work so she had some idea of what was going on and of course the neighbours on either side of me were also able to hear it. I was almost becoming afraid to go out anywhere because it was easier not to go through all the interrogation sessions. It was bad enough with Roger knocking me around, while he was questioning me about everyday things like walking to school and the shops, without complicating it with extramarital activities.

On my visits to the antenatal clinic in Bradford-on-Avon, I had to drag Amy on the bus even though there was a car in the drive when he worked nights. I pleaded with him to let me take the car.

'No,' he said, 'I can't trust you. If you take the car you can pick up some man along the way.'

'Look at me,' I laughed. 'Why would any man want me in this condition even if I did want one.'

'Well, you're not taking it – it's not my fucking baby so why should I care?'

I gave up asking and trudged on. I tried to keep all this from Mum and pretended that everything was OK because I didn't want her to worry. I was still not thinking about what dreadful repercussions this may have on my children.

*****

One day as I was putting out the washing in the back garden, Roger started up again with his questions. This time it was money: he wanted every penny I had spent accounted for.

'I earn the money here. Why should I have to keep you and pay the bloody rent to your father who's loaded anyway?'

I didn't bother to answer and as I started walking up the garden, he threw an iron bar at me. It would have caught me in the head if he hadn't shouted as he threw it. Fortunately, I looked round and tried to jump out of the way, but it hit me across the back of my legs.

Sometimes he just crept around, listening through doors, because he was paranoid about people talking about him. One evening he picked me up and heaved me straight against a brick wall. That night, I made up my mind to visit the doctor next day. When I got to see him, he agreed that Roger may have a mental disorder and wondered if I could suggest to him that he seek help.

'That would probably be more than my life's worth, doctor.'

'Well, in the meantime I'm going to give you some antidepressants to help you get by. Don't worry, they won't hurt the baby.'

*****

When Roger was in a good mood, he expected to spend hours making love, which was not always what I wanted during pregnancy, but I still loved him and wanted to make this marriage work, so I went along with all his wishes – even putting up with buggery, which was not what I wanted but he forces it upon me. It sometimes occurred to me that what he was doing was rape but I wouldn't dare tell anyone, and besides, there was no law against it as we were married.[2]

I was still determined to be the perfect wife, because I now felt that I should have tried harder in my first marriage. The house was always tidy and spotless. In fact, I had become a compulsive cleaner because if anything wasn't to his liking, it caused another row. His meal was always ready for him when he got home from work.

One night in bed, after hours of interrogation, he became so aggressive that he tried to strangle me. It seemed to go on forever but was probably only a few seconds – but that was probably how long it would take to die and that was what I thought was happening. I managed to stick my foot in his balls so that he loosened his grip for long enough for me to grab the children from their beds and run downstairs but he was only just a few feet behind me as I ran and I was still in his range.

I ran next door to my neighbours' even though it was about 1 a.m. I didn't even know their names as I had always been too embarrassed to have much to do with them. They had already heard all the noise and called the police. After an hour, the police turned up, but once they knew it was just a 'domestic' call, they didn't interfere.

Meanwhile Roger was standing on the doorstep, shouting abuse at the two policemen and me.

---

[2] *In 1969, buggery between husband and wife against her wishes was not classed as rape. According to Wikipedia: 'In December 1993, the United Nations High Commissioner for Human Rights published the Declaration on the Elimination of Violence against Women. This establishes marital rape as a human rights violation. [...] In the United Kingdom, such a category of rape was only recognized by a 1991 House of Lords decision known simply as R v R (1991 All ER 481). Whilst most parties agreed with the House of Lords' motive in making the decision, there were many (for instance the writer Patricia Hirst in her Textbook on A-Level law) who were of the opinion that the decision involved post facto criminalization, since the House of Lords were imprisoning spouses for doing what was once, according to the law, their right.'*

'Will you come in with me?' I asked one of them, 'while I get some things?' Paula, Amy and I were still in our nightclothes.

'No,' he replied, 'we're not allowed to do that.'

So my neighbour, who had a phone, called a taxi for me and I drove over with the children to Mum and Dad's. It was about 2 a.m. when we got there and I had to wake up Mum to pay the taxi. The next day she got in touch with the police and asked for help – but they told her the same thing.

'I suppose you'll give me some help when he's killed her,' she told them.

*****

After he'd had a couple of days to cool off, Roger came round to see me.

'I'm so sorry. I don't know what comes over me. I promise I'll never do it again. Will you come home now.'

Of course I forgave him and went home with him, although Mum begged me not to. Things were always better for a while after one of his big rages but these respites never lasted long and as I was further into my pregnancy, the risk to my baby and me increased.

One afternoon he erupted again, convinced that the baby wasn't his. I felt as if I was really fighting for my life as he had me up against a wall with his hands around my throat again. The cross and chain that I always wore was cutting into my neck. I didn't know how I found the strength or breath to get away from him, but I did and ran upstairs where the children were cowering. I pushed some clothes into a suitcase and managed to drag the suitcase and children to the bus stop and got on a bus to the station, a train to Bath and a bus to Mum's.

This time, Mum begged me not to go back to Roger.

'Think of what it's doing to those children,' she said. 'Even if you won't think of yourself. And then there's the damage to that little one inside you.'

'Yes I know, Mum, but I do love him. I just think he's ill and after I screwed things up with George I really want to make it work this time. When he calms down this time – and I know he will – I'll talk to him about seeing a doctor, I promise.'

*****

As always, he turned up a few days later with the usual apologies and didn't even seem to remember half of what he had said or done. There were tears as usual and he vowed never to do it again.

'If I come back, will you promise to come and see the doctor?'

'Yes, I'll do anything.'

I told him I was already on anti-depressants to try to cope. 'Perhaps they'll be able to help with some of your problems and your anger.'

'Yes, if you come back with me now.'

So once again I packed up our things and, much against Mum's wishes, returned to Trowbridge.

June was surprised to see me back.

'After you left,' she told me, 'one of my children Julie came in and said, 'He's done it this time, Mum, he's cut her throat.' '

'No that's not what happened.' I showed June the marks on my neck. 'That was from the chain I always wear round my neck. It was cutting into me so it was bleeding. I had been crying on the bus and all the other passengers were looking at me. Still, at least this time we've got an appointment to go to the doctor's, so lets hope they'll be able to help.'

The doctor made arrangements for us to see a psychiatrist. While waiting for the appointment, things were OK for two weeks, which seems to be about the length of time Roger could manage to contain his problems.

'I want to tell you something,' he said one day. 'I don't know how you'll feel but I need to talk to you about it. While I was in the Navy I had several experiences with men. There was never any penetration, only foreplay and sucking, which is perhaps why I've wanted to do it the other way with you. For a long while I was confused about which way I thought I wanted to be.'

I was speechless, but I assured him that I was not going to leave him and encouraged him to talk about it as I sensed that that was what he seemed to need. He then told me that he had had another experience with a man in a public toilet since we had been married.

I tried to be understanding and listened when he told me these things. On another occasion I was horrified – although I tried not to show it – when he told me that on occasions he had worn some of my underwear and clothes when I was out – not that an awful lot would have fitted him, but this was just another thing that made me wonder about his mental health.

Maybe it would have been easier if I thought of him as simply being a sexual deviant – or kinky to use a Sixties expression, which, now that it was 1969, was already starting to sound dated – but maybe I would rather think of it as psychological damage, which could be healed with the right treatment.

So we went to see the psychiatrist, and after he had listened to everything, he prescribed Roger tablets with regular appointments to follow.

Chapter Twenty-Five

Lana

It was six weeks before our baby was due, and I had arranged for Mum to come and stay with the two children while I was in hospital. Unfortunately, while on a weekend away with Pop, she had had a nasty accident. She had passed out in the en-suite bathroom in the hotel in the middle of the night. Pop had been asleep and unaware of this until she came around and managed to call him, but her foot had been jammed against a hot water pipe and burnt very badly; at one point they were talking about skin grafts but finally decided against them. It took months for her foot to heal.

One Saturday, Roger drove the girls and me to Bath to see their father and when we returned in the evening he decided to go and sort out some of the rubbish that needed burning. When I looked out of the window I could see that he had built the bonfire close to our neighbours' hedge. He came in to get matches, and when I mentioned this to him he took no notice. But a short while later he flew in through the back door.

'Quick! A bucket of water!' he shouted.

'You bloody idiot!' I said as he was filling the bucket. 'I told you not to light it there.'

As I had predicted, it was about to burn down the neighbours' hedge.

After he had managed to get it under control, he came in with the usual evil look in his eyes.

'Don't you ever call me a bloody idiot again!' he screamed and, in spite of my advanced pregnancy, started beating me, punching me in the head and stomach. After that, he didn't speak to me again until the day of the birth.

*****

Mum came over as often as she could, although after a while she stayed because her foot was so painful. Pop by then knew the state of my marriage, and blamed me for putting more pressure on Mum when her foot was hurting so much, although I felt this was unfair as the foot incident had nothing to do with me.

I never knew when Roger was going to be at home, as he had obviously stayed a lot with his parents who lived close to where he worked. But on Sunday, early in the morning of the day the baby was due, he was at home and asleep in the bedroom. I was downstairs with Mum when I went into labour.

'What are you going to do about Roger?' said Mum. 'You haven't spoken for six weeks.'

'I'll have to go and wake him and let him know.'

Roger and I had always talked about him being with me when the baby was born – except of course during periods when he was convinced the baby wasn't his. So I went to wake him up.

'Your baby's going to be born today.'

'How do you know?'

'Well, I have done it twice before, so I do know what to expect.'

I had left it quite late to tell him and by then I was in terrible pain with the close contractions. After not speaking to me for six weeks, he had decided then – at that time of all times – to spend at least thirty minutes cross-examining me about how many men I had had since we had been married – and throughout the interrogation I was in agony from the contractions.

'Are you taking me,' I said finally, 'or shall I get Mum to get an ambulance?'

'You go in an ambulance and I'll follow so that I can get back.'

Mum phoned the ambulance and we hurtled from Trowbridge to Bradford-on-Avon with me screaming and the ambulance man telling me to pant. The driver radioed through that he would need a stretcher waiting for me and then he put the blue light and siren on. I was rushed into a delivery room and they got my clothes off me somehow and the baby was born very quickly.

They had taken her away to be put in an incubator because she was very blue. I was extremely upset because Roger had sat outside not wanting to come in. I had hoped for a boy because it was what he had wanted. To add insult to injury, I was given a telling off by the midwife because she wanted to know why I had left it so late and she told me that the baby could have died because she should have been born sooner.

I felt like telling her that I had been forced to stay sitting on the bed being asked questions by an insane husband, which was how I was now beginning to think of Roger, but I was too tired and just said it happened too quickly, which wasn't true as I started labour at 6 a.m. and she wasn't born until 11 a.m.

Roger finally came in to see me after he had been to see the baby in the incubator.

'Maybe she is mine,' he said. 'After all, I think she looks like me.'

He didn't stay long and said he would come back later. Although I spent a week in that hospital – most of the time on my own, not like the other mums with husbands and families visiting – Roger didn't come again after the day she was born. Mum came when she could but she was still suffering badly with her foot. She brought Pop with her so he could drive her and all I got from him was another dressing down because of the trouble and pain I was causing her.

This wasn't the way you expect things to be when you have just had a baby, but at least my baby was fine in spite of her birth and her father's beatings. After eight days, Mum left Roger a note to let him know when I was coming home. She said he had been back to the house several times but was away most of the time.

*****

Mum came to take me home and stayed for just a couple of days. On the first night, I left Roger a note downstairs to ask him not to make a noise or put the lights on in our bedroom because of the baby.

He came home that night and we talked in the morning.

'I've been living at home with my mum and dad,' he said, 'and I'm going back there to think things over.'

He had looked at our baby, who, in fact looked so much like him that there was no doubt who the father was. We had decided to call her Lana. He was still paying the bills but Mum left me money for food etc. and went off with Pop. She had been off work for months with her burnt foot.

Roger returned a week later.

'I've decided to stay and give this another go,' he announced – not a word of apology this time about how he had treated me.

Things were OK for the first couple of weeks and then life resumed its usual pattern: he was questioning me almost every moment of the day, who I had seen and spoken to, at what time and where I had been. I did visit a couple of friends, although I hardly ever invited them to our house because I knew he didn't like it. I sometimes spent the day with my friend Carol, and she often told me about the problems she had with her husband Eric Jones, although he was not violent like mine. She said she had trouble getting money from him for food or clothes and shoes for the children, or anything else for that matter, and that he was always coming home laden with 'things' and she had no idea where he got them from.

But when Lana was six weeks old, I met Eric who seemed very nice – a tall, gentle, placid man. Paula and Amy were at school by this time but Lana was in her pram in their garden screaming as usual, because unfortunately she never seemed to stop crying. I was actually exhausted. He picked her up and managed to rock her to sleep, which I hadn't been able to do and I thought, why is she complaining about this man? He seems fine to me.

Roger visited the psychiatrist at regular intervals. I usually went with him and sometimes had sessions on my own, to get a picture of how he saw our lives progressing. Dr Williams was a large man with ruddy cheeks who seemed to be a chain smoker. He said there was no cure for Rogers's illness, but it could be controlled with medication. They didn't give any particular name to his illness, but later on decided he had schizophrenia.

I was unaware of any of his family history, as I didn't see his parents, who in any case wouldn't have anything to do with me. His mother didn't marry until she was thirty-five to a man ten years younger then herself. She had Roger and his twin sister at thirty-six and fourteen months later another son, and I later found out that Roger's twin had mental health problems and so did his father.

*****

I was still on anti-depressants to help me cope with life with him. I have a photo from about this time. I'm standing with Roger and my three children in the back garden of the house I was brought up in from the age of ten. Roger holds on to Lana, who is in my arms, while Paula and Amy stand coyly in front of us. Roger, a good six inches taller than me, smiles moodily into the camera; he's wearing a brown woollen polo-necked jumper, still vaguely fashionable, while I'm in a Quant type outfit with big black and white diamond-patterned top. I'm smiling too – just about – but in reality my expression is blank. It's as though I'm not really there.

When Lana was a few months old, Roger's obsession over money became even worse. The housekeeping was barely enough to live on; he hid his money each week under the carpet in a spot he thought I knew nothing about; and refused to pay Pop the rent: he had got it into his head that nobody with money is entitled to it because he had to work for it in a dreadful rubber factory.

He started siphoning petrol out of cars – but only if they were big and expensive – and then graduated to shoplifting because big shops could afford the loss, and after all, he was entitled to, wasn't he? If we took my girls to Bath to their father, he would drag me to Woolworths while he stole things and forced me to create some kind of diversion while he did so. I then had to go back to the car and wait for him with Lana. All this terrified me and I was so afraid of being caught.

Mum, whose foot was a lot better by then, still came over from work some nights and stayed over. One morning, when Lana was five months old and I was boiling nappies in a Baby Burco boiler, Roger started his usual constant round of questioning. On it went, mostly about previous men in my life. I tried to answer him to stop the kind of full-blown incident we usually had if he hadn't taken his medication.

He pushed me on to the boiler and when the lid slipped inwards, the only thing that prevented me from getting seriously scalded was that I managed to grab hold of a chair and pull myself up. After I had hung the washing on the line, he grabbed me as I was walking in from the garden, pushed me against the wall and stood in front of me, asking me repeatedly to tell him in detail about the other men in my life.

Lana was in her bouncer and she was screaming.

'Please let me go – she's hungry,' I begged him. 'Please let me feed her.'

'She can wait until you tell me the truth about how many fucking men you've really had and what men you're having when I'm not around.'

'There are no men when you're not around. How do you think I could possibly manage it with everything I have to do with three children, the house, shopping, laundry and meals to get?'

He just got angrier. 'You've got the life of Riley, doing what you like and expecting me to keep you.' He had the weight of his whole body pressed against me and his hands were on either side of my head on the wall and he was relentless with the questioning and the baby was screaming in the background and this went on for two hours.

Then he just stopped and moved away.

'I'm going out. I'll see you later on.'

His voice was calm as if that was perfectly normal.

*****

After he was gone and I had been able to look after Lana, one thought kept hammering away in my mind: I can't put up with any more of this.

I looked in the cupboard for the aspirin, which I bought in bottles of a hundred for my headaches and migraines. The bottle was about three-quarters full. I put Lana in the pram and walked to the shops up the road.

'A bottle of a hundred aspirin please.'

'We're waiting for more stock – we've only got bottles of twenty-five.'

'OK, I'll have one of those.'

I couldn't ask for more than one bottle, as it might have looked suspicious. On the walk home, I crammed aspirin into my mouth. With what I had at home, it would be about a hundred, enough to kill me and take me away from this impossible life.

Roger was back in the afternoon as if nothing had happened earlier. It was as if he were two different people. He had his meal and at 5:30 p.m. was about to leave for work.

'I've taken an overdose,' I said, 'so hopefully I won't be around in the morning.'

'What have you taken?'

'About a hundred aspirin.'

'Oh you'll be all right. Go to bed early and get a good night's sleep.' With that, he left.

*****

When Mum came later in the evening, I had her meal waiting and by this time all our conversation seemed very far away. In the night, I got up and see to Lana when she cried and by that time, my ears felt like they had cotton wool in them and there was a distant sound of bells ringing.

Mum had to leave on a very early train so she was gone before Roger came home. When he saw the state I was in, he called the doctor.

'You'll have to go straight to hospital,' said the doctor when he arrived. 'I'll call for an ambulance.'

'Why does she need to go to hospital?' said Roger. 'Won't she be OK in a while?'

'No she won't. They won't even be able to pump her stomach now. It has all gone into the bloodstream.'

I could hear this conversation going on as if at the end of a very long tunnel. The ambulance arrived and I was taken to Bath. The drive was dreadful –I was always travelsick, but this of course was much worse – and although I vomited on the way it was only chocolate that I had eaten with my Mum the previous evening as I had had nothing else.

In the hospital, I answered their questions as well as I could and then I remember them hammering a needle into my wrist and putting me on a drip.

*****

The next three days were a blank and when I did come round, my only thought was: am I still here? I had hoped never to wake up again to the hell I was living in. They told me that it had been touch and go whether I would survive. They also gave me a lumber puncture to see whether I had brain damage. Fortunately, there was no damage to my brain, for which I was grateful. I had to keep living, even if it meant listening to Mum wittering on about what she would have done to Roger if I had died. All this I could have done without.

The hospital sent a psychiatrist to see me as they did with all attempted suicides. He explained that they did this in case I did it again. When I left the hospital, he also explained that normally someone of my age wouldn't have been so badly affected by the aspirin but they were mixed with the anti-depressants that were already in my system.

I told him the reasons I took the aspirin and why I was on anti-depressants in the first place. I told him about Roger. I told him about my life. He listened to my story and said that he was sure it was OK to let me go, and didn't have any suggestions as to what I could do.

Chapter Twenty-Six

The Man Who Won't Go Away

'I don't remember what I do a lot of the time,' Roger said. 'Please come home and I promise to keep taking the medication and try a lot harder.'

'I'll think about it.'

I did think about it. Of course it was Pop's house we were living in (although Roger was still refusing to pay the rent) so I had to go back – there was no alternative. Roger came to the hospital on Sunday with Lana (Mum was looking after Paula and Amy) and asked the nurse if I could go home – which I did, in dressing gown and slippers, just as I had come in. I still didn't feel well and they had told him to look after me for a while until I felt stronger. The night he got me home there was a Western on TV, which triggered off another round of questioning.

'Didn't you say you once went out with a real American Indian, Janey?'

'Yes, but it was a very long time ago.'

'What was he like in bed? Was he better than me?'

'Look Roger, please don't start on all of this now. I really don't feel all that well and you promised you'd try harder.'

On that occasion, for once, he stopped.

*****

I tried to live with him as quietly as possible for the children's sake, and because Dorothy, his mother, had had so many problems because of his father, Ronald's, mental problems she had left him after twenty years of marriage. I didn't know too much about what those problems were, but I did know that Ronald was a bit of a lech and on one occasion I had to tell Roger he had tried to touch me. He was also always saying that Dorothy was trying to poison him. I wondered if it all ran in the family as Roger and his twin sister also had mental problems.

It was Christmas 1969, and Roger's mother Dorothy, who had never seen her granddaughter, finally decided to visit us, which I hoped might help our marriage. The visit went fine and I even got on well with her for a time. (Some time later after this particular visit, when Roger wasn't around, I went to see her with Lana and told her how Roger had been treating me – and she was actually quite shocked.)

After Christmas, the next bee in Roger's bonnet was that it was my fault that he came out of the Navy and that his life was going nowhere, so he decided to join the police. He was eventually turned down, because, so he told me, he was married to a divorcee. Although that may seem incredible, he showed me the police's rejection letter and it did imply that that was why they were turning him down. Although, of course, it may possibly have been their polite way of doing so.

Then he decided that we should emmigrate to Australia and start a new life over there. We even started the application process. When we were getting near the end of the processing, I went to see Dr Williams, Roger's psychiatrist, on my own to see what he thought.

'He would definitely be better away from his family's influence,' he said, 'but of course there is never going to be a cure. On the other hand, he can always seek psychiatric help in Australia.'

I went home and thought about the implications and about Mum and I had already worked out a plan for getting me and the children back if it became impossible out there. I dreaded telling Roger that I didn't want to go, and all my fears came true when I finally told him. He beat me black and blue with his fists, hitting every part of my body (but not where it could be seen.)

I tried to keep quiet because of the children, but I was not the helpless victim type – I tried to fight back, though I was no match for him, of course.

'It's just you and your fucking family as usual,' he screamed, 'trying to bugger up my life and make sure I don't get on! And anyway there's nothing wrong with me, I'm not taking these any more. You're just trying to get me locked up.'

With that, he threw all his pills at me.

*****

Life was unbearable. The interrogations and assaults were then virtually daily.

One night, he came home at 10.30 p.m. and Lana couldn't sleep, so I had let her play in the living room. As always, he started questioning me and started to get angry. I moved towards him to try to put my arms around him to calm him and as he flung me away from him, he threw his arms in the air and smashed a large light fitting. Glass flew everywhere. I bent down to pick up Lana who was screaming and even though I was trying to comfort her and check that she hadn't been hurt, he carried on hitting me.

Another night when he was screaming and hitting me, Paula came down from her bedroom and pushed herself in between us.

'Please don't hurt my Mummy, Roger,' she pleaded.

Amy always stayed upstairs out of sight when there were big rows, but when the doctor sent her for tests, because she appeared to be going bald, we discovered that she had been pulling her hair out from stress.

*****

When Roger was in the Navy, he was training as a fitter, so in one of his better moods I sat and talked to him about going on a government training scheme.

'How will we be able to manage?' he said. 'The money's very poor.'

'If you want to do it and get back to your trade, we'll manage

137

somehow. I'm going to look after my friend's daughter for a few hours a week and she's going to pay me, and you haven't been bothering to pay Pop the rent anyway.'

He decided to look into it: the course was in Bristol but there would be quite a long wait.

Since the marriage had been deteriorating, I had been seeing John Mattson, the minister who married us, and he had advised me to separate from him and get a divorce.

'I don't say this lightly,' he said. 'We both know about the vows you have taken, but this is an impossible situation for you and it's probably doing untold damage to the children.'

I had found a solicitor, Simon Halford, in Trowbridge who worked alone, specialising in separation and divorce, and I went to see him one morning. I assumed that Roger had followed me, because as I sat talking to him, the door to his office suddenly hit the wall with great force and Roger grabbed him by the lapels of his jacket.

'You leave my fucking wife alone,' he yelled. 'She doesn't need any advice from you!'

The terrified secretary had called the police who arrived very quickly and warned Roger never to intimidate the solicitor again or they would take further action. When Roger was in one of those moods his strength was unbelievable: he had just hauled the solicitor right over the top of his desk when the police arrived.

I decided to leave the papers for the separation until he was on the course in Bristol, which meant carrying on for a while longer. In the meantime, he just kept on and on about how he was never going to let me go. The men at his workplace sometimes taunted him because they knew he was married to a divorcee with two children. One morning when he came home from a nightshift, he crept into the house so I didn't hear him and the first thing I knew, he was dragging me out of bed by my hair.

'Who have you had in this bed last night?' he screamed.

It was difficult for me to say anything at all because he was dragging me around the bed, looking for somebody else's hair.

'Don't try to lie to me!' he shouted. 'One of the lads saw a car parked on our drive on the way to work. Now tell me who it fucking was and I will kill him.'

'They are winding you up,' I managed to say when he finally let me go, 'because you go into work and talk about us. Why would anyone even pass our house on the way to work as we live in a crescent? You'd have to drive in at one end and out the other for no reason at all.'

*****

By then I was aware of how much insanity there was in his family. Roger's mother had gone back to his father after eight months, hoping things would be better, but they had just become worse and his father Ronald kept getting in touch with Roger at work.

'Can you come over?' he would say. 'I can't eat anything – your mother's trying to poison me.'

So as well as trying to deal with Roger, he kept taking me over to Melksham in Wiltshire where they lived. The only thing they talked about was Claire, Roger's sister, who was now in a mental hospital. Her problems were very similar, I learnt, to Roger's, although she had taken it to an extreme by crashing her car trying to kill herself.

*****

When Roger left for Bristol on his training course, I finally got a little peace with the children: he only returned on weekends.

For me, the crunch came one bank holiday weekend when he said he had to go back and it was pretty obvious that he had become involved with another woman, although he denied it for a while. At least it made me feel that I had done the best that I could in this marriage and after all his accusations of me being with other men – to the point where I couldn't pick my children up from parties because he would say I was carrying on with the man in the house – he was the one who had actually been unfaithful. I had so desperately wanted to be the perfect wife and for our marriage to work.

The papers with the date for us to go to court for a legal separation hearing were delivered to him in Bristol. As it was early in the week, I was taken completely by surprise when he crept up behind me one evening, grabbed me and punched me in the face.

'There! If you're going to court you might as well have something to show for it.'

After a lot of raving about how he would never leave the house, he left again.

*****

By the date of the hearing, in autumn of 1970, Mum and Pop had been living together for some while, Mum having left Dad and moved to Weymouth. Pop hardly had a civil word to say to me because he was only interested in the stress I was causing Mum, so he wasn't too happy that Mum was going to look after the children while I went to court.

It was a dreadful day. We hadn't been married long enough for a divorce (it had to be three years) so my solicitor had to prove mental and physical cruelty. We had witnesses who have come to court – friends and neighbours who had heard and seen it, and also our GP and psychiatrist. The case was only halfway through by the time they stopped for lunch, so I went into Trowbridge to get a coffee. Roger strutted up to me.

'You're not going to win this,' he said. 'I will sort the rest of them out now.'

It seemed that the GP and psychiatrists gave their evidence first and were allowed to leave, so Roger had been wandering around through the lunch hour threatening the other witnesses – so much so that people were scared and I thought the case would never end. The courtroom should have been closed, but the judge said he wanted the case finished that day, so we were there until 8 p.m. He finally gave me the separation and Roger had fourteen days to collect all his belongings.

My solicitor got me a taxi home. Mum had been worried to death, thinking the court closed at 4 p.m., not knowing where I was. For the next few days I lived in a state of fear as I had no idea when Roger would come.

He arrived one night, creeping up on me as usual. Grabbing me by the lapels of my cardigan he picked me up off the ground and swung me around so that my body hit every piece of furniture and the wall. As soon as he had put me down, I ran into the garden and shouted for my neighbour to get the police who, because I had the separation order, stayed until he had gone, albeit with a threat.

'Don't think you've seen the last of me. You're still my wife.'

Chapter Twenty-Seven

Eric

Things calmed down after that for a while. I changed the locks and started thinking about how I was going to live. The judge's order was for Roger to pay all the household bills and two pounds a week maintenance for Lana. I was supposed to get £4 a week maintenance for my other two children, the maximum amount for each child being £2,10 but I didn't ever know whether I was going to receive this or not. I had about one pound a week from my friend Carol for looking after her children sometimes. So I decided to take a female lodger from Trowbridge College, a very nice sixteen-year-old girl named Vicky. We got on very well and the children liked her.

I had become friendlier with a few female friends now I was able to leave the house when I wanted to, and they were able to come and visit me. Although I had to call the police out once or twice when Mum was with me, as Roger would suddenly shout something from outside the back door and I would be terrified that he was hiding in the garden.

One night I was stupid enough to go out for a drink with him after he asked if we could talk about trying to see if we could have another go at our marriage. After several hours of unproductive argument, I knew it wasn't going to happen, so I asked him to drive me home. While driving he became really aggressive.

'Stop!' I shouted. 'Let me out! I'll walk the rest of the way.'

'I'll let you out. Who'd want a whore like you anyway.'

He stopped the car and I started walking down the road (there was no pavement) when I realised just in time that he was heading straight for me! I just managed to jump into the hedge in time.

*****

Every week I spent a day with Carol. She lived on a council estate a long walk from my home, and she asked her husband, Eric, to walk me home to make sure things were alright. Having listened to Carol's side of the problems in their marriage, I got to hear it all from Eric's side. He seemed so nice and gentle (compared to Roger) and I really wondered why she moaned so much about him. He was tall and good-looking with thick dark hair and a dimple in his chin.

A few weeks later, Eric shocked me by saying, 'If I get a divorce from Carol, would you marry me?'

'No I most certainly wouldn't,' I said. 'I really have had enough of marriage.'

But the following evening, Eric arrived on my doorstep asking if he could come in. I didn't see any harm as Vicky was with me – we were in the kitchen looking at catalogues – then I washed my hair over the kitchen sink. Suddenly there was an almighty crash as Roger came through the back door, shattering glass and wood everywhere. I instantly realised that he must have been following me and watching every move I made at night.

'What the fuck do you think you are doing here with my wife?' he shouted at Eric, dragging him into the hall.

Vicky just stood there rigid, the children were coming down the stairs screaming as Roger and Eric fought in the hall and I was trying to see to the children with my soaking wet hair.

Roger was not a fair fighter and booted Eric in the testicles, and jabs his keys into his face, leaving through the front door while Eric was in agony on the floor.

An hour later, Roger came back again.

'I've been up to Carol's to tell her what you were doing,' he said with a manic look in his eyes. 'I told her you were down here fucking my wife.'

He then refused to leave the house while Eric was there, and Eric in turn, refused to leave me with Roger. It was a stalemate: they both stayed all night in my front room.

Meanwhile, I had been trying to calm my children down, as well as Vicky of course, who was only a teenager.

The next day when Roger had left, Eric went home to find that Carol had packed his cases and put them on the doorstep. She wouldn't speak to him, and a neighbour told him that Roger had been shouting obscenities from out in the street for all to hear.

Eric came back to me but I said, 'There's no way you can stay here. He'll kill one or both of us,' and I sent him to a B&B closer to town.

After that night I was terrified, not knowing when Roger might break in again, and for a few nights I slept in the lounge, thinking that if he broke in I could get out of the window and run to the phone box.

I hardly saw anything of Mum as Pop did his best to keep her away from me now that they were together. Finally, when I decided that things had gone quiet, I went upstairs to bed. That was the first night that Roger broke in again. He was amazingly quiet and I didn't know he was in until he got to the bedroom. Then his hand was over my mouth and before I could make a sound and he tore my panties off and tried to force himself on me.

I managed to get his hand away from my mouth while I was struggling with him and bit him really hard on the shoulder. He had to stop or I would probably have bitten a piece out and then he seemed to have had enough for the night and left quickly.

Through all of this I carried on seeing Eric as a friend. He worked as a driver, delivering parts, and I usually saw him in his lunch hour for coffee or for rides in his work van with my youngest (the other two were at school). Otherwise I would have been alone most of the time, although Vicky was good company when she was not at college or at home on weekends.

The last time Roger broke in I was in bed but fully dressed in case I needed to run. I was lying on my stomach with my head to the side and he used karate-style chops to my neck and shoulders and left me screaming until Vicky finally came in. I couldn't move and she went to get an ambulance. The ambulance man managed to get me on a stretcher and I was taken to hospital. Vicky was left with my children to look after and as she was unable to go to college, she managed to get hold of Mum. Then of course the college decided to move her.

After I have been examined and X-rayed in hospital, they said I had been extremely lucky and that nothing was broken, but that the pain from bruising is usually worse and that I would probably get arthritis when I was older. At twenty-five, after a few weeks of pain, you forget about that and I had little idea what agony it will cause me later in life.

Mum was very good when all this happened although Pop was quite abrupt and abusive, as if it was all my own fault.

*****

I then found myself living on my own with the children, terrified most of the time and not knowing how I would manage financially. Roger wasn't paying the rent or bills, nor the maintenance – and maintenance wasn't guaranteed for the other two children. I had a chat with Eric as he was just about the only friend I could talk to. I decided to ask Dad (George) if I could go back to live in Bath with him, as he had the house to himself since Mum had left and their divorce was in progress.

Dad agreed and the children and I moved back to Combe Down in Bath where I spent so many years. Eric often came from Trowbridge to see us and a close bond was forming between us, although there's nothing sexual. We had talked about getting together at a later date but I had to wait until the three years of marriage to Roger were up before I could get my divorce and although Eric and Carol had been married for seven years, there were no real grounds for divorce.

One evening at about 11 p.m., six months after I moved to Bath, when Dad was out and Eric was visiting, there was a knock on the door and I had an awful feeling about it as nobody ever called.

'Who is it?'

'It's me,' came Roger's voice. 'Can I come in and talk to you?'

146

'I don't see the point. Everything's been said.'

I motion to Eric for him to go upstairs and out of the way.

'Just let me come in for a short while and then I will go, or else I'm going to stay out here all night."

Roger persisted, begging and pleading.

Stupidly I let him in. He sat down for a while and we chatted, and only then did it start to dawn on me that he had still been following and watching me a lot of the time.

'You've got somebody here you're sleeping with, haven't you?' he said.

'Of course I haven't.' It wasn't a lie as I hadn't slept with anyone.

All of a sudden he jumped off his chair and rushed out of the room and up the stairs. He grabbed Eric, saying, 'I knew you were here,' and gave him a good beating, then rushed down the stairs again yelling at me, 'I knew you were fucking lying. You've been having it off with him all along, haven't you.'

I tried to protest but it was pointless. He gave me a couple of hard slaps around the head and left.

After settling the children, Eric and I talked long into the night about what the outcome of all this would be.

'I know you said no once before,' he said, 'but if we were both divorced, would you marry me? I love you and I want to marry you and I will adopt your children and bring them up as my own.'

I hadn't really intended to marry again, but I didn't like living on my own, and it was so nice to be with someone gentle, after all the violence I had been through, someone who didn't question my every move.

'Even if I say yes,' I said, 'it will be ages before my divorce comes through and how are you going to get yours?'

'Well, if we're going to get beaten up for something we're not even doing we might as well do it, and Carol can divorce me for adultery.' He hesitated. 'Do you think George would let me live here with you and would you be happy with that until we are able to get married?'

'I'm sure Dad would let you live with me but I don't like the example it sets for the children, so we will have to explain to the older ones, why we can't marry yet and that we will as soon as we can.'

*****

So that was what we did. My solicitor tried to get my divorce through more quickly by applying to the judge on the grounds of forced sodomy, which is illegal, and the fact that I wanted to marry because of the children. He didn't agree to it, however, so Eric and I lived together for a year in total.

That year was probably one of the most peaceful in my life, and it might have been better to stay that way. But given that my eldest two children Paula and Amy kept asking when we were getting married, and it wasn't easy for them because they didn't have a normal family and a dad like the other children, I felt I had to get married as soon as possible.

We wanted a firm foundation for our family life with a church, and after my minister John Mattson advised me to divorce Roger (in spite of having married us) I had been in touch with him when I got back to live in Bath, but didn't feel at that time that I could go to the church. However, when the divorces were over, and Eric and I were able to get married, we went to see him together to discuss it with him. We knew he wouldn't be able to marry us, but we asked him if he would be able to do a blessing.

'I'm sure that under the circumstances the church members will be happy for me to bless your marriage,' he said.

Our marriage in May 1972 was a very quiet affair. Having done my best to be a good wife after a fairly large second wedding, I felt that a quieter third wedding would be better. We married in Bath register office with just the children and two witnesses, followed by the blessing at Manvers Street Church. I am grateful to John for the blessing as that was the part that made it feel right. After we were married, we all became part of the church and became very involved with church life. As this was my spiritual home from the age of five, most of the congregation knew me, so we had plenty of support.

We had booked a honeymoon in Jersey, but this was cancelled by the travel agent at the last moment so instead, we spent it on a market garden belonging to some Christian friends. Although I didn't realise at the time, this was actually the start of problems between Eric and me, as he went off every day and left me, but I tried not to make too much of it.

Before Eric and I were married, we talked about whether Amy, my second daughter, should at the right time be told that she had a different father. We also talked it over with Mum and decided that as so few people knew about it, and there was no one who would be likely to tell her, it would be better for her and the others if we said nothing. We could not have known what a dreadful decision that would turn out to be.

*****

So by 1972, I was twenty-seven years old and already on my third marriage with three children by three different fathers, although my children weren't aware of this at the time.

We consulted a solicitor about adopting the three children to make them legally Eric's. My first husband George was quite happy for us to do that as long as he could still see them, to which we were quite happy to agree to as they were too old to cut off contact with him. He was also only interested in the fact that there wouldn't be maintenance to pay.

'Oh good,' he said, 'now I'll be able to afford a car.'

Lana, my youngest, knew Eric far better than she did her father and really thought of him as her dad. Of course, Roger's reaction was going to be different because it would still give him some reason to see me. By now he had found himself a new girlfriend named Valerie with a face like a cabbage and who was ten years older than him. He had done what he had always said he should have done in the first place – found himself a dog of a girlfriend who at least would be faithful – and he seemed to have stuck to it this time.

We invited them out for a meal one evening and then I said, 'How would you feel about Eric adopting your daughter?'

'No I wouldn't even consider it,' Roger said immediately.

'Why should he?' said Valerie. 'Roger loves her.'

We tried to give him all the good reasons; among these the suggestion, of a psychiatrist off the record, to whom Eric and I had spoken, that his condition could be hereditary, and that not having contact with him could be better for her. Of course, we had to put this to Roger as tactfully and diplomatically as possible and it was not easy to make him understand the problem. Our trump card was really that by now Lana regarded Eric as more of a father to her than Roger and that, from that point of view, was best for her.

When Valerie went to the ladies I followed her out.

'How do you feel about Roger?' I asked her.

'I love him,' she said, 'and I would like to marry him, but he still loves you.'

'Well then help yourself and me as well. You persuade Roger that the adoption would be best. That way you would get him completely away from me.'

'I hadn't thought of that.' She looked at me, thinking for a few moments, and then seemed to make up her mind. 'I will talk to him and then get him to contact you.'

Roger got in touch with us about a fortnight later to say that he and Valerie had discussed it a lot and he was now prepared to let the adoption go ahead.

Eric and I had talked about having a child of our own and I said that we could probably just about manage financially to have a fourth child.

'I am used to having to work,' I said, 'so I don't mind doing whatever I have to do to help, but it will be difficult in the time I'll have off to have a baby.'

We talked more about it, bearing in mind the lack of room living with Dad, but even so, we decided to try for another child as the age gap would be too great if we were to wait too much longer.

150

*****

During the first year of our marriage I was to find out a lot more about Eric than I ever had in the year we lived together. I realised he was probably on his best behaviour in that year, but I started to discover that what my friend Carol had told me about him was indeed true. I married him because he was a very gentle sort of person, and none of that changed. In this marriage, I was never subjected to any violence either physically or verbally, but I knew from the beginning that he was unable to manage money and could get into debt very easily, so from the start I took over the finances. But what I hadn't really been aware of were the lies and stealing.

My knowledge of that all came gradually, and in the meantime, we got along reasonably well – except that living with my father was becoming more difficult. Finally Dad decided to pass the tenancy of the council house over to me and said that he would find somewhere to live in Devizes where he worked. One of the reasons for this, apart from the space, was that Eric and I would be able to buy the house as this was what the Council have started to do. So all the initial paperwork was completed and left for the Council to sort things out. Besides, the house was now very cheap to buy because of the number of years Dad had lived there and they were offering special mortgages.

All the lies were to start very slowly with Eric. He had money to go and buy something and then he would manage to lose it. I believed him and things would appear and people would have given them to him – I was gullible enough to believe this. Then he told me all sorts of stories about his life in the Merchant Navy and about other things he had done which I found out eventually to be untrue. He also liked to have jobs for which he could go to work suited and pretend that he was something he wasn't. While he was working as a salesman for an electrical firm (he never managed to keep a job for very long), he managed to have some excuse to be out all day, and for having to go out to see customers at night.

As time went on, I no longer felt I could trust him and my sense of loneliness and a feeling that I was being neglected – which when I think about it, started even on our honeymoon – intensified. He brought his boss Graham home to meet me and was quite happy to leave him with me for hours on end. Unfortunately, Graham was a real charmer and as I still hadn't found the love and security I was searching for, I began a very short-lived affair with him. Yet I did feel very strongly about our marriage blessing in the church and I confessed that I had slept with Graham almost immediately to Eric – and I did have my reasons.

'If you want to leave me I will quite understand. I didn't mean for it to happen but you seem to have lost all interest in being with me since we got married."

'I don't want to leave you as long as you promise me it's over between you and Graham,' said Eric. 'We will try to work at the marriage together.'

We had been going to classes with John at Manvers Street Baptist Church as we were soon going to be baptised. I discussed this with Eric and we agreed to start again.

'Will it be something you'll throw up at me all the time?' I asked.

'Of course I won't.'

And in my heart I knew that he wasn't that sort of person. I thanked him and felt that I had made my peace with God.

In spite of the affair – or perhaps because of it – Eric and I agreed to a new start and the first thing he does was, quite understandably, to change his job.

In November 1972, Eric and I were baptised at Manvers Street Baptist Church. We were very active in the church at that time and I was working at home as a childminder as I had my own three daughters to look after. As a result of all this, I tended to ignore all the warning bells telling me that something wasn't quite right, such as the things that appeared in the house apparently from nowhere.

In the back of my mind, I must have been aware that he was stealing and lying about it, but weeks and months went by until one day he received a summons to appear in Crown Court. It seemed he had been involved in a dodgy car deal, which of course he hadn't told me about, and he only just managed to keep himself out of prison.

Chapter Twenty-Eight

Andrew

In the beginning of 1973, I was expecting our first child (my fourth), which was due in September, so I was unable to carry on my night work in a home for mentally handicapped children in Combe Down in Bath. In later years, regulations would not allow it to be run as it was. The home catered for children up to age sixteen and I worked alone all night with 45 children in three dormitories. They all had to be taken to bed, but many didn't stay there and created all kinds of havoc. I had been punched and kicked, and some needed showering and cleaning up, especially after they soiled their beds or smeared excrement over the walls. They could also be violent, especially several of the bigger boys. It could be quite a dangerous place and I didn't want to risk this now that I was pregnant again.

We were always short of money and Eric kept changing his job, although he never seemed to be out of work; I met him on paydays but he always borrowed money from someone which needed to be paid back at the end of the week. And we also had loans because we had been improving the house as we were going to buy it.

When I was about seven months pregnant, there was an advertisement in the *Bath Evening Chronicle* for several evenings at Pratt's Hotel for people to train as models, male and female.

'I'd like to have done it but I can't see how I can,' I told Eric. 'But you could go down and do it.'

Male models were needed for all sorts of work, and as he was six-foot with black curly hair and a really good body, it seemed like a good idea. He agreed to go and find out about it and how much it would cost.

At eleven in the evening, when Eric had been to the hotel, he arrived home with the man who placed the advertisement and was apparently going to run the course. There was no promise of work and I soon discovered that in fact it was a big moneymaking scam.

The man he had brought home was Michael Howard. He had a David Niven moustache and a posh, plumy accent and said he was fifty-seven, but we never did find out his true age.

Eric of course, was the only male at the induction session, probably because even though we were past the liberated Sixties, it was still not something men were prepared to do. But Eric and Michael had struck up an instant friendship. Eric was hugely impressed by the fact that he had a title – Lord Howard – and had brought him home to stay with us as the modelling training course ran for three nights.

In the course of the week that Michael stayed with us, we found out a little of the truth behind his phoney aristocratic veneer. He had recently been released from prison, and in fact had no place to live. His only family was one daughter who lived in London and she had very little to do with him.

He regaled us with stories of his con tricks over the years and at the time we couldn't help but find him very entertaining. Some of his con tricks had been reported in the press in previous years (the ones that worked, that is) and he had even been named 'The King of Conmen'. When we met him he had been trying any stunt to make money but with very little success.

After he had left, things settled back into the usual routine, although Michael had promised to come back. Eric and I had several arguments because I had chosen to lend him money from my children's saving for funding for this continuing scheme with the models, as he was sure it would work. We had talked it over with Michael and he was going to set up some other recruitment meetings in Bristol as he knew someone who could run the courses, though obviously with all these kinds of courses there was never any guarantee of work.

'You won't let me have money for anything, yet you're prepared to lend it to him,' said Eric.

'Well, I've only done it hoping that he'll be able to get enough people to run a proper class and hopefully you might be able to make some money,' I replied. 'He does actually have some good contacts.'

Eric agreed that if you had some training and a portfolio of photographs and you've got the right looks and body to get work, it might be a good investment.

We didn't hear anything from Michael for months, during which Eric kept reminding me about the money. Meanwhile, he moved from job to job as we tried to keep up with our debts, until we were settled enough to continue with the purchase of the house.

In September 1973, our son, Andrew, was born. This was a good time for all of us, and for a short while life seemed OK. The only thing in my life I was struggling with was Mum's apparent desertion of me. Since my divorce from Roger, Pop had stopped her from seeing the children and me almost completely, and when she left home to live with him, she didn't even take a single photo of any of us with her. She rang me twice a year and came to visit by train. Pop wouldn't bring her or come himself and they were only living in Weymouth.

I found this very hurtful as they wouldn't have been together if I hadn't looked for him. I might have been able to understand if it was some new man in Mum's life, but he was after all, my own father. This just made my feelings about men even more confused, given the fact that at first he wanted to sleep with me and this was really why I had engineered the meeting with Mum.

*****

Seven months later, at the beginning of 1974, Michael turned up again on our doorstep. He called us the family he never had, and wanted to spend a few days with us. He had a Jaguar and was renting somewhere to live out in the area, and had another modelling scheme running in Bristol. Of course there was no sign of the money I lent him. The few days turned into a couple of weeks until I had to be brutally frank and asked him to leave.

Eric and I were unable to make ends meet, so I applied for a night job at our local hospital, St Martin's. I was offered a position on the maternity ward, but the Health Department wouldn't let me start until our son Andrew was nine months old. After Andrew was born, Eric and I knew we didn't want any more children so he had a vasectomy. It seemed to make sense, as I knew I had a job to go to and he had a job with an insurance company with a car.

This, we thought, would be the time to buy the house. Since we had first applied to the Council, the policy of selling council houses had changed. It could now only apply to those accepted before a change of councillor. We went to the Housing Department to get things on the move but couldn't give them dates of when George Hicks signed the house over to me, or when they valued the house and gave us a price. However, as they couldn't find our file – or so they said – they refused to go ahead with it. We got in touch with our local MP who tried to do something but failed, so we then found ourselves in a council house we couldn't buy and a millstone of debt around our necks for the work we had done on it.

This was a massive blow, and I found the strain of looking after four children and Eric (who still had to be watched permanently with money that went missing and things that suddenly appeared at home) almost unbearable and couldn't wait to get back to work to try to sort out the mess.

Eric by now had taken a job with a shower company, and had been asked to go to the Ideal Home Exhibition as a salesman. This lasted about four weeks and at the end there was a big dinner and dance for all the staff. Andrew by now was six months old and up until then I had never left him, but I got an overnight babysitter for all the children while I went to London. Our marriage had been going through a really rough patch and this was a chance to get things on the right road again.

We had a good weekend and managed to do some talking, leaving the party early and going back to our room. Although there hadn't been a lot of sex since Eric's vasectomy, because we have been told to use condoms until they had cleared the tests, we were both keen to make love after our separation. It was a wonderful night but halfway through Eric said, 'Bugger this thing,' and threw the condom on the floor.

I didn't give this much thought at the time, but on the Monday after we arrived home we received a letter from our surgery asking us to go in as the vasectomy unfortunately hadn't worked. Eric went into hospital to have it done again under general anaesthetic and they found that the houseman, who had performed the operation originally, hadn't even cut the right tubes. The surgeon who should have done it first time around had broken his leg the day before.

When my next period didn't arrive after the weekend away, I knew in my mind that I was pregnant. There were still no fast, reliable pregnancy tests, so I went to my doctor.

'Oh no,' he said, 'I don't expect you're pregnant, there are other reasons why this would happen – you've got a young baby and a lot of stress at the moment.'

The test was negative and the following month when I went back to him the test was again negative, but in my own mind and body I knew differently. Sure enough, on the third visit the test was positive.

'Well,' he said, 'as it was the fault of the vasectomy and because I know you've mixed with someone with German measles I would recommend a termination.' (I had had German measles myself, but then when I was pregnant and had been working at home as a childminder, one of the children in my care also had German measles.)

'How can I do that now? I'm twelve weeks and the baby is fully formed. Maybe if you'd believed me sooner...'

'Go home and talk it over with Eric,' said the doctor. 'You don't really need to put your body through another pregnancy and have another child only fifteen months apart.'

Eric and I discussed it for hours and John Mattson, the minister from our church, came up to talk with us as well.

'Whatever decision you make will be OK with me,' Eric said in the end, which didn't help me one bit.

With regard to the German measles, I know all the possibilities, but it is possible that I will have an immunity to it as I had it at twenty-seven.

And as the baby was then over twelve weeks, I found myself unable to have a termination. We tried to claim compensation from the hospital where the original mistake was made, but the houseman who had done the operation had left and of course all doctors stuck together in situations like that. Our solicitor advised us that if we went to court and lost, it could cost us a lot of money, so we gave up the fight. This, of course, then left us with no house to buy, a pile of debt and me unable to take up the position in the hospital maternity unit.

One bank that we owed money to continually hassled us and resorted to sending around the heavy boys to threaten us as well. Life was really very difficult when one day I saw an ad in the paper for a herdsman on a farm in Upper Basildon near Pangbourne in Berkshire, with a tied house.

'Didn't you tell me that when you left school you went to North Cadbury to train in Farm Management?' I said to Eric.

'Yes. I did a couple of years there.'

'Can you milk cows?'

'Yes of course I can.'

'Well, take a look at this advert.'

'Do you want me to apply for it?' he said after reading it.

'Well, we've really got nothing to stay here for now and the money's a lot better so you might as well.'

Eric phoned the next day and was asked to go for an interview in two days' time.

Chapter Twenty-Nine

Down on the Farm

The house and farm were in lovely countryside, a few miles from Pangbourne and quite close to Reading. Eric was offered the job, so we packed and left without telling anyone in August 1974. Our second child was due on Christmas Day.

In October, I found my fifth pregnancy difficult and tiring with the other four to look after – so much so that I was given a home help. Eric wasn't getting on well in the job and to add to our problems, one of our creditors had found out where we were living and a bailiff had turned up on our doorstep. I managed to put up an item of jewellery that was a twenty-first birthday present from my Mum as security until I was able to get the money together to pay them. We thought we had managed to get away from everyone, but even Michael Howard turned up on our doorstep one night with nowhere to go.

Having spoken to the farm management, it was obvious they would prefer that he looked for other work. Of course, there was the house problem, but we started looking. The hospital consultant decided that, as my fourth child was born very quickly and we were living such a long way away from the hospital and they expected me to have a big baby, I should come into hospital on the evening of 19 December so I could be induced the next day. They also said that for various reasons, I would need to stay for about ten days.

I then had the problem of who would look after the children. I wrote to Mum and asked if she could come and stay. She replied that she wouldn't leave Pop for that long, so I suggested that he come as well, but she said he wouldn't do that. I told her that the farm had refused to give Eric time off and if she wouldn't come her grandchildren would have to go to foster families. But neither Mum nor Pop nor the farm management appear to feel any compassion for my children.

In November, Eric applied successfully for a job as a school caretaker. The position was available towards the end of December but the house to go with the job wouldn't be completed until mid-February 1975, so they were going to put us into a temporary house, and Eric would have to move while I was in hospital. Mum turned up on the 19th with presents for the children and was with us when they were collected to go to two different homes (social services had been unable to find anyone who could take the four together). It was very upsetting seeing them go and I could never forgive Mum for not looking after them for me.

Chapter Thirty

Jackdaw

On 20 December 1974, Eric and I had a daughter, Julie. Having five children by four fathers in three marriages by the time I was twenty-nine wasn't really the sort of life I had hoped to have but I was not to realise for another twenty years the damage that my life was to cause my children.

Eric brought the children in to see me on Christmas Day, but that was all I saw of them in twelve days as the farm made him work until the last minute of his employment with them and of course he had the removals to see to. He then had to start work at the school immediately in January. It was a special needs school adjoining the primary school our children would be going to.

While we were in the temporary house, (three miles from the school) Eric had to get our children to school and back and I was left without transport. Our daughter suffered with colic at night the whole time we were there. For the first time, I suffered postnatal depression and seemed to cry all the time. In some ways, this wasn't surprising. Mum must have suffered some pangs of guilt because the day I came out of hospital, she popped in to see us, but Pop sat in the car outside.

During the first six weeks of Julie's life, I got very little sleep, staying downstairs and trying to stop her waking the others. Then after six weeks of living in one habitable room, with the surrounding rooms filled with boxes and no stair carpet, the removal day came and we were finally able to settle down (I had hoped) to an ordinary routine life.

Unfortunately, that was wishful thinking.

It was obvious to me within the first two weeks that we were not going to manage on his very low wages, even though we were only paying a very small amount of rent, so once again I found myself looking for work and applied to a hospital for a job as an auxiliary nurse. We were living in Tilehurst in Reading, so I used the Yellow Pages and picked out a hospital named Ballidon because it was only three miles away, close to where we had just moved from.

It was a small hospital for geriatrics and terminal cancer. The matron said she was desperate for staff and, after interviewing me next day, said she would be pleased to take me. I knew I could arrange the hours around when Eric could look after the children. I passed the hospital medical but they wouldn't let me start work until the baby was twelve weeks old. This soon passed and I worked a variety of shifts either nights or evenings and weekends.

*****

All seemed to go well for a while. Then things started to go missing from the house and once again things started to arrive that I hadn't seen before. Eric always had an answer for these things. There were boxes of keys which he assured me would open anything he wanted, boxes of medals, military buttons and many other items and Eric always said that he had bought them in second hand shops.

Then there was a break-in in our garage: all our electrical garden tools were stolen (or so I had thought) but something about it seemed very odd.

I had a very good friend, Jill, from when we lived in Upper Basildon.

'Janey,' she said, 'I think Eric may be taking all the things from the house and selling them in the shop on the Oxford Road in Reading. He may even have engineered this so called break-in of the garage and sold them as well.'

'I hadn't thought of that.'

'Well, come on, let's drive down and see the owner and find out, so you've got some idea what's going on.'

Jill was very tall and had an authoritative presence and when we got there the owner seemed to think she was a policewoman. To my amazement, he knew Eric very well and it was soon quite clear that he had brought everything that had gone missing from our home and garage. The most upsetting thing for me was a pendant that my children had saved very hard to buy me for Mother's Day.

I felt that Eric was just one more man who had betrayed my trust and feelings just like the rest. I confronted him about all of these issues and he said, 'I'm sorry, I don't know why I do it.'

'What do you do with the money?' I asked but he wouldn't tell me. 'I'm trying to look after the children and work because you don't earn enough and then you steal and just waste the money. And where do you get all the boxes of things you have collected and why do you do that?'

'I don't know,' he said. 'I just seem to have to do it.'

'I think you need some help Eric. Will you come and talk to someone about it, if we are to make this marriage work?'

He agreed and I found myself once again visiting a psychiatrist, Dr Grayson. This very nice man, after a long talk with Eric, said, 'Well, I think it's quite clear that you're a kleptomaniac and you just can't help taking and collecting things like a jackdaw does – hence the boxes of things and of course the stealing from your own home is just for money that burns a hole in your pocket until you have spent it.'

'Can you help?' I asked him.

'Well I can try.'

*****

This started a series of visits, but none of them really solved the problems. Our garage was used mainly for storage, so I didn't go out there often, but one day when I did, I was horrified to find huge stores of things like toilet rolls and cleaning fluids, all obviously stolen from the school where Eric was caretaker. I confronted him with this when he came home from work.

'Oh it doesn't matter,' he replied, 'there's loads of stores over there. I order it and I've got an arrangement with the caretaker in the school next door and we sell on the things together.'

'This is your job and our home and lives you're playing with,' I protested. 'In any case, you're bound to get found out sooner or later.'

These words were to come true sooner than I expected. Eric had been at the school about a year when the headmaster came to see me.

'I know what's going on with the stealing and I can't let it go on any longer. I feel very sorry for you and your children so I don't want to have to sack Eric and make things worse for you, so if you can tell him I've been to see you, I'll give him time to find another job.'

He even asked if I would like to take over the job, but I said no, thanking him for his trouble and kindness and waited for Eric to come home from work. By then I was really upset.

'The headmaster has been, and for mine and the children's sake, he's not going to call in the police or sack you, but we have to move on as quickly as possible. Look what you have done to us now. I am working all hours and looking after five children and you put us in this position. It's not just a job you've got to find – we won't have anywhere to live either.'

'I'm sorry,' he replied, looking very sheepish. 'What more can I say?'

He managed to get a job in a factory, and with both our earnings and the fact that there was a house for sale just up the road owned by the manager of the Bradford & Bingley who needed to move fast, he arranged a 100% mortgage including an insurance top-up. The house was put in my sole name because I didn't trust Eric. As the mortgage was more than we could afford, we had to work even more hours.

Chapter Thirty-One

Old Flame

I was feeling quite desperate soon after this move, and wrote and asked Mum to ask Pop if he could help us for a while. He did come over with Mum and stayed for a cup of tea. Things were quite strained and money wasn't mentioned but Mum wrote to me later saying that he wouldn't help because we seemed to be doing O.K. It would be a long time before I saw them again.

To add to our problems, after we moved, Michael Howard turned up again on the doorstep, driving a big Jaguar and with more schemes in his head. He was involved with some garage, which meant he had cars at his disposal as he was supposed to be selling them. But as usual, he had nowhere to live, so he ended up sleeping on the put-u-up in our dining room. He still had big ideas about Eric modelling and took him off somewhere to get a portfolio of photographs done.

He told us that he had a girl he wanted Eric to work with on stage, which of course would involve nude work. This is where I drew the line. When we lived in Bath, and I was childminding, I had looked after a child named Rosanna whose mother Anita had been a stripper. Anita and I had become friends and I had gone out with her sometimes to clubs where she worked, so I knew only too well what these places were like. There was pornography as well as ordinary strip shows and quite often the clubs were raided by the police.

Michael was often at home with me while Eric was working. He spent his life thinking up ways to make money. He seemed unable to accept that his life as a conman was over. Things had changed drastically since his last term in prison. He used to get away with murder – not literally of course – but once journalists had written stories about how people had been conned, it wasn't nearly so easy for him to talk people into things. But he was good company and very amusing, always telling a great story – and I had to admit that on days when I was on my own, I liked to be entertained. He played the piano by ear very well, and we had some enjoyable times together. He was very endearing in spite of his criminal lifestyle.

*****

Eric's job at the factory, like all his other jobs, didn't last too long and he decided to take a franchise on an ice-cream van.

Meanwhile, our marriage was going slowly downhill and I had become very restless. I took advantage of Michael's offer to look after the children to go off to Bath to look for Bob, whom I had never really been able to forget since the age of fifteen.

I found him by going to his mother's house, who still lived in the same place. She was a tiny woman in her eighties, who fussed over him and did everything for him. I've sometimes wondered whether this may have contributed in any way to his OCD. Bob was now living in a bungalow in Weston in Bath where he originally lived with his second wife when they had both been working. I didn't know he had married again until I went to see him in his bungalow. She had left him and he was once again unemployed, still suffering terribly from OCD. I was now thirty-one and as always, let my heart dictate my feelings and actions rather than my head. My heart told me that Bob was still the love of my life and once again I had an affair with him. Understandably, Bob was not happy with me coming to Bath when I could manage, and kept asking me to move in with him.

Meanwhile, at home, Michael was telling me about the girls that Eric was carrying on with while he was at work; and of course the money situation was dire, as I had no control over what Eric was doing. He thought that everything that came over the counter of his ice-cream van was his. Michael showed me a photo of Eric's latest girl.

'He said she's got a face like the back of a bus but big tits, but the problem is that she's only fifteen.'

When Michael told me this, I felt very badly about the girl, as she was very young and he was just using her.

On top of all this, we had a fire in our house, forcing the children and me, along with Michael to be put up in a hotel (although Michael was not gay, there was never any hanky between us). Eric stayed at the house because he had to plug in the ice-cream van.

'He has arranged to see that girl while you're away,' Michael said to me. To be honest, by that time I didn't really care much.

When the house was ready for us to move back into, the insurance cheque was sent to me. I had decided to move to Bath, but not live with Bob as he only had a small bungalow, so I bluffed my way into renting a private house in Weston in Bath, around the corner from him. I wanted to ease the children into the new situation gently.

'I think it would be a good idea if we have a trial separation,' I said to Eric. 'I don't want to sell the house, so see if you can rent out a couple of rooms to help pay the mortgage.'

He agreed to do so, although he was unaware of the affair I was having and didn't know that I knew that he had been having an affair. My knowledge of this affair had finally made me decide on the separation and I didn't feel at all guilty about leaving him. The house in Bath was furnished but Eric moved the things I needed to take with me in a hired van.

'I'll keep in touch,' he said, 'and come and see you when I'm not working.'

I immediately registered a claim for housing benefit and benefits to keep myself and the children, and I also put my name down on the Council housing list, the house agent believing that I had a private income. I got the three older children settled into school and Bob was introduced as a friend.

I had never been just at home without doing anything and was soon very bored. Bob came around most days, but because of his illness, it was usually afternoon before he arrived and, because of the OCD, just being with him was very difficult. For instance, he was constantly washing because of his fear of contamination. Then not long after we arrived in Bath, Michael turned up. I was still very fond of him and I had a spare room so he stayed.

One of his tricks was to open accounts all over the place for groceries, or at the butchers, off-licence and even the hairdressers, all of which he arranged for me to use, so the financial burden for me was suddenly much better. The accounts never got paid of course, because he always had plausible excuses – after all that was his trade, and life was rather different then.

Bob objected to all this on moral grounds, but was quite happy to come around and eat with us most days. I, on the other hand, was not at all uneasy about what Michael did, which was the main reason why Bob and I started to row, because he was quite happy to take whatever Michael provided. We always seemed to be arguing about it and the fact that Michael was there at all. Yet ironically, the other advantage for me in having Michael stay is that most nights I could go around the corner and sleep with Bob.

*****

I kept in touch with Eric and he had visited, as had other friends of mine from Berkshire. The worst problem of course was that when you went back in life, things were never the same. Two of my five children were still very young and all my friends' children were older, so my friends had been able to go back to work. I had found out from Bob that he eventually divorced his first wife after she left him for the second time when she was expecting his son. He had never had anything to do with the child. As for his second wife, he had told me that he married her for the company, and then when she wanted him to take a job managing a news agents with her and he wouldn't, their relationship began to deteriorate.

There were problems back in Reading with the house. I hadn't paid the builders so they had been to court and got a charge on my house and also Eric hadn't kept the mortgage payments up to date, and I was wondering what to do.

I left Michael with the children and went around to stay with Bob. His OCD was at a critical point where almost everything in his mind was contaminated, so we sat in the only available place, the settee. He wanted me to move in with all the children to his one-bedroom bungalow because he thought the council would then be obliged to re-house us and started to go on about my not sorting out living with him and complained about the fact that Eric still visited me.

I had finally had enough and got up.

'It's better if I go home rather than argue with you.'

'That's right, you go home to Michael. I know he must be fucking you.'

I was so shocked that I slapped his face before I even realised what I was doing. I turned around to leave and Bob grabbed me from behind and pushed me into the corner. His eyes were glaring and dark and evil looking. I had never seen him like that before. As he moved away, I staggered up and got out of the front door. Holding my head and crying, I managed to get home. I was clear in my mind: tonight will have to be the end of my relationship with Bob.

Chapter Thirty-Two

David

Eric was no longer working on the ice-cream van and, although I had no idea why, we talked about having another go at our marriage and he came to stay with me in Bath and we worked for a while on a hotdog van.

Michael, meanwhile, had become involved in a shady deal with some solicitor and was talking about bringing diamonds into the country. He went off on his travels and we received the odd postcard from Swaziland and a transfer charge telephone call from there as well. I was left to deal with all the trades people whose accounts he had never paid. But as they weren't my debts, and I wasn't responsible for them, I just told them that he was in Swaziland.

Eric and I decided to move back to the house in Reading and see if we could pick up the pieces. I managed to get the arrears of the mortgage put on the end of the term and got a job in a hospital, working as an auxiliary nurse as I did before, while Eric did a variety of things including working on mobile food vans.

*****

When we lived on the farm in Upper Basildon, I had met a man, through a friend, named David, whose father had a franchise with Citroen cars. He had several garages, including one in Grays Inn Road in London, and a farm and horses. David was six months younger than me and we had struck up a friendship which resulted in a short affair before I went back to live in Bath.

He was a very gentle, understanding person. He loved my children and they felt the same about him. He belonged to the Round Table and at Christmas was always Santa Claus on the sleigh. He was also a very good car salesman in his father's business.

On my return to Reading, I met up with him again from time to time through our mutual friend and our affair started again. It was mainly a respite from life with Eric who once again was always doing things to make life stressful. We had a 50p meter for the electric, but when they came to empty it, he had broken the seal on it and there was only one 50p in it as he has been taking the money and re-using it. The Electricity Board threatened action against him, so I had to come to an arrangement with them to pay off the debt and they put an extra heavy-duty seal on the meter.

My stress was added to further when I found out he had been claiming unemployment benefit while running the ice-cream van. The people who owned the van had told the Benefits Office because he hadn't paid them any of the rental costs for the van or the bills for the wholesale materials. This inevitably meant that the DSS and the owners of the ice-cream van took him to court, which put an even greater strain on us financially, and this was exacerbated by the problem of trying to get all the money from Eric so I could keep the bills and mortgage paid.

So my affair with David gave me some kind of relief from all the strain of work and home life and because he could afford to take me out.

*****

Eric decided to do a BSM course to become a driving instructor, which meant that he would be away for a week. Things between us had become so strained and tense that I just didn't think I could take any more. He didn't bother to speak to me before he left nor phone the children or me while he was gone. My friend from Upper Basildon helped me find a bedsit while Eric was away and moved all of Eric's things into it. When he came home, I was even more relieved that I had decided to break from him, because he had failed the BSM course and was out of work again. He left, but fortunately we remained on friendly enough terms for him to come to see the children.

Being on my own meant that David spent a lot of time with us, which of course his family was unhappy about because I had been married three times and had five children. David and I were thirty-three and he had never been married, and I wasn't exactly what they wanted for their son. David's father even sent him to work in the London garage in the hopes that it would keep us apart, but it only made him more determined and he drove from London every day, staying at my house.

'All this is really not good for the children,' I told him. He was sleeping downstairs and leaving early in the morning, but even I didn't realise what my life was doing to them.

'You must make up your mind what you want,' I said to David. 'If I come with you permanently, my father has said that he will cut me out of the business altogether and even the car belongs to the company.'

'Well, if it's really what you want to do, you have enough experience to get a job and a company car in another car showroom.'

Working and sorting out the children had become impossible so for one of the few times in my life I had to go on to benefits, which I really hated.

*****

Christmas 1978 was a turning point in my life. David spent the day with his family, although he seemed to spend less and less time with them and his father still kept him working in the London branch.

On Boxing Day, he brought food and champagne for the evening and all the children were allowed to stay up. He looked after me and the children as I was ill, but after midnight, Paula, my eldest daughter (then fifteen), who had become very difficult with the rest of the family, had an enormous row with her sister, Lana, and hit her so hard that I really thought she may have broken her jaw. Paula found it hard being part of a large family and had often said that she wished she were an only child. There had been other fights between Paula and her sisters and I was getting to my wits' end.

When my friend Jill from Upper Basildon visited on New Year's Day, she discovered that I hadn't been well over Christmas and said that if I didn't phone Mum to ask for help, she would. She did in fact phone Mum, and my parents came up from Poole to see what they could do to help. As a result, Paula was taken off to live with them.

On the first Sunday in 1979, Michael Howard turned up on my doorstep again needing somewhere to stay. His Jags had always been on loan to him, but this time he had run out of steam and as he didn't have any transport, he needed me to drive him to the Bell Inn at Aston Clinton in Aylesbury, where he was to have lunch with an old friend of his from prison.

The friend was a man named Brendan O'Toole, who had been written about in newspapers over the years as the 'Prince of Conmen'.

'Of course,' said Michael, 'you are invited to lunch as well.'

'The trouble is I don't have anyone to look after the children.'

I plucked up courage to phone David to ask him if he would come and look after them for me. It meant cooking them lunch etc. but David was a good cook and the children loved him anyway. He very generously said he would come and Michael and I set off on the Sunday morning.

As soon as I met Brendan in the bar and our eyes met, my stomach turned over and my heart missed a beat.

He was to be the greatest love of my life.

Part Three

Into the Fire

Chapter Thirty-Three

Brendan

He was warm and friendly with the classic Irish gift of the gab. He was obviously much older than me, with a high domed forehead and twinkling blue eyes and an easy manner that all added to his charm. We had lunch and later went back to Brendan's hotel room and he kissed me. The whole experience had a magnetism I had never felt before. I telephoned David to say I would be late because we're staying on for dinner if it was OK with him.

'Of course it is,' he said. 'Just drive carefully home.'

During the day I spent with Brendan, I learnt that he was staying at the hotel on a stolen credit card and that he was wanted by the police for a whole host of offences related to all sorts of crimes. His attitude was that it was only the big banks that suffered, not individual people. I was still very naive at this stage in my life and although I was thirty-three, apart from my involvement with Michael, I had never been involved in any real crime.

When we were leaving, Michael and I arranged to meet Brendan again at a small village near Pangbourne the following week and then we returned to Reading. Michael left the next day and arranged to come back the following week.

On Monday afternoon, David rang me at home and asked if I could pick him up at the station, which I did.

'What are you doing home now?' I asked.

'Well, I've done it. I've told my father what to do with his job and left the company car, and I've bought the papers to look for a job.'

I was speechless. I didn't know what to say because I knew that the only person I wanted was Brendan, and I couldn't wait to see him again.

I had never been in love with David. He was a good friend, and very fond of my children and I would have had a go at life with him if he had made up his mind about me or his family sooner.

I waited a couple of days and then said to him, 'You have really left this too late, David, and it would be unfair of me to lead you on.'

I explained what I felt when I met Brendan. However, this did not put him off and he was convinced that I would get over it.

*****

I met up again with Brendan when Michael returned, and he asked me to go up to London by train and meet him for a weekend. Michael said he had nowhere to go so he would stay at my place with the children. At this point I seemed to have lost all sense of reason and the only thing I could think about day and night was being with Brendan.

To my shame, my children took second place in my mind and I just wanted someone to stay with them so I could do what I wanted. I took the train from Tilehurst to Reading up to London on 5 January 1979 and Brendan met me at the station. He took me to the hotel he had booked us in at and explained to me about the names we were booked in under, as this was a stolen credit card. We went out elsewhere to eat as he explained that it's best not to run up too much on one credit card in one place. Instead, I used outside phones to ring home and check that the children were OK.

The next day, we went shopping all over London where he used different cards, and in places like Marks & Spencer he bought the goods and got me to take them back to get cash refunds, as neither of us had very much cash. He bought lots of things for my children and a suitcase to put them in.

All this, although I knew was wrong, gave me a great buzz and made the adrenalin flow. We laughed a lot together and had more fun than I had had in years.

He told me about his Irish roots and said that he came from Limerick and had one sister. He led me to believe that there had been a lot of money in the family and that when his parents died when he was seventeen, he had had too much money too young. He had been used to living the extravagant life. He used to ride horses and rode as an amateur in the Grand National.

He had lived all over the world, in Paris, America and Canada but had lived the longest in Spain. He was married for a few years at the age of thirty-six. He spoke fluent Spanish and told me about his writing as a freelance journalist and about things he had written for the magazine *Tit-Bits*.

'I will bring you up to London again,' he said, 'and we will go to the newspaper offices in Fleet Street and the Wig and Pen where the journalists all drink.'

When we were back at the hotel, we were unable to keep our hands off one another. I had never felt like that about any other man in my life. Brendan making love to me was like being in another world, and yet it was not the only attraction. I just felt as if I never wanted to be without him again. When the first weekend was over we went back to Reading together so Brendan could meet the children, but at this point I didn't want him to stay because I didn't think it was fair to the children. I already had Michael sleeping on a put-u-up in the dining room and David kept on calling to see if he could change my mind. Eric was also still in contact as we were in the latter stages of getting a divorce. I was expecting the divorce to be finalised at the beginning of March 1979.

*****

The next time I met Brendan, we went to the Waldorf Hotel in London and he became very edgy when we came back in after dinner, because they spoke to him by name (whichever one he was using, which in this case was Mr Godber), which he thought strange with all the people there. Then he decided that it was probably because they thought I was his wife and there was a large age gap.

'It was my birthday on the tenth,' he said to me.

'How old are you, Brendan?' I asked.

'If I tell you, you probably wouldn't want to see me any more.'

'Of course I would. It doesn't matter to me how old you are, I just want to be with you.'

'You are only thirty-three and I've just turned fifty-five.'

We spent a lot of time talking about what we were going to do as we had no money and we didn't know how we could make it by earning a legitimate living. I of course was still living on benefits and the interest on my mortgage was being paid.

'Can't you go back to writing and work for a living if you come back and live with me?' I said.

This, he explains, would be very difficult as he was wanted by the police and didn't have a National Insurance number or anything else legal for that matter.

'Well, you can still come and live with me anyway,' I said, 'and we'll work out what to do then.'

'I've got an idea,' he said. 'I'm running out of credit cards and cheque books that I can use.'

'What idea?'

Earlier, he had showed me how to use bleach and brake fluid to take the names off of cheque guarantee cards so he could re-sign them so as not to have to try to copy a signature.

'Well, you know David keeps pestering you to go to that hotel in Reading for a dinner and a night with him. We could arrange it so you get his credit cards out of his pocket and I'll get a room in the same hotel for a night and you can bring them to me.'

'How can I do that?' I said. 'It wouldn't be right to do that to him, and anyway that would mean me sleeping with him. Wouldn't you mind?'

'Of course I'd mind,' he said, 'but I know it wouldn't mean anything to you and I really do need them, until I'm able to get other cards and cheque books, or figure out some other way of making money.'

182

When I next spoke with David, I agreed to spend a night away with him. Michael was still around to stay with the children. Brendan phoned me to let me know his room number and I racked my brains as to how I was going to manage to do what I was supposed to do.

*****

David and I arrived at the hotel in Reading in the early evening. He wanted to go to bed with me before we went down to dinner. I was dreading this but I knew I'd have to just put up with it. After we had got up from bed we were going to shower and get ready to go for dinner. I managed to persuade David that I wanted to shower alone so I could get dressed and have time while he was in the bathroom.

I searched his jacket pockets for his wallet and found the small case full of credit cards. I took it and shouted through the bathroom door to him,

'I'm going down to the bar to get us some drinks,' and disappeared out of the door as quickly as I could.

It was a large Post House Hotel and it seemed to take forever for me to run through it until I found Brendan's room.

'Here are his cards,' I said. 'Now you had better make a fairly quick exit before he realises their missing and reports it.' I gave him a quick kiss. 'I love you – phone me tomorrow and let me know where you are.'

I then flew back along the corridors to the bar and got some drinks to take back to our room.

David was ready and waiting for me when I got back. 'Where on earth have you been?' he said.

'I had to wait in the bar.'

'Why didn't you just phone room service?'

'I didn't think of that.'

We drank our drinks and went to dinner. The rest of the night wasn't easy as David was aware of my relationship with Brendan and was still insisting that Brendan was no good for me, and that he, David, would be able to give me and my children a better life. My conscience did prick me a little as the children had known David since they were little and were all very fond of him. David's feelings for us all were such that although he knew about Brendan, he hadn't ever thought of going to the police.

It was only when we were ready to leave next day that David noticed that the small wallet of credit cards was missing. He reported this at reception and of course they looked around the hotel in case it had been dropped. All the details were then given to the police and we left. David dropped me at home.

Brendan phoned to let me know where he was.

'I won't ever ask you to do anything like that again,' he said. 'I went through absolute hell knowing you were sleeping with someone else.'

Then David phoned me in the evening and said he wanted to come to talk to me the next day about his interview with the police. When he arrived I could tell by his manner that something was wrong. He looked at me and said, 'Why did you do it?'

'Do what?'

'Take my credit cards of course. I had given it a lot of thought and came to the conclusion that it had to be you.'

My stomach heaved. 'Have you told the police about your suspicions?'

'No. I haven't told them who it was that was staying with me. You did it because of Brendan, didn't you?'

'Yes, and I'm really, really sorry. You have always been so good to us and you didn't deserve that, but my feelings are in such a state about him, that I would do anything for him. Are you going to tell the police now?'

'No,' he said. 'I will always be your friend and around if you need me, but I really think you are going to get hurt.'

Chapter Thirty-Four

Credit Card Wedding

I was taking off to meet Brendan – we were off to Heathrow Airport with the intention of going to Southern Ireland. We couldn't go anywhere abroad because I didn't have a passport, and of course this was home territory for him. I phoned Michael at home to see how the children were and after talking to Brendan I said, 'It's no good, I can't go away from the children. I'm being a dreadful mother as it is, but I can't leave.'

So instead of getting a plane, we left the airport and drove into London to eat (Brendan always carried an Egan Ronay Good Food Guide) and he asked me if I would marry him.

'Yes of course I will. As soon as my divorce is through.'

After finishing lunch and shopping for things for home and the children, we travelled back to Reading.

While all these trips were going on and we were eating in good hotels and restaurants, we were also doing quite a lot of drinking (which I hadn't done since I was a teenager). When he had cash, Brendan went to the bookies for an odd bet. I thought nothing of this at the time, as Brendan had grown up with horses.

Eric came to see the children and had a go at me again about what I was doing and all the problems ahead. After he had gone and I had tried to think logically about things. I did wonder what we were going to do, without jobs and money and with four children still at home. My benefits didn't really allow for feeding an extra adult and most of the time I had Michael staying as well.

I decided that I shouldn't let my heart rule my head, so I sat Brendan down.

'This is an impossible situation,' I said, 'and I must try to do what is best for everyone.'

We hugged and kissed and shed many tears, but he understood and packed his bag. I drove him to the station.

I busied myself for the next day or two getting things in the house sorted out and of course I still had Michael to keep me company.

Then Brendan phoned to see how I was.

'I can't get you out of my mind,' he said. 'I love you so much.'

He told me that he was in London, staying at the Lancaster Gate Hotel.

'I'm trying to get on with my life,' I said to him, 'but I'm not doing very well. I will never be able to forget you and I will always love you.'

*****

After the phone call, I sat in the lounge talking to Michael, who of course had known Brendan on and off for years.

'All I did was take you to lunch with the man,' he said. 'You weren't supposed to bloody well fall in love with him.'

'I didn't do it on purpose. It was something that just happened and now I feel as if there's no point to my life at all.'

'Well, if he really means that much to you, you might as well go to him and bring him back and figure out some way of working things out.'

I didn't need to be told twice. I packed a small bag, jumped into the car and headed for London. At the hotel reception I took a chance on the name he would be using.

'I've come to see Mr Godber – I'm his wife.' I had got the name right and they gave me Brendan's room number. He opened the door, pulling me into his room and hugging me so tightly I could hardly breathe. We almost ripped the clothes off each other, as we just couldn't wait to make love.

After we had got up and got dressed, we talked again about what we

186

could do, but could come to no long-term conclusion, only that we had to be together. I rang home and assure the children that I would be back the next day.

Within a couple of days of my return from London with Brendan in February 1979, Michael decided to up and leave, and got on with his next wild scheme. Brendan and my children got on well together, especially after he got them a Labrador. I should have learnt from the dog that Brendan's temper was sometimes out of control. The dog soon learned to do what she was told or she got beaten or kicked until she did, but of course this was done in such a way that I really didn't see any of the bad bits until I wondered why the dog growled at me when I tried to move her.

*****

After my divorce came through, we planned to get married on 5 March 1979, but we didn't want to tell anyone because we still didn't know what to do about my claim for benefits or whether different offices might tie things together and let the police know about Brendan.

Nothing about our wedding was normal. Brendan had purchased my wedding ring on one of our shopping sprees in London with a stolen credit card.

'Promise me you won't change after we are married,' I said to Brendan on the day.

'Why would I change?' he replied.

'Because people always seem to after their married.'

And I should know. With hindsight, I think it's because they tell you very little of the truth about themselves before you are married.

I took my youngest child Julie to nursery at lunchtime and then we went to a public house close to the register office and asked the landlady and a friend of hers, neither of whom we had ever met before, to be witnesses. We spent our wedding night in a hotel in Oxfordshire under someone else's name, paid for on their credit card.

We had been married for three weeks before we told anyone, and only then because one of the neighbours stopped her daughter coming to our house because she thought we were living together.

I heard very little from my parents except when they brought my eldest daughter Paula to me in the school holidays, and although they knew that I had married again I had told them that Brendan was a freelance journalist – I thought this was at least half true as this was in the fact the case many years ago.

From the time we met, we had celebrated our anniversary every month by going out for a meal. Brendan consulted the Egan Ronay Good Food Guide, found somewhere far enough away from where we lived for it to be safe to use a card and off we went. This continued until one evening in May, when we were in a restaurant out in the countryside.

We had finished our meals and we were ready for the bill. I always sat opposite Brendan, so I could watch what they did with the card before bringing it back for signing and whether they were making a telephone call.

'They're phoning,' I said to Brendan. 'Take the car keys and go.' (We never parked outside.)

'What are you going to do?' he asked.

'Never mind me. I'll get a taxi. Just go quickly.'

And he left.

When the owner came over to the table where I was still sitting he asked me where Brendan had gone.

'I think he's gone to the gents.'

'I think it's more likely that he has left, as this card is stolen.'

I gasped and acted really shocked and surprised.

'How did you get here?' he asked.

'By taxi.'

'Do you know him well?'

'No,' I replied, 'I just met him tonight in a bar.'

'I'm going to have to call the police. What are you going to do?'

I was afraid he might try to keep me there so I said in a nervous, anxious voice,

'Can you ring for a taxi for me please as I'm a married woman with children at home and I don't want to be involved in this?'

'I can understand that,' he said and rang for a taxi.

'I'll go and wait outside for it,' I told him.

The restaurant was so deep in the wilds that there were no street lights so it was pitch black outside. As I was standing there I saw a vehicle crawling towards me without any lights and then realised it was Brendan. I got into the car quickly.

'Why the hell did you hang around?' I said. 'I told you to go home.'

'I just couldn't go and leave you there.'

He drove into the lanes that run through the woods, then put the lights on and went like hell. We worried all the way home, fully expecting to have the police waiting for us there, but all seemed to be clear and quiet. Indoors we clung to each other.

'If we get away with tonight, that's the last time we do it,' I told him. 'Promise me you'll get rid of all the cards and go straight now.'

'I promise. I'm never going to risk anything else now that you're my wife.'

Miraculously we got away with it that night.

Chapter Thirty-Five

Jeremy Thorpe and Me

Since the time we got married, we had spent a lot of time looking at all sorts of businesses we could go into if I sold the house, because property had gone up and I would have quite a bit of capital. That way Brendan could work with me without anyone actually knowing anything about him. But one thing that had started to bother me was Brendan's gambling. He always seemed to be betting on the horses and whenever there was racing on TV he would be glued to it. He had also, without my realising it, opened accounts at bookmakers that I didn't know about at the time. On Saturdays when he was watching the racing all afternoon, quite often David came around to see the children and me. He had accepted the situation and was still a good friend.

We had put my house on the market and after travelling all over the country, found a fish and chip shop in Treherbert in the Rhonda Valley in South Wales. Property there was cheap and we could afford to buy this without a mortgage and the owner had agreed to teach us the trade. There was a three-bedroom flat above. Meanwhile, we still needed money and Brendan had an idea about how we might be able to make some out of a court case in June 1979.

In 1967, the Leader of the Liberal Party, Jeremy Thorpe, then aged thirty-seven, was in the limelight for nearly a decade. Thorpe was a homosexual and had had an affair with Norman Scott in the early 1960s. In 1975, Scott wrote to the press telling this story but also alleging that Thorpe had tried to have him killed to keep him quiet. Scott also sold letters from Thorpe to the press. Because of all the media attention Thorpe was forced to stand down in 1976 as Liberal Leader. He was subsequently charged with conspiracy to murder on 20 November 1978, and after a 31-

day trial he was cleared of the charge on 22 June 1979.

Before the trial began, Brendan said it might be possible for me to write an article for a magazine if he was found guilty and decided on the German magazine *Der Spiegel*. Before the end of the trial he had managed to get *Der Spiegel* to pay for us to go to London and stay in a hotel for two nights, but the part of the deal I didn't know about until I got there was that I was expected to go to the house Thorpe was staying at and talk to him with a tape recorder running in my bag. I was absolutely terrified.

'What am I supposed to say to him?' I asked. 'That's if I even get to speak to him.'

'Don't worry, we'll tell you what to say and what to ask him,' I was told by someone from *Der Spiegel*.

The evening that I was put in the taxi to go to see him, I was so frightened I didn't even remember the address. Fortunately, they had told the driver the address when they put me in the taxi. When I arrived at a large house in a row of terrace mansions and ring the bell, I expected a minder or underling to open the door to try to prevent people getting at him, and to be asked who I was and what business I had with him. I was literally shaking in my shoes because I had been expecting to have to try to talk my way in, but to my complete amazement, Jeremy Thorpe himself opened the door. I said whatever it was I had been briefed to say – that I would like to talk to them about the trial – and then he just smiled and invited me in.

At this point, I could hardly believe what was happening. After all, I was basically a housewife with five children, on my fourth husband with three failed marriages behind me, and with a poorly paid job to earn a bit of extra money. Yet there I was in the house of one of the most famous people in the country and at that moment it was just him and me.

I must admit that in a suit and make-up I scrubbed up well and could look the part and although I didn't really have a clue what I was doing. The two men from the magazine had briefed me well and had taken a calculated risk that I would look less intimidating than they would in carrying out this mission. But, as you can imagine, I was still completely terrified.

'Mary, can you come down?' he called up the stairs.

His wife Mary Thorpe came down and the three of us sat in a room and chatted. I was completely in awe of them and of my surroundings and all I could register was that it must be the living room and it had very high ceilings. I sat on a settee just inside the lounge door and they sat on two armchairs facing me.

I talked about the things I had been told about by *Der Spiegel* and asked whatever questions they had briefed me to ask and the whole time I was expecting them to notice that I had this machine in my bag recording every word he said.

The Thorpes were both very pleasant. We chatted about the possible outcome of the trial and he seemed completely unfazed, as he was adamant that he was not guilty. I was unable to get anything very specific out of him, but that was not surprising as I had never done anything remotely like that before. In any case, I was on autopilot as I was terrified that they might realise that I was keeping my handbag on my lap as there was a tape recorder running in it. I had visions of them ringing the police to arrest me.

I was there about ten minutes and then they politely ended the interview and they both came to the front door together to see me out. After I had left, I had to hail a cab myself to get back to the hotel. The magazine was very pleased with what I had on tape. Brendan and I went home next day and when the jury retire to deliberate for fifteen hours, we imagined there would be a guilty verdict. When he was cleared I actually felt a little relieved as he was so charming, but of course, at the same time, we were upset as the story was now of no use to *Der Spiegel*.

However we managed financially and progressed with the sale of the house and buying the shop.

Chapter Thirty-Six

Stranded in Wales

We visited Treherbert again and met a couple with a guest house who were very friendly and also had young children with one about the same age as my oldest that was at home, Amy. We were due to move in September 1979, but the school term started a couple of weeks before, so as Amy, who was coming with us, was at comprehensive school, we arranged for her to stay with these people for two weeks before we arrived.

Selling my house was on track and we had decided to buy almost everything new in Wales so we had a big sale at the house some weeks before and almost everything was bought, even the cooker. Most people were prepared to collect things just before we left, but the cooker was taken weeks before and I had to cook for the family with a slow cooker and one small camping ring.

We then discovered that the third bedroom over the shop had been built over the house next door, which created legal problems, but we were assured that it shouldn't take too long to sort out. We phoned the guesthouse and book rooms for the rest of us as we had no alternative but to go because the house had been sold. Then we hired a transit van to take with us all the things we had kept, and left for Wales. After breaking down just before the Severn Bridge, we finally arrived and settled into the guesthouse. Amy was at school, so the first thing to do was to sort out schools for the other two, Lana and Andrew, as my youngest, Julie, wasn't yet school age.

At this point I made one of my biggest mistakes ever. I opened a joint bank account with Brendan into which I put the cheque I had received for my house. As this was now a joint venture, I wanted to make everything ours between us. I really thought that it was going to work out well. But then we saw the solicitors dealing with the purchase of the shop and found out that things weren't as straightforward as we had been led to believe. It might take weeks to sort out, if they were able to sort it out at all.

'What are we going to do about money?' I said to Brendan. 'All the time we're staying in this guest house we're using capital and we'll end up without enough money to go ahead if we're not careful.'

I then agreed with Brendan's suggestion that we look for a house and try to claim benefits until we were able to work. A few days later, we met a lady named Norma in the local pub.

'It must be costing you a lot of money staying in the guest house,' she said after hearing our story. 'I've got room in my house. It would be a lot cheaper for you to come and stay with me.'

We accepted gratefully and moved into her council house. The problems with finding a house soon became obvious. Most of them were built on hills and suffered from subsidence.

During these first weeks in Wales, I started feeling very sick and unwell.

'I think I'm pregnant,' I told Brendan.

He was delighted, but obviously bothered about the situation we were in. I visited the doctor and my pregnancy was confirmed, but I was so sick that I couldn't get out of bed most of the day, so he prescribed tablets for me. They didn't really help much, but I took them anyway. I had never been like that with any of my other pregnancies – I was almost unable to put my feet on the ground until the evening without being sick, so Brendan was left to get the children to school and collect them and feed them. However, I didn't seem to see much of him during the rest of the day, and I suspected he was spending his time either in the bookies or the pub. We had still only been in Wales for a few weeks when Brendan collected the children from school one afternoon, went out again and didn't return.

That evening Norma asked me where he was, and I say I don't know. Later that night I found a short note under Brendan's pillow saying that I would be better off without him.

*****

The next day, no matter how ill I felt, I dragged myself out of bed, see to the children and go straight to the bank. I had been awake all night with the terrible thought that he may have taken all my money, although he had left my car.

I told the cashier I wanted to close my account and that I wanted it in cash. She asked me to wait a minute so I took a seat and then the bank manager called me into his office.

'I'm sorry to tell you but your husband has been coming in for days taking out cash, and yesterday he took half of what was left.'

'Well then, just give me what's left now.'

'Are you sure you want it in cash?'

'Yes.'

I had no idea what I was going to do. When he had given me the cash, I went back to speak to Norma, explaining that Brendan had left me and the children and that I didn't really know what I was going to do, as I didn't have enough money left to buy anything as I had planned.

'Please don't worry,' she said, 'you can stay with me until you've worked something out.'

I explained to the children as best I could, because of course they had no idea about Brendan's criminal history.

I accepted what Norma said and settled myself down to think. The furniture we had brought to Wales with us (the children's beds and some other bits and pieces) were stored at the shop and all my friends were in Berkshire. Getting in touch with them didn't seem like a good idea because they warned me in the beginning and now I was pregnant as well, and still feeling really ill – and I also had a cough and sore throat.

That evening Norma's son Alan arrived. 'Right, I want you all out of my mother's house now,' he said, much to my amazement.

'Where can I go at this time of night with four children?'

'I don't care. Just get out now.'

Outside it was raining, just as it has been most of the time since we arrived.

'Come on,' I said to the children. 'Get together what things you can and get in the car. I've only got a small car,' I added to Alan. 'Can I come back for the rest of our things?'

'Yes, but don't leave it too long. I'll put them in the shed.'

By the time we were all in the car it was 7 p.m., so I drove to the nearest phone box and rang social services. I was put through to a duty officer who was unsure what to do.

'Stay where you are until I come for you,' she finally said.

It was only thirty minutes but it seemed like an eternity sitting in the car with the children who were naturally very upset.

'I've managed to find one room in a hotel for you for tonight at least,' she said, 'and we'll try to sort something out tomorrow.'

The hotel was in fact a pub with sawdust on the floor and a room or two to let upstairs. We were given a room with two beds in it. The three younger children shared a double bed and I shared a small bed with Amy, who was fourteen and a half years old.

'I'll try to find somewhere more appropriate for you tomorrow or the day after,' said the social worker.

'Can we get anything to eat here for the morning?' I asked (fortunately we had had dinner).

'No. There's a shop down the road and you can probably buy something there.'

After she had left, the situation began to sink in, Brendan had left me in Wales with four children and expecting his child, and taken half my money with him. His farewell note was quite pathetic and when I looked at things clearly I realised he had been gambling and drinking the money away and couldn't face telling me and of course I had no idea what we were going to do.

The only person I had to talk to and give me any support was Amy, which was hardly fair on her at her age, but she was my rock for months to come.

Chapter Thirty-Seven

Refuge

Amongst the things we had brought with us were a cassette player and a few tapes. Amy went downstairs to buy a bottle of dry martini and a bottle of lemonade and to borrow some glasses.

'Mum,' she said when she came back, 'they looked at me as if I was from another planet when I asked for Dry Martini, and I don't think they've ever heard of it. It's a real spit and sawdust down there.'

They had sold her a cheap bottle of sherry instead. The younger children were very tired and we put sloppy love songs on the cassette player (including Brendan's favourite, 'Chanson d'Amour') and they soon went to sleep. Amy knew how desperately I loved Brendan and I blamed myself because I thought he hadn't trusted me enough to talk to me. Now I had no way of finding him. We sat for ages drinking the awful sherry, with me crying and desperate. Eventually we slept fitfully in the small bed. The next morning, we were at a loss what to do, so we walk to the shop and bought bread, butter, bananas and cake. We borrowed a knife from the people downstairs to put butter on the bread and I made banana sandwiches and cake for lunch.

The social worker re-appeared in the afternoon. 'I've found you a place in a women's refuge,' she said. 'At least it will be better than here.'

We piled into the car and followed her. At the refuge, we all shared one large room with a single bed for me and two sets of bunks for the children. We were shown where things were and how they arranged food. At first the other women seemed quite hostile towards me, maybe because I was not a battered wife and I had a car.

In the next few days, I became quite ill with the cough and sore throat and I was still feeling sick, so one of the women suggested I go to the doctors, and told me where it was.

'Leave the children,' she said. 'We'll see to them.'

The doctor put me on antibiotics and within three or four days I was feeling much better and not coughing all night.

As the women gradually got to know the position I was in, I found they were very nice and we all helped each other.

I started to wonder how I could find out where Brendan was and I made a few calls to Fleet Street and spoke with someone who knew him years ago. I didn't know why I imagined he could help me, but I got him to promise that he would get in touch if the papers heard that he had been picked up anywhere.

Meanwhile the council in Wales were arguing with the council in Berkshire as to who should be responsible for housing the children and me. The Benefits Department had also managed to track me down as well because I had cashed my benefit up until the week I cleared the cheque for my house and then I posted my benefit book back. They wrote that they knew I had been married and not declared it because they had a copy of my marriage certificate and gave me a day and time when they wanted to see me in their office. I went to the appointment and explained that I hadn't really thought it would matter, as my husband hadn't been working and that if I had declared it we could actually have claimed more. They advised me that what I had done was still fraud and I would be hearing from them again when they have decided what they intended to do.

*****

After Brendan had been gone for a couple of weeks, I heard from the police that he was in Bristol, having been picked up for using a stolen card, with quite a lot of money on him. He had told them that the money was mine and they wanted to check. They said that there was also a car that he bought that was now in one of their car pounds.

The girls in the refuge were brilliant and looked after my children while I went to Bristol. The police wanted to question me but they let me see Brendan first. We had a short while together in one of the police cells. In spite of everything, I clung to him and my feelings were just as strong.

'Don't say anything to them,' he said. 'I've told them that I will put my hands up to everything as long as they leave you out of it.'

We said a very tearful goodbye and I was taken to a police interview room. They asked many questions about the fact that there had been lots of reports from people that Brendan had always been with a dark-haired woman for the six previous months. They knew that I was married to him, but we obviously didn't want them to know that I had been with him when he had been doing anything criminal.

'How should I know who he was with?' I replied. 'There are very many dark-haired women.'

They questioned me for an hour although they promised Brendan that they wouldn't. But I did as Brendan had told me and said nothing that would involve me.

The next few weeks were taken up with trying to do the best that I could for the children (having only told Amy what was really going on) and running backwards and forwards to Horfield Prison in Bristol.

Feeling very alone on those journeys and having no one I could talk, to I got in touch once again with Bob. Although when I left Bath, we hadn't parted happily, I still felt that he was one of my oldest friends, having known him since I was fifteen years old. We spent time together and I told him about Brendan and the baby I was expecting. I also told him that I knew Brendan was likely to go to prison for a very long time.

'Look at the practical side of things,' he said. 'You've already got five children. Do you think it's wise to have another one next year to bring up on your own?'

By next morning he had persuaded me to book an appointment the following week at an abortion clinic. Of course, I didn't keep the appointment. This was Brendan's baby that I was expecting and he was still the love of my life. I had every intention of waiting for him. I really wanted this baby.

By November, the councils had decided that Berkshire should be responsible for us and we were given a council house in a small village called Frilsham about eight miles outside Newbury. Amy and I moved the things we had taken to Wales in a hired Luton van back to Berkshire. The house was in a dreadful state, an old Rayburn being the only means of heat or hot water. We had no idea how to work it and filled the house with smoke several times before we mastered it. We carried one small portable fan heater around with us while we got beds put up for the children and we bought basic things second hand, so that we were able to travel back to Wales to collect the other three children.

Over the next month Amy and I worked hard together to sort out the house and arrange schools. Christmas was fast approaching. I was also trying to visit the prison in Bristol where Brendan was on remand which wasn't easy as I had to travel from Frilsham in Berkshire, there were the children to sort out, and of course money was very short. I also had to find a solicitor for him for when he appeared in Crown Court at the beginning of 1980. While worrying about Brendan and his court case, I head from the Benefits Agency that they were going to take me to court in January for fraud because I had married and not declared it.

Chapter Thirty-Eight

Trial

Mum and Pop were going to bring Paula to stay for Christmas. I had been continually lying to Mum about where Brendan was, saying that he was working abroad. Mum arrived at Frilsham with Paula, though Pop stayed in the car. I hadn't told Mum about my pregnancy and hope she wouldn't notice, but of course one of the first sentences to me was,

'Are you putting on weight, Janey, or are you pregnant?'

Reluctantly, I told her I was pregnant and this didn't go down very well. Having to keep up the happy-go-lucky pretence that everything was fine wasn't easy. Fortunately, Mum didn't stay very long, but it didn't end there because I had to keep up the pretence for the children, and only Amy knew what I was going through.

Christmas went well for my children and me, given the stress I was under, but I was quite relieved when Paula was collected (a lot of questions had been asked about Brendan and I had made up a story about him being a journalist working in Spain; this story seemed best as he *had* been a journalist and had lived in Spain) and I could start to think about the urgency of seeing the solicitor about my own case as well as Brendan's. In January 1980, my case came up in the Magistrates Court and I explained why I hadn't said anything about my marriage.

'How did you manage to live on the money?' one of the magistrates asked.

'With difficulty, madam, and mostly on egg and chips,' I replied.

In spite of all of their supposed understanding and the fact that we could have actually claimed more money, they decided that technically it was still fraud. They put me on probation and made an order for me to pay back the money. They had decided that other people could learn lessons from my case.

Of course the repercussions of this were to affect my children as later in the week, a friend rang and asked if I had seen the local paper. I replied that I hadn't because I didn't buy it.

'Well, your case is on the front page,' she said, so the older children had to face this at school.

Besides all these things, they were taking money from the benefits. I was getting then to pay back the debt before it was paid to me.

*****

Although Brendan had been picked up with quite a lot of my money still with him, my solicitor had been unable to get it back, because they had to wait for a High Court judge to decide whether any other person that he had defrauded has a greater claim for compensation. However the police had decided to release the car he had bought and said that I could collect it from the pound in Swindon. It was just one more chore for me to get to Swindon to bring it back and sell it.

Because of the shortage of money and the cost of my trips to Bristol to see Brendan and the solicitor in Reading, I took a part-time cleaning job (in spite of my pregnancy), which I continued until the end of March. Times were hard and I didn't know how I could get through it.

In February 1980, the time had come for the solicitor to find a barrister for Brendan's case in March. He discussed it with me and said there was an exceptionally good man in London named David Whitehouse. He made an appointment for him and me to go to his Chambers and see him. Mr Whitehouse, of course, had all the prosecution papers, but asked me to go through everything I knew since I met Brendan. He said he would look into this case and asked if I was prepared to go into the witness box. I said of course I was. My solicitor and I left with a date to go back to see him when he had had time to go through all the papers to see whether he could make any case for Brendan.

When we returned to London the following week, I was utterly shocked at what Mr Whitehouse told me: having dug up all he could about Brendan, he had found that for the previous twenty-five years, Brendan had actually been sentenced to a total of twenty-five years in prison. He had of course been out some of the time because of parole etc. He said that he thought the only way he could try to make a case for him was to use the fact that he met me and I was expecting his baby, and so it was a case of his being 'saved at the eleventh hour' and been given a chance for a new start – even though he was fifty-six years old.

'Are you prepared to be grilled in a witness box?' he asked me.

'I'll do anything it takes to get him as short a sentence as possible,' I replied.

I left with my solicitor that day feeling as if I was going to be having our baby on my own in May, and would probably be on my own for a very long time afterwards.

*****

The next two or three weeks before the trial were very difficult. I was cleaning for other people to have money to run the car and visit Brendan, and I was still lying to the neighbours and my children's school friends about where my husband was.

Amy and I were also decorating and sorting the house so that it was ready for when the baby was born. I was still lying to Mum and Paula on the phone about where Brendan was. The children had also suffered in school over my prosecution by the DSS and, living in a village, people talked a lot. Fortunately at this time Mum and Pop never visited.

The day of the trial finally came. When we arrived at Bristol Crown Court, my solicitor said that we couldn't possibly have been given a worse judge. His name was Desmond Vowden and he was known to be particularly hard.

We had the last conversation with Mr Whitehouse, who went briefly over everything with me and made sure that I was confident about everything that was going to happen.

The prosecution case didn't take too long as Brendan had done as he had promised and cooperated with the police investigation. There was also the £3500 that Brendan still had left of my money when he was arrested. The police seemed to think that it should be used as compensation for his fraud.

I was the only person to go into the witness box for the defence. The police asked me some questions but it was actually Judge Vowden who spoke to me mostly, after he had heard everything that David Whitehouse had to say, which was that after the dreadful record Brendan had before he was with me, this might be the time to give him a chance. He also made the case that the money had been mine from the sale of my house, so I had a prior claim to it. After Judge Vowden had questioned me about our relationship and whether I thought I would be able to keep him on the straight and narrow, he did his summing up of the whole case.

'Either I put you away for a very long time or I give you a last chance,' and decided he needed time to think about this and adjourned his decision for a week.

The next week felt like a month. It dragged on because if Judge Vowden decided on prison, it would be a very long sentence. The day finally arrived and I was back again at Bristol Crown Court. It was a nightmare waiting as the judge was held up and when we finally got into court and Brendan was in the dock waiting to hear what was going to happen to him, I was in a cold clammy sweat and feeling sick. Judge Vowden dragged it out, going through everything again. Then said he had decided under the circumstances (myself and the baby) to put Brendan on probation for two years. On hearing this, I started to cry and really thought I might have fainted. He also made an order for the police to return my money to me.

I thanked David Whitehouse and my solicitor and went to collect Brendan, as I had driven myself up that day, just in case he was coming home. Brendan hugged and kissed me, then grabbed my hand.

'Where's the car? Let's go.'

We ran as fast as I could manage (I was seven months by now), to where I had the car parked.

'What the hell was all that about?' I said, once we were out on the road, driving home.

Then he told me.

'Scottish law is different from English law and as some of my offences were in Scotland they could have been waiting to re-arrest me if they had felt so inclined.'

Chapter Thirty-Nine

Kevin

The homecoming was wonderful, but after a couple of days we had to think again about what we were going to do to earn a living.

Brendan had drawn to my attention a newspaper article about a woman who had found a small shop and opened a baked potato bar.

'Why don't we try to do the same in Newbury?'

'Well,' I said, 'we don't have enough capital to set it up with and I doubt whether we could find premises we could afford.'

We scanned newspapers and agents and managed to find a very small shop about twelve foot square and a tiny shed a few doors away (for storage) in a small arcade of shops, which were all owned by the same man, for £25 a week. He wanted to rent it on a week-to-week basis but Brendan managed to persuade him to give us a seven-year lease. Armed with this, he made an appointment with the bank manager, fed him a story about coming back from abroad and somehow managed to borrow money, unsecured, for us to start up this business. It was put in a joint account ready for our use when we need it.

The shop needed a lot of basic work – scraping off old wallpaper and general decorating and cleaning. The problem was that I was not far away from having the baby so it was really hard work.

Brendan had managed to source all the equipment and workmen we would need and things were all going well. In the middle of May 1980, my sixth and last child was born, a boy, Kevin. Brendan was over the moon as it was his only child, but home life changed drastically for me and my other children. Everything now revolved around Kevin and my other children could never do anything right and Brendan became very nasty towards them. On visits to his probation officer, he admitted he treated my children diabolically, but seemed unable to help himself.

*****

We planed to open the shop on August Bank Holiday. I had been available as much as possible, taking Kevin with me, but I still had to look after the other children and I left Brendan to sort out most of the paying. Then a bank statement arrived and I found that the account was almost empty, there were bills to pay, the shop wasn't finished and Brendan had gambled away the money.

'What the hell do you think we're going to do now, Brendan? If we can't finish the shop, we can't make payments off the loan.'

He just did his usual thing, which was to say how sorry he was and that he didn't mean to do it.

I made a clean breast of it to the bank manager, explained what Brendan was like and what had happened to the money and asked if he could lend me enough money to get the shop finished and opened as otherwise he was unlikely to get any of the money back.

He thought about it for a while and then said, 'I feel that you can do this and I'm prepared to lend you the extra money once you've taken this form for your husband to sign to take his name off the account.'

He wished me luck and even came around to the shop to see me when we were open. The opening of the shop was even better than we could have imagined, probably because it was something different, and we were really busy with a very good turnover. I employed a lady to help me with the baby in the shop, taking him for walks and feeding him. Kevin was born with a cleft palate, fortunately only the soft palette at the back of the mouth, but it had made feeding him very difficult right from birth and he would have to go into hospital to have it repaired.

*****

Although there was now no shortage of money, life with Brendan was becoming very difficult. He would start an argument over anything; I thought some of it was to cover up for his own inadequacies such as his gambling and drinking during the afternoon when the shop was closed. He had a real Irish temper and swore profusely.

We had very little time together as a family because the shop was open through lunch and during the evening hours Monday to Friday and all day on a Saturday. We lunched out most Sundays, but because it was difficult to get cleaners for Sundays, we sometimes had to clean the ovens ourselves on a Sunday.

Brendan always drank too much at Sunday lunchtime and one Sunday afternoon when he was in the storeroom, a drunken man came into the shop.

'Are you open?' he asked.

'No I am afraid we're not,' I replied.

Just then Brendan, rushed in and yelled,

'What the fuck are you doing, talking to my wife?'

Before the man could speak, Brendan caught him by the lapels of his jacket and dragged him out into the alleyway and into a corner, where he beat and kicked him unmercifully. I was absolutely horrified: I had never seen his temper quite that bad and I didn't know what to do, so I took the first-aid box and a bowl of water outside and bathed some of the cuts and checked that he was breathing and managed to roll him onto his side. All that time, Brendan was yelling at me to leave the no good bastard alone.

'He didn't do anything,' I tried to tell him, but he wouldn't listen. The man had had some sort of raincoat over his arm, so I covered him with it and we left.

I drove home and the whole way Brendan kept shaking and screaming at me about this man, until in the end I stopped about a mile from home.

'Get out!' I said. 'I can't stand any more. Perhaps a walk will calm you down.'

Amazingly, he got out and slammed the door. I started to move away, but I was so cross that something snapped in my head and I stopped and

211

reversed the car and I really had hoped I would hit him, but he saw what I was doing and managed to jump over the wire fence into the field. I put the car in gear and screamed off home.

I realised that day that there was a very fine line between love and hate – in fact, because of how much I loved Brendan, the line almost merged into one. When he got back that Sunday, he took a few things, including the week's takings from the shop, and left.

*****

Being left on the Monday without transport I was unable to do very much – apart from getting the children to school – as I was eight miles out of Newbury, and I wondered what on earth I was going to do about the shop.

I had a very good friend, Angela who lived just outside Reading, and she dropped everything and came over. I was able to borrow her car and put a note on the shop door to say we were closed due to illness, but I didn't want the shop closed any longer than necessary as it would be bad for business.

Angela had been unable to work for some while for health reasons so she offered to look after the children while I tried to find Brendan. It was impossible to run the shop and the home without help, and although Amy, now fifteen, was marvellous, I had her education to think about.

I searched through Brendan's things for clues, having had no luck with the bookies or pub landlords, except one who told me that Brendan spent the Sunday night there. He also told me how much time Brendan spent there and at the bookies across the road and how much money he had been spending.

By then it was Monday evening and children are aware there was more trouble, but they were much more relaxed because Brendan wasn't there to keep shouting, bullying and pushing them around.

As Angela and I were checking through his pockets, she made a discovery.

'Look, Janey, I've found this card with a jockey's name on it. It's written on the back of a pub card in Lambourne.'

'Oh of course. It's so obvious – why didn't I think of it?'

After our evening meal I drove to Lambourne. When I walked into the pub, Brendan was in his favourite place, propping up the bar.

'What the fuck do you want?'

'I need you to come home so we can get the shop opened up.'

'Well, I'm not coming. I'm sick of it.'

'So am I. You're not pulling your weight. You're always gambling and drinking when you should be working and I've got our baby to see to, who never sleeps at night, and I'm the one up at six every morning cooking fillings for the potatoes in the shop.'

'Well, that's your problem. I'm not coming back.'

Part of me would have loved to just leave him, and I knew it would be best for my children, but the other part of me thought that I still desperately loved him and that I couldn't manage without him. I spent a couple of hours talking to him and also in a way using our son to make him feel guilty.

'OK,' he said finally. 'I'll come home tomorrow and we'll give it another go.'

He arrived home on Tuesday afternoon and we re-opened the shop the next day. We had seen the consultant at the John Radcliffe Children's Hospital about repair to Kevin's palette – the operation would be in October. I would be in hospital with him for ten days so I needed to get things worked out. Brendan had said he could manage the shop. We had started buying hot fillings from cash and carry (although we had lost trade because they were no longer home-made) to lessen my workload. And although by then, Amy hated him, she said she would help him. Finally I got in touch with an agency, Country Cousins, who arranged for someone to live in for two weeks to look after everything at home.

Chapter Forty

Compulsions

On the morning of the hospital admittance, I rang to check bed availability and they told me the operation had been cancelled because of a bed shortage. I explained my situation and the arrangements I had put in place. They just said 'sorry, we can't help that'. I got off the phone in tears.

Brendan was absolutely furious and phoned them himself, insisting on speaking to the surgeon, who was absolutely wonderful and said that they had been told that he didn't want any of his cleft palette patients cancelled. He apologised for the stress we had been caused and said bring him in as agreed.

It had been very hard ever since Kevin was born, but the day I carried him to the theatre door and handed him over to a nurse was dreadful, even though I knew that a lot of children had worse problems than my son.

It was during this time in the hospital that one of my own long-term problems began: compulsive eating. It had plagued my life ever since. It started to a degree when I brought the baby home from hospital after his birth; he was unable to feed and the doctor could find no reason for it. It wasn't until my midwife found that he was dehydrating and suggested on the phone that I try feeding him off a spoon. He took the milk from a spoon and I rang her back.

'I know what's wrong with him,' she said. 'I will arrange for you both to go back to the hospital.'

In those few days I put on half a stone with my compulsive eating from stress. I got it under control then, but at the return to hospital for his operation, it returned with a vengeance.

*****

After Kevin's successful operation and recuperation, I tried to work in the shop as much as possible. Takings were dropping when I was not there because as soon as Brendan could, he closed up shop and went to the bookies. Amy told me how much of the work she had had to do while I was at the hospital, which made me feel very guilty.

Brendan's temper was getting worse (I later realised it was mostly when he was losing money) so there were many arguments and fights when I accused him of gambling away our money or spending it on booze. He was dreadful to my children though, expecting them to help with scrubbing potatoes and getting the older ones Amy and Lana to look after the younger ones while I worked. I took the baby with me whenever I possibly could.

With Christmas of 1980 fast approaching, I suggested to Brendan that we go to Ireland to see his sister Maureen. I had only ever spoken to her on the phone. We booked an overnight crossing for Christmas Eve, opened the shop lunchtime and then left for the ferry. The crossing was appalling and the children and I were really ill. We drove to the hotel not far from Limerick (where Brendan was brought up), which had a varied programme for the children at Christmas. We were booked there for four nights, with all the usual Christmas entertainment and food. It rained constantly so Brendan took the four children to Limerick Races on Boxing Day and I stayed at the hotel with the baby who was seven months old.

After that, we moved to a hotel close to Dublin where we met up with Maureen and her husband Pat. During these few days my eyes were opened about my husband's former life. Maureen revealed that most of what Brendan had told me of his life was a complete fabrication. He was the youngest of a family of five, not just one sister as he had told me, but he had had nothing to do with the others (only Maureen) because he was the black sheep of the family. He only went back to them when he needed money. They had virtually washed their hands of him. There was a bond between Brendan and Maureen and he had kept in touch although she admitted he usually wanted something when he contacted her.

Brendan had told me he had been brought up in Limerick and that the family had money (not that they worked for it) when in fact they were all brought up in Dublin where his mother had owned and run a small hotel. His father had been an engineer. I thought this lie was because Brendan wanted to be regarded as upper class whereas in fact his mother had to work very hard for the money that enabled them all to go to boarding school.

One of Brendan's sayings was 'I managed to survive a Catholic upbringing' and in that respect he had actually been telling the truth: Maureen told me what dreadful lives they had at these schools that were run by nuns and monks.

She also said that he had used the name Brendan O'Toole since he was seventeen and that it was not the family name.

'Did he actually go to Trinity College and get a BA which he always said he has when he gives lessons in English Literature or Spanish?' I asked.

'Of course he didn't, because in our day Trinity College wasn't open to Catholics.'

'Was he in the Army as a tank driver in the war?'

'No, Brendan could have done anything he wanted to. Our mother offered to pay for any career he liked, but he never wanted to do anything in particular except be a 'gentleman' and of course gambling and drinking was a problem even then.'

When I confronted Brendan with what I had learned, at first he was furious with me for asking Maureen and also furious with her for telling me. When he had calmed down he told me more about his life at home and at school, and said that he changed his name because he didn't want to be like his father, who was a gambler and drinker whereas his mother had worked so hard.

'But it seems I'm just like him,' he admitted, 'and changing the name made no difference.'

*****

217

We were back to work in the shop on 2 January 1981. I did work as much as I could with the business, but takings were down, and I didn't know whether it was because the novelty of the baked potato bar had worn off or if there were other reasons. I knew they dropped a bit when I stopped cooking, because people kept mentioning it. We started to do toasted sandwiches and pizzas as well to help with parties of people where one person didn't like potatoes. Brendan managed the shop on his own sometimes when I couldn't make it. It was one Saturday in January when I got a phone call from a friend.

'I thought your shop was open all day on Saturday, Janey.'

'It is.'

'Well, it's not today because I've just been round there.'

Brendan first of all lied about it, and then when he realised I knew (and after a huge row), I found out that quite often if I was not there, he closed up and went to the bookies.

'Well, the only thing to do,' I said, 'is to put the lease on the market while we've still got books that show good figures for our first six months and we've got just over six years on the lease.'

We had some really violent rows in the next two months while we were trying to sell. One day we were outside in woods near where we lived and he had been drinking and got really physical towards me because I blamed him for the mess we were in again. Because he was hitting me and Kevin was crying in his pushchair, one of our neighbours called the police. They still didn't get involved in domestics and when they were sure the baby was OK they left.

We were lucky it didn't take us very long to sell the lease on the shop, but this left us again without an income. Brendan actually applied for a part-time job selling wood-burning stoves in someone else's shop and miraculously, with his gift of the gab and a few lies, he got it.

*****

I went back to work as an auxiliary nurse evenings and nights while we looked for another business. Having looked in all the business papers, we decided that a fish and chip shop still seemed like a good idea. We found a new shop on an estate in Reading (it was just a shell) where the planning application for a fish and chip shop has been turned down twice, but as planning applications were still cheap, we thought it was worth trying. Brendan wrote a brilliant letter to go with it that covered all the problems. We got planning permission and the lease for the shop and all we needed was the money to fit it out.

'Now you can go and see that bank manager, and get him to lend you the money,' said Brendan.

I had made the appointment with Mr Wilson, the bank manager, but when I went I wasn't terribly optimistic as I needed to borrow a lot more than for our first venture. Although he was very nice and congratulated me on how I had sorted the money out with the first shop, I sensed there was a problem coming.

'I'm retiring in six months' time,' he finally said, 'and if I wasn't I'd lend you the money, but if I do now I'll be in big trouble for lending that sort of money without security. Do you have anyone who would stand guarantor for you?'

'No,' I said and then remembered. ' ... Strictly speaking that isn't true. My father is a millionaire but I don't really have anything to do with him.'

'Well, would it perhaps be better to swallow your pride and ask rather than not do anything?'

'I don't know.'

I had sworn to myself that I would never ask him for anything or get involved with him ever again, although I couldn't really explain why to Mr Wilson.

'Go away and think about it,' he said, 'before you make any rush decisions.'

Chapter Forty-One

Pop Goes the Weasel

I went home to discuss with Brendan what Mr Wilson had said, but I couldn't tell him that the main reason for not bothering with Pop was because of his continuing sexual advances towards me. (He would still take any chance he could get when Mum was out of the way to make advances towards me, if only in the things he said or the way he would kiss me goodbye.) Brendan and I spent several days talking about what Mr Wilson said and Brendan finally persuaded me to talk to Pop. I phoned him and arranged a meeting in Newbury for a meal.

We met as planned and I told Pop about the fish and chip shop we wanted to open and the guarantor that I would need to borrow the money. He came to look at the place with me and I quickly started to sense that he was raising objections simply to prove that he had control over me.

'I don't like leasehold properties. It's always better to own a freehold.'

I point out that this would cost even more money.

'It's quite a distance for you to travel every day and you've got the young one and the other children.'

Along with the lease of the shop, the Council had given us the chance to buy our house, so I talked to him about this as well.

We were sitting in the car and still talking when he suddenly started trying to kiss me and grope at me. I knew then that if he had any input into our lives this was going to be part and parcel of it, and I knew that if I told Brendan what the problem was there would be a fight and, as Pop was in his seventies and not particularly robust, Brendan could do no end of damage to him.

So I decided to take what help he offered and to handle the personal side as best I could.

'Well, will you help me?' I asked him.

'I've helped family before and have got no thanks for it in the end, but what I will do with you is this – I'll give you a private mortgage to buy your house and you can sort out your own financial position with your jobs or we will look for some nice fish and chip shop with accommodation that I can buy so that you're able to live with the job without the travelling. This is the way I started my business after the war with a partner and I bought into that first business. Well, what do you think?'

'I'll talk it over with Brendan and ring you in a day or two.'

We parted in the usual way, with Pop giving me a kiss and me trying to hold his hands as he always seemed to have more than two that were trying to maul me. I discussed it with Brendan and although he thought it would be a shame to move from our house in Frilsham in Berkshire (although it had been in a terrible state when we moved in, we had spent a lot of time and money doing it up and it became a very nice semi with woods all around it) he also thought we ought to grab the chance of living in something where the business and home were together, as we had tried to do in Wales.

I phoned Pop the next day and although I felt as if I was selling my soul to the devil, I told him of our decision.

'Good,' he said, 'now we can start looking.'

I already felt trapped because I knew that it would end up being what he wanted and my life would be controlled by him.

*****

Brendan and I bought *Dalton's Weekly* and another paper that dealt only with the fish and chip trade. Our search started again but meanwhile, we had put the lease of the shop we had taken back on the market with the planning permission for a fish and chip shop. We managed to sell that lease but the paperwork took so long that we had already moved before we received the money.

We found several properties we were interested in, but every time Pop looked at them he founds some reason why he didn't think they were suitable. Then he found a property near where they lived in Dorset. A fish and chip shop with a restaurant and the people who owned it suggested that I went down and work in it for a while. I decided to spend a week with my parents and then some time in the shop.

I left for the week with a very unsettled mind. I was worried about leaving Brendan and Amy to look after home, knowing he treated my children badly even when I was there. I was dreading what it would be like without me. I was in a catch-22 position: I couldn't tell my parents what Brendan was like and I couldn't tell Brendan what my father was like.

Pop picked me up early in the morning.

'Now we can spend the day together,' he said. 'I told your mother I wasn't picking you up until the afternoon so she won't be expecting us early.'

'What was the purpose of that?'

'Well, I want to spend some time with my girl.'

'I'm staying for the week, so you'll have plenty of time with me.'

'Not that sort of time. That isn't the sort of time I want with you.'

On the way, he parked up several times and put his arms so tightly round me it felt like a brace. For a small, elderly man, he seemed very strong. He tried getting his hands into my bra and into my knickers and the whole thing was the start of a nightmare.

'I'm your daughter,' I kept saying, 'I don't want you doing this sort of thing.'

'Well, as we've never lived as father and daughter why should it matter?'

'It does matter a great deal not only to me, but what about my mother?'

'Oh, she doesn't really want to know any more.'

'No, but I am sure she wouldn't think much to you trying it on with me.'

This seemed to work for a while at least. He drove to a hotel in the

New Forest where he said we were going to have lunch. He walked in with his arm around me.

'I wonder what they're all thinking,' he said after we had ordered. 'Probably, look at the silly old man, with that lovely young woman.'

'I don't expect they're interested. It's just your ego. Your son said you were a womaniser.'

As we ate our meal he tried to persuade me to let him book a room for the afternoon. I was horrified though by now, not surprised, at anything he might do or suggest. My job was to keep him under control and to get what Brendan and I needed out of him – I had no other choice.

'I think we'd better drive straight home to Mum after lunch.' I was also looking forward to seeing Paula.

Pop was in a foul mood when we got back to the car, but later as he was driving he said,

'I'll take you and show you the business. I've just had the office refurbished.' Part of his business was the four funeral directorships he owned. 'We've got three chapels of rest in this one.'

'That would be good. I'd like to see it.'

By the time we got there, the staff had all left.

'I'll ring your mother and let her know where we are.' He told her we wouldn't be long and took me around the chapels and the other parts of the building and then back to the main reception area which was quite luxurious.

'Sit down for a minute.'

'We'd better not, Pop. Mum will be waiting and I've already got to lie to her about the beginning of the day and I don't like it.'

I sat down for a minute and as he turned around towards me I realised he has his hard penis out of his trousers and forced it into my hand. I screamed and we begin to tussle. After a struggle I made him tidy himself up and leave the office to head home. By then there was a lot of traffic about and it was a slow process.

'Where on earth have you been?' Mum said when we arrived. 'I expected you ages ago.'

It was good to see Paula again. She was at the grammar school in Poole taking her A levels, but to be honest, her relationship with me was about the same as it was with Mum: the only person she was interested in was herself. And life back with Mum and Pop that week was a nightmare; I had to contend throughout the week with all Pop's advances and Mum's drinking, which started in early 1980 and was slowly getting worse.

I spent part of every day in the fish and chip shop near their home and at the end of that time, Pop made an offer on the property and had decided to employ us. This was the start of him controlling me again.

I returned home to find that things were even worse than I expected. Brendan had spent most of his time in the bookies or the pub with Kevin either with him or left outside. Amy would come home from school and have to see to the meal and the children as Brendan had driven the car home drunk and left it at an angle in the garden and would be asleep in the chair with the baby screaming on the floor.

'I came home one afternoon, Mum, and he had even wet himself,' she said.

One evening while I was away, Brendan was so drunk he tried to hit Amy, resulting with him chasing her around the house, in and out of the front and back doors, shouting foul language at her. He was so drunk he ended up falling down. I regretted terribly subjecting my children to that environment.

I expected things to progress with the shop premises that Pop was buying but things went wrong a couple of weeks later when the vendors changed their minds and decided not to sell. So the search began again.

Chapter Forty-Two

Another Kind of Batter

When Brendan was in prison in 1979, he had made friends with a fence (receiver of stolen goods) who was still serving a sentence. This friend Guy had a mother, Joan, in her seventies living in the West Country, who in turn had a very elderly mother in her nineties for whom she cared. Brendan told Guy we would try to visit her, which we did one weekend. She was really pleased to see us – and determined to feed us as much as possible.

When a property in Somerset was advertised, we thought it would be good to view it. I had been brought up in Somerset so the territory was familiar to me, and I felt it would be better than another episode like Wales.

Brendan wasn't particularly pleased when Pop said he would pick me up to view it, but as I pointed out, he encouraged me to get involved with my father and this always led to him taking over everything. Having visited the fish and chip shop, which had ample accommodation for the family, (although it would not have been the location I would have chosen) Pop was the one who looked at all the books and went ahead with the purchase.

The sale was completed on 7 December 1981, and knowing that this wasn't an ideal time to move with children, I had already wrapped up all the Christmas presents as we wouldn't have much time after we had arrived.

The previous owners worked with us for a while until we were familiar with the business. They also had a large Alsatian dog, which we later found out, kept away the rats. This was the first problem to be sorted out. Much worse was to follow. The whole family arrived for lunch on Christmas Day, which, apart from all the work, wasn't a good idea with the amount that both Brendan and Mum drank.

With Christmas over, and the decision made to take on someone to live in to help with the children and house, I thought that for once in my life, things might be straightforward – no chance of that. Of all the applicants for the job, I thought it was better to employ someone slightly older, although Lindsay didn't come from a large family like some of the young ones. This proved to be another mistake: the children managed to take advantage of her vulnerability and run circles around her. I was constantly called from the shop because she had fled to her room and I found her crying on the bed.

None of this was any good for Brendan's temper. He took it out on the children and me, and shouted at Lindsay which frightened her to death. She said she had worked in another fish and chip shop in the town so we decide to swap roles, she would serve in the shop (while Brendan fried) and I would go back to the house. This lasted a couple of days until Brendan came to me in a furious temper.

'For Christ's sake will you get out here and serve? They're queuing out to the door and she hasn't got a clue.'

This was the last straw and Lindsay left. I then employed a woman approximately my own age named Christine who had a child the same age as our young son (nearly two) and brought him to work with her. She looked after my son, the house and the others when they were at home.

Brendan's temper didn't improve: a fish and chip shop was hard work and he started going out every afternoon gambling. Pop paid us a weekly wage to run the shop and the takings were to be put in the under-floor safe until he came to collect them. I had to put up with Pop turning up when he felt like it, though Mum rarely accompanied him. I could see she was not looking too good, though, and knew that the drinking was getting worse but there was nothing I could do.

*****

One Sunday evening, Brendan and I went to a local hotel for a meal. I asked him about the gambling. He denied it and as the evening wore on and he drank more, he became more and more aggressive. As we started to walk home, he became quite violent with me. After he had knocked me to the ground a couple stopped to ask if I needed help.

'No thank you, I'll be OK.' I didn't want anyone else involved with Brendan.

They left and Brendan gave me a parting kick and walked off home, leaving me on the ground. The people who passed by must have rung the police, or called in at the police station. When the police arrived I was still on the ground and Brendan had disappeared.

'Do you want us to drive you home?' they asked.

'No thank you, I can walk home from here.'

Brendan had gone to sleep and I had to knock on the door until Lana let me in. Amy, now sixteen, had stayed in Berkshire to carry on with her job training.

All this took place in January 1982. The following weekend after Sunday lunch, Brendan was drinking heavily. A row started up between us about the money he was gambling away. As he became more and more aggressive, Lana shouted, 'I'm going to call the police,' and picked up the phone. Brendan snatched the phone from her and threatened her with violence if she dared to phone. He then knocked me to the ground. The children stood around screaming and crying, as he proceeded to kick me in the body and the face. I stayed curled up on the floor and he left the room and went upstairs.

The children went quiet, wondering what would happen next. Brendan came downstairs, gave me one last hard kick in the back and left the house. After I heard the door close, I dragged myself onto the settee and asked Lana to phone the police. I had had enough. She was naturally afraid, but I assured her he wouldn't be back.

When the police arrived they asked if I needed to call someone to stay with the children while they took me to hospital. I called Christine who had been working for me in the house, and she kindly came down and waited until I came home.

At the hospital I was checked over but they said nothing was broken, that I was just badly bruised. By then my face was swollen and one of my eyes had completely closed up. The police took me to the police station and photographed my injuries.

'Will you prosecute when we catch him?' they asked.

'Yes, I will. I've put up with enough now.'

They took me home because I was in so much pain and said they would take a proper statement the next day. The hospital had given me strong painkillers, which I took before going to bed, although this didn't stop me being violently sick in the night because the pain was so bad. Christine had stayed to get the children to bed and promised to be in as early as she could on the Monday.

On Monday morning, Lana helped with getting the other two off to school and she and Christine came in to see to the youngest. The police rang me to say that they had caught Brendan and that he was in custody.

I couldn't open the shop and knew that I would have to phone Pop. To make matters worse, Brendan had taken the previous week's takings that I had stupidly not put in the safe. Pop arrived with Mum and although they were both horrified at the way I looked, he seemed more bothered about the loss of his takings and what was going to happen to the shop than about me.

The police had given me the number of a solicitor and I had made an appointment, but I told Pop that I would have an advert put in the job centre for a young person to help me in the shop. There was a government scheme where Pop can claim part of their wages if they were under eighteen.

I was unable to open the shop for two weeks because of my body pain and the state of my face, and Pop didn't even care enough to pay me while I wasn't working, or bother about whether I could afford to feed the children. In those two weeks, Brendan went to the Magistrates Court and was remanded in custody. I visited the solicitors (by taxi, as I was unable to walk very far) and made statements.

I interviewed several girls from the job centre and managed to find a girl named Pauline who proved very capable and we ran the shop well together. Although Pop got most of the assistant's wages back from the government each week, he still cut my wages, because he said he was paying two of us and now it was just me. I argued that he still expected me to do all the heavy work and cleaning up at night that Brendan did, but this made no difference to him. He knew I couldn't do anything about it, because my home was with the job. We had only moved at the beginning of December 1981 and I could hardly believe that things could be so bad two months later.

Brendan was brought to the Magistrates Court once a week to be remanded in custody while the police and my solicitor were getting the case ready for hearing. Had things been sorted out swiftly, life at this point might have taken a turn for the better, but because the legal system's wheels were very slow, Brendan obviously persuaded his solicitor to write to me, although all other correspondence had been through my solicitor. This letter threw me into turmoil. The letter pleaded with me to go and see Brendan the next time he was in the cells at the courts and to speak to him. It also said how devastated Brendan was at what he had done to me and begged me to reconsider and not carry on with the prosecution. I was devastated at the whole situation because I still loved him, but also knew what it was all doing to my children.

Chapter Forty-Three

What Comes Around

When we moved to Bridgwater, I had joined the local Baptist church, not with Brendan of course, because he was Catholic, and after the beating that Brendan had given me, Will, the minister, sent Mary from the church to visit me. Both she and her husband Ted picked up the children for church while I was out of action.

Right from the beginning of this bad period, Mary had been coming twice a day to see what she could do for me, so it was Mary who found me in tears the day the solicitor's letter arrived. I showed it to her and she was kind and understanding, but sensibly said that she couldn't advise what I should do.

I decided to go to see Brendan, although I felt that getting his solicitor to write to me was rather below the belt. Brendan was desperately apologetic.

'I can't believe I did that to you,' he said, 'but I promise I'll never do anything like it again if you give me another chance.'

'I don't know if I can take that risk again, and I have the children to consider. Of course there's also Pop and the property does belong to him.'

When he was taken up to the court, I left with a lot to think about. I knew that I still loved Brendan and still wanted him. There was of course our son Kevin, who was only a couple of months away from his second birthday. I sat down with the three of my four children who lived with me (Kevin was only two years old and too young to understand) and spoke quite frankly with them. I explained what had happened and said, 'He doesn't have anywhere else to go, do you think we should give him another chance?'

They were very confused, but between us we decided to give it another go. My solicitor wasn't happy about my dropping the charges and the police were very annoyed. I explained to them that they would probably find with all domestic violence cases, they would get a lot more women going through with prosecutions if they didn't take so long about it.

Pop was furious about Brendan coming back.

'I don't want to set eyes on him,' he said, 'and I don't want him anywhere near the shop.'

When Brendan got home, Pauline, who was running the shop with me, said, 'What are we going to do when your father turns up without notice like he frequently does?'

'We could work out a series of rings on the bell that we could ring through from the shop to the house, so Brendan can go upstairs.'

Things were very difficult, what with all the bell ringing and Brendan having to ask me for money, which he found hard to handle, as I knew he would, and me knowing that all the time he spent out in the town he was still gambling. That situation lasted for less than three weeks, and one evening when I had popped into the house from the shop, I found he had managed to pack his things, steal more money from the takings, and leave by the back door – I imagined by taxi.

The shop continued to run but although trade had increased after Brendan beat me up and it had appeared in the local newspapers, people lost sympathy when I dropped the charges against him and took him back and trade started to drop again, which didn't please Pop. He still turned up and expected me just to drop everything and go out with him for meals, which I was obliged to accept – until one night when we had eaten and gone back to his car, he put his arms around me and pulled me to him. The car park was dark, so he tried his usual trick of trying to get his hand into my knickers. I snapped and slapped his face.

'Remind me never to buy you expensive meals again,' he said.

'Don't worry,' I replied. 'I won't ever be coming out with you again. We'll keep this strictly business.'

And this time I meant it.

*****

Just after Kevin's second birthday in May 1982, I received a phone call from the police to say that Brendan had been picked up doing what he had always done, living on stolen cheques and credit cards.

Brendan went to court and was given a sentence that meant with remission he would be out again in October 1983.

Living on my own I became very depressed. My doctor prescribed Ativan anti-depressant tablets and even suggested that if I didn't get a grip, I should put my children in care for a while. This of course frightened me enough to make me keep going with the help of friends. Unfortunately I was becoming dependent on anti-depressants and sleeping pills. Pauline and Christine, who helped with the shop and house, managed to help me keep the shop afloat.

During the months up to August 1983, I longed to leave the shop. I was totally worn down with trying to keep it going and taking Kevin to visit Brendan. I was also getting drunken phone calls from Mum, who by then was in a pretty bad way.

After I had finished with Eric, my friend Angela had become involved with him but their relationship had got into difficulties; I had managed to help her with her problems with him and she didn't stay with him. Then, when I was at my worst with the depression, she arrived from Berkshire to stay with me. The staff managed the shop and Angela the house and children.

I also had visits from a couple of my ex-husbands who, on the pretext of visiting their children, seemed to think that as I was alone, I might be interested. Roger came, asking me to have another go with him, even though he had remarried. Eric, who of course knew Brendan, came down to stay for a while and took me to see Mum while Pop was away. She really did look ill and I wondered what the real cause of her drinking was.

Bob, who was my first love (and I then felt my best friend), came to stay for a while as well. I didn't really know why I kept going back to him for friendship, but I did when I was in the refuge and when I almost decided to terminate my pregnancy after Brendan had left me in Wales. I think it is because he goes back so far in my life. When I visited Brendan I told him about all these visits and he was pleased that I had some support – when he wasn't drinking all his jealousy and paranoia disappeared and if I told him something he would believe me – but he did write to Amy in Berkshire to say that he was worried about me as he thought I was too thin and looked ill.

One thing I was deeply ashamed about: Amy and her boyfriend visited from Berkshire at the weekend as often as they could, and on one of these weekends when we had had quite a lot to drink, her boyfriend was lying on the settee with his head in my lap and I was running my hand through his hair. Later that night, when we had all gone to bed, he crept into my bedroom and whispered, 'I've come to give you a big cuddle,' and being starved of affection and due to a lot of drink and drugs, I let him into my bed and before I realised what was happening, we were making love. It was brief – over almost before it had started – and then he crept back to his own room.

On Monday morning I visited my GP and explained. He was very understanding and gave me the morning-after pill and said that if it didn't work and there was a problem he would get it sorted out for me. I was lucky and it did work, but it was something that was to cause trouble some years later.

Chapter Forty-Four

Cold Turkey

The takings for the shop were getting worse and I had to let Pop know that I didn't want to stay, so although I didn't want anything to do with him, I asked him to call. Before he even knew why I was ringing he tried to win me over to him by dangling a carrot in front of me.

'You are married to an old man. Why don't you just let your old dad look after you and you wouldn't need another one? I have got to have some one to leave this property to.'

I was furious. 'You can't bribe me into bed with you. What do you think Mum would feel if I told her all this?'

He didn't reply and I got the impression he didn't care.

'Don't wave your money at me,' I went on. 'You think you can buy anything and as far as I am concerned you can stick this fish and chip shop up your arse. I want to leave here and I think it would be better if you evicted me and hopefully the council will house me.' (I had put my name on the list as soon as we had arrived.) 'And then I will be back to where I started before you got involved in my life.'

'How can I evict you? What will people think? You are my daughter.'

'Pity you hadn't thought about that before.'

'I will talk to your mother,' he said and left.

It would be years before he allowed me to see Mum again. Pop stuck to what he had said and refused to evict me and told me to look for somewhere else to live and he would put the shop on the market. It wasn't what I wanted, but I just had to get out of the shop.

The house hunting wasn't easy – there was still the shop to run and time was very limited. I was still on anti-depressants and sleeping pills and the worse things got, the more I took. Pop managed to find something wrong with every house for which I sent details. He was still controlling me. How I wished he would just evict me and let me get on with my life. I was also trying to keep up my visits to Brendan with Kevin, so that he didn't forget his dad. Finally Pop agreed on a house in a village about five miles from where we were living.

'I'm going to buy it in your mother's name,' he told me, 'and then she will rent it to you.'

*****

While still in the shop, I had a visit from someone I didn't recognise when I opened the door. He introduced himself as Guy (the person with whom Brendan was in prison and whose mother we visited) and said that as he had been released and heard that Brendan was inside, he was returning the visit. He was very tall and good looking with a high forehead and piercing eyes, but as I was busy in the shop I was rather distracted at the time and thought no more of it.

In August 1983, we moved out of the shop into and the house owned by Mum in the village of Stoke-sub-Hamdon, near Martok. Although she phoned now and again I didn't see her as Pop has given her the option of him or me, and of course she had to stick with him – he was her whole life. There had only ever been him and the man she had married when I was five; the other years of her life, she gave to Nan, because of the way life was when she had had me.

We had to change everything when we moved, including schools and doctors, because our old doctor was out of callout range. I visited our new doctor, a man without a bedside manner, to ask for repeat prescriptions of Ativan and the sleeping capsules I had been taking.

He looked at the Ativan and said abruptly, 'You know you're addicted to these, don't you, and I'm not going to keep giving you them like you have been having them.'

He gave me a prescription without any further discussion or advice.

When I got home, I sat down and thought about what he had said. There had never been any medication I had been addicted to as I had a very high tolerance to all medication – I found this out over the years as I had suffered from the age of seven with very severe migraines. I then decided that no one would speak to me as this doctor had and I immediately stopped all the medication. I was later told that this could have had very serious effects or even killed me.

However the withdrawal symptoms from the Ativan were dreadful. After the children had gone off to school I would go back to bed, pull the clothes over my head and shake for hours. I eventually got up to make a cup of tea at lunchtime and sat holding it in both hands while I shook and tried to keep the tea in the cup. Over six weeks, it gradually got better, although it was probably a year before I was fully over it. This was truly a ghastly time in my life. After the initial six weeks, I took the pills back to the surgery and sat opposite the doctor, threw the pills at him, flinging them in their packets at his face – and said, 'How dare you speak to me as you did and offer me no help whatsoever!' I didn't wait for his reaction – I just walked out.

Soon after that, I changed to the surgery in the next village. I was of course, just waiting for October 1983 when Brendan was due to come home.

Chapter Forty-Five

…Comes Around

When the day finally arrived, I took Kevin and went to collect Brendan. In the beginning, things seemed wonderful because he was back, but soon they were back to the way they had been before. We were back to the original thing that his son could do no wrong but my other children he treated really badly.

One morning that stuck in my mind was when I was still in bed after working a nightshift. Brendan was supposed to be seeing the children were sorted out and sent to school. Lana, who was still with us and at secondary school, suddenly came racing up the stairs, slammed the bathroom door and locked it, shouting: 'If you don't leave us alone I am going to go outside and tell everyone all about you.'

She was talking about his criminal life and his prison sentences; she knew this would probably work because wherever we lived, Brendan hated for anyone to know anything about this, which was why it was such a strain always living a lie.

Brendan wasn't working and of course he was claiming benefits, but I had taken a night-duty job in a residential home for the elderly, which meant that I had to leave the children with Brendan and I felt very guilty, as I knew how he would treat them. Of course, it was not long before all the gambling and drinking started again. He would go off to the nearest village where he knew several bookies and money would disappear from my purse and he would blame it on Andrew, my older son. When I confronted him about his gambling he still denied it, but of course, in his drunken state he forgot to remove the betting slips from his pockets. I tried talking to him and offered my help. Quite often, he cried and said that it was an illness, which I agreed with. We talked for hours to work

241

out how he could tackle it. Then I thought things were starting to get better and he was not going out all the time; he had even started to write a book as he was a journalist many years ago.

Then there was a surprise in the post. He had opened accounts with quite a few bookmakers and was doing his gambling by phone. The rows started again then and I became very frightened of him, because with the gambling, the drinking always got worse. If he lost, he would go to the pub to drown his sorrows and if he won he had to buy everyone a drink. In the pub around the corner from our house, the landlord would close the doors and serve after hours, so I never knew what state he would be in. After the beating I had taken in the fish and chip shop, I was always worried for the children's safety and mine. By the beginning of 1984, things had deteriorated so much, I was starting to think about divorce.

*****

One evening Lana had gone to babysit for someone in the village and it was one of my work nights, which Brendan was aware of. Several days later, I received a phone call from a restaurant in the next village where we knew the owners.

'I'm sorry to bother you, Janey, but could you come in and pay the bill from the other night when Brendan was here? He said that you would come in and settle it.'

I was absolutely furious to think he had left three children (our son wasn't yet four) on their own and gone out to eat and drink. After a terrible row in March 1984, I saw a solicitor to arrange for a divorce. He told me that someone would come to the house to serve the papers. I knew when it was going to be and waited, absolutely terrified.

When the doorbell rang, I showed the gentleman into the lounge where Brendan was sitting and went into the kitchen/dining room where the children were. I heard Brendan let him out and return to the lounge. Later in the evening, Brendan left the house and didn't return for hours. I rang the owner of the pub who said that Brendan was there getting drunk.

After the children had gone to bed, I just sat waiting, shaking and wondering what was going to happen next. By midnight, I was really scared because I knew what Brendan would be like with the amount he would have drunk. Soon after midnight, I decided to lock up and go to bed. At 2.30 a.m., he finally returned and upon realising he couldn't get in, just stood outside with his finger on the bell. He rang it for about an hour, by which time the children were all awake and shaking with fear, as I was. I encouraged them all to stay in bed and hoped he would go and sleep in the car, but then I heard the sound of breaking glass. We had small diamond-shaped mullioned glass panes so I knew that getting in wouldn't be easy. I rang the police, who came along and told him to leave us alone for the rest of the night.

In the morning, he waited until the children were at school and Kevin at nursery, before making an appearance. I was waiting for a violent outburst, but was surprised by the fact that it was only verbal; he said that he was not leaving whatever I said. Remembering how he left when we were in Wales, I got the only money that I had out of the bank and very stupidly carried it around with me wherever I went.

We lived in the same house but didn't speak for a couple of weeks and he must have worked out that I had money in my handbag. One Monday morning when I was about to take Kevin across the road to nursery, he asked,

'Can Daddy come with us?'

'I will come if you want me to,' said Brendan.

As we were all going together, I left my handbag behind the settee and we went across the road. When we had got inside the nursery, Brendan said goodbye to our son while I was seeing him in and managed to leave before me. I could feel my heart thumping when I left. Brendan must have run all the way to the house, as he was nowhere to be seen.

Indoors, Brendan was upstairs, and I immediately went for my handbag and of course the money was gone. Brendan came down with a suitcase packed.

'Will you take me to the station?' he asked.

'I will when you give me my money back.'

'I haven't got your fucking money. I didn't know you had any.'

'Don't give me that one. I know you of old and that's all I have at the moment to feed your son and the others.'

'Search my things if you don't fucking believe me.'

This told me that he must have had it somewhere on his person. I knew that if I tried to find it on him, I would be in for a beating, so very stupidly, I got the car. He loaded his things and set off for the station. It was going over and over in my mind to drive to the police station and get them to do something about it for me, but I knew that he would run before I got to the police station (our car didn't have central locking) as the parking was quite a way off from the entrance. Instead, I just took him to the station and left him.

I went to my friend Mary, as she lived close by. I rang the police and told them what had happened, but realised it was probably going to be too late for them to do anything. I then had to put my thinking cap on again to do something about money and to get more work to support the children.

*****

Not long after Brendan left, perhaps about a month, the police rang me to say that he had been arrested again as he had gone back to his old ways once he had spent my money. My best friend Mary became a lifeline for me at this point – and for many years to come: I seemed to spend more time in her and her husband Ted's house than in my own, when my children were at school, that is.

I tried to speak to Mum, who only got in touch with me occasionally when Pop was out. One day I phoned and was answered by a strange voice, who said, 'I am afraid Cec and Iris are out. I am Rubina, who is this speaking?'

I told her and she went into raptures about how she wanted to meet me.

'Excuse me for asking,' I said, 'but who are you?'

Rubina turned out to be Pop's[3] wife, who was staying with them after spending some time in hospital. This was yet another bizarre side to Pop's life, as much the fact that Mum put up with her, as that she put up with Mum.

*****

Soon after Brendan had been arrested and was on remand in prison, he wrote to me and asked me to go and talk to him, as he didn't want a divorce and he still loved me. I gave a lot of thought as to whether I should go or not, as my brain told me one thing and my heart something else. My heart won and I made arrangements to visit Brendan. When I arrived in the visiting room, I really just wanted to throw my arms around him, because in spite of everything I still loved him desperately. But I knew that for the sake of my children, if not for myself, I couldn't let the marriage carry on.

We sat opposite one another and he held my hands and told me that he loved me more than he had ever loved anyone in his life, except our son of course.

'Yet you took every last penny that you knew I had,' I said, 'and left me to sort out all of the children.'

He also told me that the DSS were prosecuting him for claiming money and not declaring the nights I had been working, but that of course was of no great consequence given all the other charges against him. He pleaded with me not to go through with the divorce and used emotional blackmail again: 'My gambling is an illness – would you leave me if I had cancer or some other illness?'

I stuck to what I had to do and said that I would be carrying on with the divorce although it felt as if my heart was breaking. When it was time for me to leave, he kissed me and I clung to him. Leaving him was one of the most difficult things I ever had to do. It was like leaving a part of

---

[3] *Cecil was Pop's real name, which he hated and preferred to call himself Jim, but Mum sometimes also called him Cec.*

me behind. I cried the whole way as I drove home, all the way to Mary's house, who wondered what on earth was wrong with me.

When she had made me coffee with a drop of something in it to calm me down, I told her that I was definitely going to carry on with the divorce but that I would never in my life be able to love anyone else again after the passion that there had been between myself and Brendan.

Chapter Forty-Six

Guy

I had kept in touch with Guy's mother (Brendan's friend from prison) and she had rung me previously to tell me that Guy had been arrested again and was on remand in prison, so I visited her as she was elderly and on her own.

In July 1984, Guy's mother rang me to say that Guy had been released on bail and would be home with her the next day. I told her how pleased I was and thought no more of it for a while.

Life was very hard, trying to work, arrange childcare and make enough money to support us.

'I think I'm going to write to Guy,' I said one day as I sat with Mary, 'and ask him if we can meet up for a drink.'

'Be careful what you're doing,' she said, 'you could get yourself into another load of trouble if you are not careful.'

'I know what I'm doing. I'll never get to feel like I do about Brendan with anyone else, and life has to go on. At least Guy and his mother have property and money.'

I wrote him a short note and he rang me soon afterwards and invited me over to have a drink one evening with him and his mother. I accepted and we arranged a day.

I travelled the short distance to Guy's mother and met Guy, an impressively tall man at six-foot-four and distinguished looking – he was fourteen years older than me, quietly spoken, well-educated and, I discovered, quite musically inclined. We sat talking about the things that had happened between Brendan and me, and I learnt something about Guy's background. He told me why he had come to be on bail this time and I was aware that he was a fence, specialising in silver, which he was also quite capable of dealing in legitimately.

I had had quite a bit to drink and when it got late, his mother went to bed. I suppose it was inevitable that I should end up in bed with him, given the fact that he had just come back from a spell on remand in prison and that there has been very little sex in my life for some while. The next morning, his mother came into the bedroom and didn't seem a bit surprised to see me there. Later, I decided it must have been a situation she was used to.

When I left that morning Guy said, 'I'll phone you some time.'

'OK,' I said, as I drove off. Well, you've probably blown that one by sleeping with him, I thought to myself. I returned home, thinking that would be the last I would see of him.

*****

About a week later, he rang and asked me out. By then I had taken a girl named Kirsty and her small child to lodge with us to help the financial position, so we were able to babysit for each other. Although Lana was old enough to look after the others, a lot of the time she was either studying or babysitting for someone else to make some pocket money.

Guy told me the reason he was on bail was because of his handling of stolen goods. His criminal life had been very different from Brendan's: he had been privately educated, was in the services and a director in the family business. He told me about his first wife and the child she had had that wasn't his. He split up from her but still maintained the family, though he soon found someone else who he lived with. He turned to crime in his thirties because his wages from the family firm were not enough to pay the overheads of two families. As time went on, he said, he found he couldn't live without the adrenalin rush. He said that he was in love with me and asked me to marry him. He said that he knew it was unfair to ask as he didn't know what the future would hold once his case comes to trial, but explained that he would see that the children and I were taken care of.

I said that I would marry him and we plan this for February 1985, to allow for my divorce to be finalised. When I agreed to marry him, I was mainly thinking about security for my children. There was quite a while between our getting engaged and the wedding and I was still not really sure if it was the right thing to do, but as I got to know him better – and he was really good with my children – I began to feel a lot for him. And once again, sex reared its ugly head: it made me think that I felt things towards him, but I wasn't sure how real these feelings were. I so wanted to believe they were based on something real, and that this time I would be able to make the marriage work.

Although Guy was on bail, he still seemed to be unable to stop himself from continuing to work. Unbeknownst to me, when I rented a room to Kirsty, she had just come out from a short spell in prison for cheque fraud (of which I was unaware). Although this wasn't Guy's normal form of work, because he was always involved with burglars, he become very friendly with Kirsty and wanted to know how she operated. Unlike Brendan, who always removed signatures on cards and re-signed them, Kirsty was able to forge any signature you put in front of her. He then asked her, 'If I buy cards and cheque books from the burglars are you prepared to use them?'

'Oh yes,' she said, 'I'm up for it if you get them.'

I asked Guy not to get involved, but he was intrigued with all things criminal; everything was an adrenalin rush for him. He had told me that financially, he never needed to work again. When he first brought back some chequebooks and cards, I knew who he had bought them from because I was beginning to meet all his friends. Guy coerced me into going out with Kirsty as she used these chequebooks to buy everything from food to furniture. Guy couldn't go himself as not only is he already on bail, but he would have been conspicuous because of his height; and Kirsty couldn't go on her own as she didn't drive.

As the time approaches our wedding day, I visited the minister of my church. Guy was an agnostic, but I still wanted the marriage blessed in church. After a long talk with the minister, and having told him all about my life and marriages, he decided that if he was prepared to bless my marriage, he should be prepared to actually marry me. He put this to the deacons and church members and then agreed to marry us in church in February 1985. This wasn't what Guy had really wanted, but he agreed to it for my sake.

I started to make phone calls to the council to get them to move Kirsty and her daughter from my house. I was still on good terms with her, but there was simply not enough room for all of us as I had two of the children sleeping in with me. They quickly found her a house and I hoped that the activities between her and Guy would stop, but this wasn't to be, because by then she was going out with one of Guy's burglar friends Bill. And although Kirsty and her daughter were housed before the wedding, everything carried on the same. Guy was going away for most of the week and I knew he was still dealing in stolen goods, even though he was on bail. When he was at home we were still friendly with Kirsty; he still wanted her to use the cards he was buying from the burglars.

*****

When our wedding day arrived in February, I worried about the reception in a hotel: all Guy's guests were of the criminal fraternity and anything could go missing. Mum and Pop didn't come, but it all went well and we went away for a week's honeymoon in Somerton, Weymouth and Brighton, although we were not allowed out of the country because of Guy's bail restrictions. I had no one to look after my children so Ted, my best friend Mary's husband, took a week off work to look after them for me – and also gave me away at the wedding.

During our week away, we talked and I really believed that Guy was going to try to change his way of life. He said he felt guilty about marrying me as we didn't yet know whether he would be going to prison or for how long. He was quite capable of earning a regular living, but I soon found that old habits die hard. Guy assumed that because I was married to Brendan I was worldly-wise in the ways of criminals.

250

'I didn't expect you to be so naïve,' he said one day.

I explained that Brendan's crimes were usually only committed on his own and that he didn't talk about it and generally didn't mix with other criminals.

I then discovered things about Guy that, had I known them before, I wouldn't have married him. He told me that usually if you were the fence, you went out to find the properties that were to be burgled and that he was involved in the burglaries himself. One such burglary involved several of them climbing through an old lady's bedroom window, and the old lady was tied up. He went to great pains to explain that he had nothing to do with this part, but as time went on, I started to doubt this.

He warned me about things that may come out in his trial. Guy had a ferocious sexual appetite and told me of a fellow criminal who stayed with him and asked Guy to have sex with his wife while he watched, ending up as three-in-a-bed sex. He didn't understand why I couldn't see the funny side of this. I also found it upsetting when he told me that she was working as a prostitute.

'Haven't you thought about what you might have caught from this and could have passed on to me?' I said.

Chapter Forty-Seven

Clink

One day I had been with Kirsty to a dressmaker with the material for her wedding dress and was taking her young daughter to her sister's. I was stopped at traffic lights as a car screamed up alongside me and three people jumped out. I soon realised that they were police officers in an unmarked car. One leaned in and grabbed my car keys.

'You're coming with us,' said the policewoman, 'we've got a warrant to search your house.'

'What about this young child?' I asked.

'Where is she going?'

I told her and she made me move over and drove me to the child's aunt's house. I was then driven home where they proceed to search my house. They had brought a van and removed from the house anything that appeared to be relatively new, including things that belonged to my children – furniture, TV, and my clothes. When I told her it was time for me to collect the children from school (Lana walked home) the policewoman said that she would go and get them; I could go with her if I liked.

We fetched them and when Lana had arrived home she asked, 'Is there anywhere they can go and stay for a while?'

I had them taken down to my friends Mary and Ted's place, except Lana who stayed to wait for Guy to come home.

When they had finished, they took me to the police station where they took fingerprints and photographs and put me in a cell

'We have got your friend as well and she is telling us everything,' they said.

They kept taking me in and out of the cell to ask me questions, like the good cop, bad cop I had seen on TV. Guy had always told me never to talk to the police, so I refused to answer anything. They kept putting me back in the cell with just bare boards to sit on. I'm offered food and drink, which I refused, but ask for the police surgeon as I needed tablets for my migraine. They kept me waiting hours for this and also hours before they got me a solicitor.

A really friendly CID man came to question me again.

'You look cold, Janey, I'll get you a blanket. Now your friend is telling us everything and she's eating and drinking, why don't you do this the easy way and just tell us where the credit cards came from? We know it's something to do with your husband and friends. Tell us what we want to know and you can leave now on bail, or even without charge as it's not you we want but Guy and whoever he's getting the cards from.'

The policewoman was much nastier than the men. She seemed to enjoy gloating over questions like, 'Who do you think's looking after your children tonight?'

All this time I said nothing out of loyalty to my husband, although later on I was to realise it wasn't worth it.

*****

'You've got a visitor. I'll bring her down to you.'

It was only later on that first evening that Guy had sent Lana to see me, with sandwiches and a few essential clothes. I was absolutely gutted that he should send my daughter to see me in a police cell, and I made sure she went away as quickly as possible. I realised later that he was afraid to come himself in case they would arrest him as well.

By 2 a.m. the next morning, they had given up questioning me and put me back in my cell, this time with a mattress, pillow and blanket, and told me to sleep: they would talk to me again in the morning. The next day, they charged me with a variety of things but mainly with conspiring to steal the goods they had taken from my house. They kept reminding me that if I answered the questions they would let me go home to my children. The whole experience was horrific.

Lana had told me that Joan, Guy's mother, was helping him with the children, which turned out to mean that she stayed with the children so he could keep out of the way of the police.

On the afternoon of the second day, I was told that I was being taken to Bath police station as the main offences that Kirsty had committed with the cheques were in that area. It was an awful journey as I was a very bad traveller, especially in the back of a car. I was checked in and put in another cell. At least in this one, I had some idea of the time as I could hear the church clock striking. It was dreadful being locked in a cell without your watch.

There was one decent young policeman there who actually found me a book to read, but once again the women officers were the nastiest. That evening I was told I would go to Magistrate's Court the next morning. By then, my solicitor had come to see me and told me he would make an application for bail, but the police were going to try to get the time lengthened that they could keep me for questioning

An officious policewoman got me up early the second morning, giving me a towel, soap, toothbrush and toothpaste and I asked for a comb. She stood and watched while I showered; the water was freezing cold. I looked a dreadful sight after having no sleep for two nights and my hair was all over the place. I asked again for a comb and although she said, 'I'll see what I can do,' I didn't think she had any intention of getting it. The worse I looked in court, the better it suited them.

Suddenly at 10 a.m. there was a mad rush to get me to the courts. Once there, my solicitor told me, 'I'll do everything I can to get you out. The police are talking about re-offending or absconding, which I'm sure a judge won't go along with.' He also said that when he had got me out he would take me to Bristol to meet up with Guy.

The waiting was nerve-wracking and I looked like such a mess. Eventually, we got into court, and the judge released me on bail, pending a Crown Court hearing in Bristol. My solicitor drove me to Bristol, left me with Guy and said he would be in touch soon.

Guy took me to get something to eat and drink, but I just had ice cream: after not eating for several days I didn't really want anything. I was very upset at how unconcerned he seemed to be after what I had been through. He was only worried about whether I had said anything to implicate him.

As this incident was very early in our marriage, and it took a very long time for my case to come to court, I was unprepared for just how much was to happen within the first eleven months of this marriage.

Obviously after this, all dealings with chequebooks and credit cards stopped, but there was absolutely no let up on Guy's other activities. I honestly believed he would stop when I married him, considering he was on bail and afraid of the police getting to him when I was in the cells, but he didn't seem to care. I had now met more of his friends who are always looking for a way of stealing or making money illegally.

One of Guy's friends, Brian, asked me if I had life insurance on Brendan in my name, which I still did. He then said he could kill him, make it look like an accident, and I would get the money.

'Who the hell do you think the first suspect would be?' I said.

Guy and Brian said that as long as there were only the three of us and we all kept our mouths shut, they wouldn't be able to prove anything. I was horrified at all this, but Brian asked me where he lived and what sort of places he went to, and reluctantly I told him, and between them they were making plans. The next time Brian came, he said he had decided it would be easiest to shoot him and throw grass seed over him. He said this would indicate to the police that he had been killed because he had grassed on someone. At this point I became really scared and when Guy and I went up to bed we have an enormous row. We had been drinking, as usual, and I said I wanted nothing to do with it and that I was going to cancel the insurance – which I did later. Life continued with Guy usually away most of the week, either just buying or selling, or doing burglaries.

In May 1985 he had been away quite a while and when he came home, he looked really ill and I knew he had been involved in something quite taxing. I then found out that Guy and Brian had been involved in a large burglary near Brighton at a museum housing meerschaum pipes, which were very valuable. The television was saying they thought it must be a London gang because of how they went in through the roof to avoid the alarms and got away across the fields.

The strain was getting to me and I was very stressed. We always seemed to have criminals in our house and one night after drinking a great deal, we had a huge row when we were getting ready for bed. At some point, I hit Guy and he turned on me.

'Nobody hits me. Now get out of my house.'

'As it's my mother's house,' I retorted, reminding him that Pop bought the house in Mum's name and we were renting from her, 'that would be very difficult.'

Guy was twice my size and although I was very drunk, I was aware that he had me pinned down. Then his hands were around my throat and he was squeezing and I couldn't breathe. Things were going around and I must have lost consciousness. I came to when I felt him kicking me in the side. The next morning when I woke up, I looked in the bathroom mirror all around my mouth was covered in blood, my neck was sore and the whole of my side was black with bruises. It also seems that in trying to fight Guy off me, I bit a large lump out of his neck, although I couldn't remember doing it.

I vowed not to drink again. I was then almost forty and it was many years before I had an odd drink, perhaps at a celebration, and I didn't eat any meat for about ten years, because we never found the large piece that I bit from Guy's neck and the thought that I may have swallowed it just made me feel physically sick. He had to make many visits to the hospital before they were able to get it healed.

Chapter Forty-Eight

Loot

On the day after the fight, he packed a bag and left, saying, 'I'll pay the bills and come to give you money. It is over.'

For most of the next three weeks I was at Mary's house, apart from when I saw to the children. I ate virtually nothing and lost two stone in weight. Guy called as he said he would and gave me money and took the bills. I didn't know what to say to the children and I was worried to death about how I would keep them if he stopped supporting us. I was still anxious about my own court case, which kept being postponed while the police gathered more evidence.

After three weeks, Guy came more often and said he was worried about how ill I looked. I hadn't told the children that he was gone because they were used to him being away, so when we decided that he should stay, they were, I hoped, unaware that we split up so soon after the wedding. Getting back together meant that I got drawn again into his lifestyle. One of my biggest regrets was that after allowing Brendan to treat my children badly, I allowed my son Andrew to go to boarding school because Guy gave me an ultimatum, 'Either he goes or I do.'

In this marriage, I never knew what the next day would bring, but a lot of it I went along with or he wouldn't have stayed with me. A night out with Guy could be tramping across wet fields with infrared binoculars casing the next place to be burgled.

We were sitting quietly one night, when he got up.

'Where are you going?'

'Wait a minute,' he said.

I followed him to the front door, which he opened, looking left and right and then went out into the garden and brought in a black sack. It was like something I had only seen on TV programmes before, and of course it was full of stolen goods.

'I don't want these things in the house,' I said but he took no notice at all.

I then got involved with the pipes. They were stored and couldn't be sold, but he persuaded me to go to the insurance company to strike a deal with them for their return. I dressed in a suit with gloves and went by train to the insurance company. I spoke with a nice gentleman and said that I could only say that I knew who had them and could arrange for their return if the payout was enough. In the end, they were never returned because Brian was too greedy and wasn't prepared to accept what they were offering.

Guy and Brian had their fingers in a lot of pies: they were involved with forged banknotes and they broke into other museums and a jewellery shop. One Saturday, he took me to a small museum when it was crowded and got me to keep guard while he went through a door and took an impression of the key.

My greatest fear was always that I didn't know what he might have in the house at any time. On one occasion, I became really frightened because they had burgled a museum that was part of a cathedral and they were talking of actually burgling the cathedral itself. Guy even took me there while he was going around again to look over it. They needed a motorbike rider and were actually prepared to involve my son-in-law, Amy's husband – the one who jumped into bed with me that drunken night. Thankfully, this plan didn't come to fruition while we were still together.

When we were married in February 1985, I had sent a wedding invitation to Mum and Pop. I knew they wouldn't come, but found it difficult that Pop wouldn't let Mum see me and thought she would at least bring the subject up with him again. She did ring me and said that she hadn't been able to do anything about seeing the children or me. She asked me what Guy did for a living and I told her he was an antiques dealer. This was as near to the truth as I could get, and at least he had a mother I could talk about which probably reassured her.

Our first Christmas together Guy was, as usual, away in London until the very last minute. I had told him that all his dodgy dealings seemed to have precedence over us and that he was putting himself at risk while out on bail. He always said that he was safe in London as he was only a very small fish in a very large pond, but I had hoped to spend a lot more time with him while awaiting his trial.

*****

In January 1986, he got notification of his trial date. The trial in the Crown Court lasted a week and although I gave evidence for him, I had been unsuccessful in getting him off as I had done with Brendan. One reason was that Guy wouldn't pay the money needed for the barrister David Whitehouse (who by now had taken silk and was a Queen's Council) and was unable to get him on legal aid; the other reason of course was that previously with Brendan, I was expecting his baby.

Guy was sentenced to five years and the case was high profile enough for it to be reported on the BBC news, so even the people that didn't know anything about it in our area (including the minister who married us and whose church I still go to) did on that evening. Life became a nightmare again. People found it difficult to believe that such a nice gentleman (as they all knew him) had an unknown side. It was also dreadful for my children at school as it was so public. As for me, I was back on benefits and looking for a job as I still had children to support.

Although Guy left some money with me, and I was able to sell the odd thing, all his actual valuables were locked and stored away as he always had to judge when it was safe to sell them. After Guy had received his sentence, I went home and wondered what on earth my next move should be.

I then remembered that he had some forged £20 notes hidden behind the electric meter and I was in a panic because I couldn't get them out to dispose of them. I went to bed worrying about this, but in the morning when I was putting Guy's things in his wardrobe, I also found a gun that

261

I didn't know he had. Having had the house raided before, and being on bail myself, I didn't know what to do. Although I didn't want to call any of his friends I felt I had to, so I got in touch with Brian.

'Don't worry,' he said, 'I'll come up and collect them,' which he did the same day.

I spent most of the first few weeks after the trial with Mary and on our first wedding anniversary, Mary and Ted invited all of us for Sunday lunch and special tea in memory of the day. These friends had known about Guy being on bail before I married him.

Chapter Forty-Nine

Thy Will be Done

In March 1986, Mum rang to say that Pop had asked her if she missed seeing me very much. He had decided to let me go to see her on a Saturday while he was at a football match, as long as I didn't bring my husband and was gone before he got home. I wanted to stay away as I was being given these conditions, but inevitably I went to see her. I was amazed and saddened at how much she seemed to have aged in three years, but she was no longer drinking, which in itself was wonderful. We had lunch together and I explained to her about Guy as I couldn't go through a lot of lies: he was going to be away for a long time unless we won the appeal.

'I shan't say anything about it to your father,' she said. 'It will be better that way.'

'Well, there's no point,' I agreed, 'as he doesn't want to see me.'

The next time I spoke to her, Pop had decided he did want to see me, so I arranged to go again on a Saturday but I was going to wait until he came home from football and had tea with them.

When he arrived, he wrapped his arms around me and kissed me as if nothing had ever happened. We sat talking and Mum decided it was time to get tea, as she was on her way to the kitchen, which was quite a way away as it was a large house.

'I'll come and give you a hand,' I say.

'Oh no, you sit and chat with Pop.'

So I had no choice. Mum had sat us on a small settee close together and I noticed that for once he wasn't smoking his pipe. No sooner had she left the room than I understood why: he was keeping his hands free so he could put one arm around me and the other one running up and down my leg.

'When are you going to meet me?' he said. 'I have told you before that you only need your old dad to look after you.'

'Don't start all that again, or I won't come at all any more.'

Then I heard Mum coming and I pushed him away, but every time she went to get something, or when she insisted on washing up on her own as well, he was all over me, hands everywhere, trying to kiss me, and going on and on about meeting me.

I drove home in a quandary. It was lovely seeing Mum so happy and yet I knew I couldn't go back to having him pawing at me and trying to get me into bed with him. He was eighty-two but seemed to think of nothing but sex and was obviously ready for it, and he had even told me that Mum wasn't interested any more. Years before, she told me she was afraid to put her arms around him as he always thought it was an invitation for sex.

But two weeks later, the situation was taken out of my hands. Suddenly, in April 1986, Mum rang me to tell me that Pop had died.

*****

Life changed drastically. Once again my children suffered as I left them with a friend, Jo, who lived in our village while I stayed with Mum. I was away for ten days, because there had to be a post-mortem (which decided that he simply died of old age) and Mum wanted me to stay until after the funeral. By then I had realised how selfish she had become. She felt that my place was with her (even though both she and Pop treated me so badly) and that my children shouldn't have precedence over her.

While I was with her, she told me that I wasn't in Pop's will: he intended to change it once he was speaking to me again but hadn't got around to it before he died. His will was a very complex affair, as of course he still had a wife, son and adopted daughter and grandchildren. He hadn't even acknowledged in the will that my children or I existed, which I found very hurtful.

Mum was aware of this and said, 'I'll make it up to you, I'll sign the house that you're renting over to you as soon as I can, and we'll sort out other things.'

The next few weeks were hectic: I was seeing to the children working, going to see to things for Mum and also visiting Guy in prison. One June morning, about two months after Pop's death, Philip, the man who looked after the garden and pool for Mum, phoned to say that she had been taken ill the previous evening. She hadn't let him call me. She rang him because he had a key, but she had to crawl down the stairs to take the security locks off. She was so ill that he had to carry her back to bed. He called the doctor who told him to give her paracetamol and he had decided I needed to go down to Weymouth to see what I thought, because he was so worried.

When I arrived, I knew that Mum was very ill as she couldn't even lift her head off the pillow to drink. I rang the doctor and said that if someone didn't come immediately, I would hold them responsible if anything happened to her. The doctor came very quickly and phoned for an ambulance straight away to take her to hospital. Mum had had a brain haemorrhage and within a day was transferred to Southampton Neurological Unit.

I contacted a family friend of my parents, who happened to be a vicar, to help me with getting the power of attorney signed as we weren't sure how much Mum understood. This was done and recorded, just in case it was ever challenged. Then Mum had a relapse and a second haemorrhage and it looked like she was going to die. The consultant said there was not an awful lot that they were able to do other than give her some new drugs that were still being tested — if I was prepared to sign. Very soon there was a great improvement and she was returned to her own local hospital. From then on, I became fully responsible for Mum's affairs as well as everything else.

Chapter Fifty

In the Dock

In September 1986, while Mum was staying with me (by this time I had moved back to the town into a bigger house) I had to contend with my Crown Court trial, the charge being conspiracy. Mum was unaware of this; I hadn't told her anything about it as I had tried to paint as good of a picture of Guy as I could. Even though he was in prison, I talked mostly about his appeal and how he would hopefully be home soon. I had been able to engage David Whitehouse, QC, for myself so although I was nervous, I was quite confident.

Amy was staying as well at the time so she was able to make excuses for me to Mum as I went very early to court for a week. On the first day I arrived, my solicitor had bad news for me. David Whitehouse had been unable to come: as the court had changed the date once so that I could have him, they weren't prepared to do it again. Therefore he had sent another barrister whom he recommended. I was terrified then as not only did he seem very young and inexperienced, but he had only had the brief to read on the train from London.

That week was a week of hell. I knew that if I was found guilty I would be going to prison, but I needn't have worried as the barrister was brilliant and on the Friday after a whole week, the jury find me not guilty.

*****

I was then in my early forties and photos of me around this time reflect the toll of the years and my five marriages. I had worn my hair in many lengths, in many styles, from late Fifties bouffant; long, trailing down my neck like a brunette Bardot; chic Sixties Italian; Seventies layered and feathered à la Linda McCartney; permed 'Big Hair' in the late Seventies and early Eighties; nowadays, though, it's more cropped and severe. Even if I smiled in photographs, my eyes weren't smiling; they were sad and strained, but there was also determination in them: I was down but certainly not out.

By May 1987, Mum and I had bought another house around the corner, which I hoped to run as a small residential home for the elderly and Amy was living there with her family. (I became a grandmother in 1985 when I was forty, when Amy had her first child, Robin. Another baby was due in a few months.) Mum had returned home and then the appeal for Guy was due to be heard in the Appeal Court in London. It was to last two days and for this, I did have David Whitehouse.

Before this, on Mayday bank holiday, my house was burgled. I was afraid to stay there with my younger children, as my patio doors were boarded up until they could be replaced, so we moved in with my daughter in the other house. After the patio door was replaced, I was burgled again ten days later.

I travelled up to London for the appeal and on the second day, David Whitehouse proved that evidence given at Guy's trial was not permissible, and the three judges said they would have to adjourn for a week to look into the law books. If he was correct, Guy's conviction was unsafe. David Whitehouse knew he was correct and thought that a week from then Guy would be released.

I arrived back from London on the afternoon of 19 May to be told by Mary that my house had been burgled again. This made three burglaries in fifteen days. I knew these burglaries had been set up by Kirsty who was involved with Guy over the cards and chequebooks, because she had been on trial the same time as myself but was found guilty because she was already on probation for the same thing. Of course, I was unable to prove this to the police and I wouldn't want to try because some of the people she was mixed up with were really nasty pieces of work. I had no idea why Kirsty seemed to have it in for me and could only imagine the reason was jealousy.

The insurance company put me through hell again while I was claiming; during the third burglary the whole house had been completely turned over: everything in my drawers, wardrobes and cupboards had been tipped out and they even ripped plug sockets off the wall looking for safes behind them. It took four of us all day to clear up.

I never felt comfortable in my house again, and eventually moved around the corner next door to the one I hoped to make a residential home. When I returned to the London Appeal Court again a week after 19 May, the judges said that although David Whitehouse was correct, they had decided to use their discretion and after prattling on for half an hour it seemed they were going to allow the sentence to stand.

Because Guy was in an open prison, the only things to look forward to was a weekend he was allowed home for rehabilitation. When I took him to Weymouth to meet Mum, who, like everybody else, thought he was absolutely wonderful, because she didn't know any details about him. He had been given a week's leave when we were able to take the children away for a week, but by then things were becoming tense between us. Being apart and prison visits made for a very difficult life, but the other reason, which Guy wasn't aware of, was Brendan.

In February 1988 I saw a write-up in the local paper about Brendan (I had heard nothing from him for four years) and Kevin had asked me, 'Will I ever see my Daddy again?'

When I visited Guy, I asked him if he thought I should get in touch with Brendan and talk about contact with his son.

'It's up to you,' said Guy, 'but he has a right to see him,' and of course he and Brendan were friends.

So I got in touch with Brendan through probation, who set up a meeting. Not only did it put him in touch with his son but with me. The same spark between us was still there, and he had always been the greatest love of my life. We met for dinner that evening and ended up having an affair.

*****

With time off and parole, Guy returned home towards the end of 1988, and I thought that after all his promises he would go straight and we could settle down to a normal married life. But things were really bad between us sexually and I didn't really want anything to do with him.

'If I didn't know you better,' he said one night, 'I'd think you had another man tucked away somewhere.'

In fact, I had spent most of the time he was in prison only thinking about him and he always said, 'You never complain.'

I never did tell him about my affair with Brendan, which eventually petered out when I realised he would never change, although we remained close until his death. Guy had only been home a couple of weeks when he packed a bag and went off to London. He took great pleasure in telling me that he had had sex with a chambermaid in the hotel he stayed in. His attitude was, well, if I couldn't get it at home, the first available woman would do.

I struggled with the marriage for as long as I could and eventually divorced him in May of 1989.

Chapter Fifty-One

Different Wedding, Same Guy

I thought that would be the end of my relationship with Guy, but life has strange ways of playing tricks on you. Although Kevin, my youngest, was now in touch with Brendan, he was quite distraught at Guy going, as he had been in his life since he was four years old.

'I waited for him to come,' he said to me one day, 'and now he's come and gone again,' and then he dissolved into tears. Mum of course couldn't understand why I had divorced him because I had hidden the real criminal side from her.

At the end of July 1989, I bumped into Guy in a coffee shop in Bridgwater. We sat and chatted and he told me how he managed to get mixed up with a girl in her twenties with two children, and while it had obviously boosted his ego, he now wanted to get out of it but had promised to go to France with her on holiday for two weeks. I said that it sounded as if she was just after his money and he agreed because he had already lent her money.

'Will you come out to dinner with me tonight?' he asked.

'OK, I don't see why not.'

Of course we spent the night together at my house. Kevin was delighted to see him, as were the other children and Mum. Once again, because of my upbringing, I couldn't just live with him because I had the fixation that I couldn't allow my children to think you could sleep with someone if you weren't getting married.

Therefore we assured my children that we intended to remarry. Guy and I talked for many hours and he agreed to go straight and earn his living as a silver dealer, which was his speciality. He promised me that

271

he wanted a normal life with me because he had never loved anyone the way he loved me. We still had the problem of the woman and her children that he was taking to France

'Well, you'll just have to tell her.'

'I don't feel I can let her children down. I'll go and tell her on the way. I promise you, I'm not going to sleep with her.'

Even though I was in my forties, I believed everything he said.

He went off to France for two weeks, but rang me several times on the way, then a few days after he left, he phoned at night.

'I can't carry on with this,' he said. 'I'm with the wrong person. I need to be with you. I'm cutting this short and I'll be back by the end of the week.'

*****

Guy was fourteen years older than me, but with his ferocious sexual appetite I think it was his charm and lust that made me fall for all his promises again.

We married for the second time, in September 1989, just four months after our divorce had been finalised. This time it was in a register office and we had the reception at home, as by this time I had a large red-brick mid-Victorian house. Mum came to this wedding because she was very pleased and blissfully unaware that every one of Guy's friends there was a criminal.

Among these was Roy, a dapper older man, who got me involved with buying and selling cars and with whom for a short time I had an affair.

Guy and I went away for a week to Malta and on our return we talked about how he was going to work. He said that because all his money was tied up in goods that he couldn't touch for the minute, it made things very difficult.

'I'll lend you money to get started,' I said.

This money of course, strictly speaking, belonged to Mum, although I was the one working with it, buying and renovating property, and then selling on, or renting.

Guy and I eventually agreed on the loan. We had only been married a couple of months when he said he would like to invite a couple from Bournemouth to dinner. The man was an antique dealer and his wife a hairdresser and I would be able to show her the hairdressing salon I had at this time, while he talked about antiques with this man after dinner. I agreed and it was arranged. After a pleasant dinner, he sent me off with the woman – to get me out of the way, I later discovered.

'I'm just going to finish cleaning up in the dining room,' I said, after they left.

He didn't reply but when I went into the dining room there was an antique table in there and I immediately realise that it was stolen, which was why he wanted me out of the way so he could get it in.

I rushed back to the lounge. 'You're already up to your old tricks. I've told you I won't have stolen property in my house.'

'It's not stolen,' he protested.

'I'm not a fool and I don't believe you. I want it moved.'

'I'll take it to my mother's first thing in the morning.'

'Oh, that's great. So you'll use one of my cars to move it and suppose you get stopped on the way there, then I'm involved.'

He said nothing. I felt so hurt that he had done this to me so soon, because he was living in my house, I was keeping him and he was using my cars. The table was moved and I made it clear that I didn't want a repetition.

By then I had three cars. Two had been Pop's, and Mum didn't drive. When Mum had recovered from her brain haemorrhages, she passed all the money to me in the hopes that she would live seven years so that I could avoid having to pay inheritance tax after her death – but unfortunately this was not to be.

*****

Soon I realised that all was not well because the only time Guy ever went off sex was when he was up to no good. He was away quite a bit again in London working. We got through Christmas 1989 and in the New Year things seemed to be better except for the lack of any sexual response from him, which of course left me frustrated and wondering what he was doing. I think perhaps it was another woman or was it his criminal dealings?

In May 1990, I asked him to come for a week's holiday with me.

'I can't,' he said, 'I've got things on the go and I can't stop now.'

'Do you mind if I go away with my friend Jo then to Rhodes for a week?'

'No, that's fine, you go.'

Jo and I went for the week's holiday and Guy was pleased to see me when we returned –that was, until I went upstairs to our bedroom. We had freestanding furniture and I could see where the dressing table had been moved and not put back in the same indentations of the carpet. I eased the dressing table to discover several parcels wrapped in newspaper. When I unwrapped them, they were pieces of antique silver. Upon looking around, I found several more pieces wrapped in newspaper hidden in drawers. I took them downstairs.

'What the hell is this? I go away for a week and you've got stolen goods in my house again.'

He tried to protest his innocence, but I said that I knew him better than that and that he wouldn't hide them like that unless they were stolen.

'Get them moved.'

There was no further discussion on the matter.

Chapter Fifty-Two

Lost Love Found

Guy still had no interest in our sex life so I was sure that all the time he was away he was doing criminal things.

By June 1990, I was again disillusioned with, life, love and marriage, but I always seemed to drift back to men in my past: on 21 June, I travelled back to look for Bob as he had been my first great love. I traced him through his mother and went to his house. He was living in Bath in a council bungalow because of his OCD. She had told me he was divorced, so I knew he was on his own, but I didn't know what sort of reception I would get. He opened the door and seeing me there, he pulled me inside, kissed me and told me how he had longed for that moment.

'I didn't realise how much I loved you until I lost you that time,' he said.

'You lost me that time, in case you've forgotten, when you nearly did me serious brain damage when you threw me against that wall.'

I could see from the heartbroken expression on his face that he couldn't bear to think about it. 'I don't know how I could have done that. You know I was more angry with myself than you. I just hit out. I couldn't help it, but I promise I'll never do anything like that again. I've wanted to see you for such a long time.'

'Well, why didn't you come and find me?'

'I was afraid of rejection.'

The feeling between us was still electric and he managed to get me into bed before I left. I was starved of love at this point in my life so I didn't take too much persuading.

'Listen, I'm married, and I want it to stay that way.'

'Well, you can't be happy or you wouldn't be here.'

I explained that I didn't need any more complications and I had my children and mother to consider. He said his OCD had become intolerable and after all sorts of treatments that didn't work he finally went to a hypnotherapist and he had been free of all the symptoms for two years. He didn't drive and had never had any interest in learning – he started lessons once but the illness made it impossible for him to continue – so he made me promise to phone him and to come and see him again.

I left wondering what madness had made me start this all over again. I thought it was because my husband was a cheat, a thief and a liar. I once said to Guy, 'You're a liar,' and he replied, 'Well, what do you expect? It's what I do for a living.' Bob was the exact opposite – in fact, he was painfully honest.

I was delayed that night getting home, stuck in the Glastonbury Festival traffic for hours. Mary, looking after my children, was beginning to think I had actually left, as she knew all about my marriage. I continued seeing Bob, even taking Mary with me so she could meet him. She thought he was lovely because at that time, he was.

*****

In summer 1990, there was more trouble with Guy. He took his mother out one day and when he phoned me he was at a police station. He said he would be home soon and would tell me all about it on his return. This time he had been caught with church silver in his car and had tried to tell the police he was unaware it had been stolen. They didn't believe this story of course, as the silver was wrapped in a choirboy's surplus.

I had already moved Guy and his belongings into another bedroom but by then, I had really had enough.

'When I remarried you it was on condition that you gave all this up and you promised me you would.'

'I realise that's what you wanted me to do.'

'Well, I think it's time you left because you're obviously not capable of giving it up.'

'Will you give me some time to find somewhere to live? I don't want to go back and live with my mother and I'd prefer to find somewhere near to London.'

'OK, but don't take too long because I don't want to be involved in any more of this.'

Time passed; nothing seemed to happen.

At the beginning of October I said, 'You've got two weeks and then I want you out.'

He left within two weeks, but went back to his mother.

'What about the money I lent you?' I asked him, 'or more to the point, Mum's money?'

'I haven't got it all now but I'll give you £1500 and the rest later.'

I felt it was reasonable to ask for it back, as I had kept him in my house from the time we remarried.

When he was finally leaving he said, 'Shall we just agree that you don't try to get any payments from me and I won't try to get any from you?'

I asked him several times later for the rest of the money he owed and he turned quite nasty on the phone.

'What proof have you got that I owe it to you, unless you're prepared to drag your mother into court? You can't prove I've got anything but I took photocopies of all your bank statements and other things while you were out, so I can prove you've got money.'

This left me speechless. I put the phone down and didn't bother with him again.

Chapter Fifty-Three

Back with Bob

Bob came down to meet the children in November 1990, and I asked them how they'd feel about him coming to lodge with us, as we had agreed to take things slowly. They seemed reasonably happy with this, so he came for short periods and stayed in the top of the house where I had a lounge with a door that led into a large bedroom with en suite bathroom. He still had his council bungalow in Bath to go back to.

Then on 10 December 1990, my mother suddenly died from a massive heart attack at the age of 69. I was devastated, especially because for the four years since Pop died, I had been with her a lot of the time. I also felt very guilty because she desperately wanted to live with me and had I known it was going to be for such a few years I would have agreed to it. I also felt badly over the way her life had gone after Paula went to live with her and Pop. She didn't drink before then and I honestly think that the two of them – my oldest daughter and my father – would have driven a saint to drink.

I phoned Bob, in need of support, and he caught a train down from Bath. He helped at that time by being at home for the children, while Mary helped me sort out things as this was something I had never dealt with before. After the funeral, Bob went back to Bath and then came to stay over the Christmas holiday.

I had many things to sort out because of Mum's death, only four and a half years after Pop's, not least the loss of a great deal of income and several horrendous days with the taxman, but that's another story.

*****

In the early part of 1991, Bob and I decided it might be better if he had his own place to live in for a while as he was concerned about giving up the bungalow and not having his own space. We agreed that he should rent a one-bedroom flat from me. I didn't want him living with me too soon after Guy for the sake of my two children Julie and Kevin, who were still at home. Having agreed on this arrangement, he gave his notice on the bungalow and moved into the flat. I spent some days with him and he spends other days at my house.

New problems arose financially as interest rates rocketed to 15% and property crashed. And the new problems inevitably arose with Bob: what I hadn't been aware of was that this terrible OCD could return when there was any change in the sufferer's life. He wanted to spend more time with me and ended up living with me, although he kept the flat on as a bolthole. His major obsession was now with me: he was jealous of everyone I spoke to or anyone I had anything to do with, including my family. He created a huge fuss over what I wore or because he said that men were looking at me. I started to find out what his temper could be like. Apart from that one incident many years previously in Bath, I hadn't really thought he had a bad temper. How wrong I was.

In this early time together, I thought it might help if he had some other interest in his life except me and his obsession about his mother dying. I knew he had a son from his first marriage he hadn't seen since he was very young, so I tracked him down and arranged to meet him in a pub in Bath. His son was instantly recognisable as he looked just like Bob. They got on well and he learned he was soon to be a grandfather. I did everything I could for him, took him to Bath when the baby was born and picked up his mother to go and visit them. I bought gifts from them for the baby as neither Bob nor his mother had any money. Bob seemed to need constant looking after and motivation, otherwise all he ever did was read books about his illness, the brain and medication.

The year 1991 turned into one big nightmare: he was constantly washing chairs and anything that his brain told him was contaminated. There were the big rituals: showering without him touching door handles or allowing his clothes to touch anything before he got to the shower.

During the day, if anyone came to the house and sat in a chair, that may have been the only chair he felt wasn't contaminated. I could see him getting more and more agitated until they left, and then he would have to start washing it.

Throughout this time, I was not thinking straight about what I should be doing financially because I was spending all my time tiptoeing around him, otherwise there were violent rows. Nothing I did ever seemed right. He would scream the most hideous abuse at me and when I retaliated (I was never any good at keeping my mouth shut) it would end up with him knocking me about. He yelled at me about the other men in my life and said that it must have always been my fault that my marriages hadn't worked.

The other major thing in Bob's life was sex. When I first went to Bath to visit him, I didn't think too much about it because we were always in bed, but he had ideas that one of two things in his young life triggered the OCD. The first was that because his father went off with another woman when he was eleven, he felt responsible for his mother and had the constant fear that his mother would die. The other was that at home, he had always been made to feel that sex was something dirty. Bob wanted much more explicit things from me sexually than I actually felt comfortable with at times, but because I was not living with him then, I was able to cope with his ways, and the hours and hours it lasted. Once he came to live with me, it became a big problem.

If he didn't get enough sex or got what he wanted, it caused rows. He could make my life hell if I didn't want sex, because I couldn't make him see that if things have been bad during the day I wouldn't be interested or when he had violent outbursts I didn't even want to be in the same bed with him. To suggest not sleeping in the same bed so I could actually get some sleep meant more rows.

There were the rituals about how and when he touched me: sometimes we had to sleep in a particular hotel before he could go to bed with me at all. He became obsessed with taking photographs of me nude. He had a lot of photographic equipment and printed his own photos as well. The more I refused the more he asked and he wanted to take pictures of us together.

When we were alone in the house one day, he kept on so much that I gave in – to my regret. The photographs were pornographic and I have always worried about what has happened to them. He kept both the prints and negatives at his own place and always insisted that no one would ever see them and that he needed them to look at when we were apart.

I spent a lot of money that I shouldn't have been spending during the property crash trying to keep him happy and amused, almost like a child, to pacify him. It didn't occur to me what all this was doing to my youngest son, and I forgot that children hear and see what was happening to their mother.

Chapter Fifty-Four

Love is Strange

I asked Bob to leave many times, but always took him back because of the good times; he somehow made me remember them more than the bad times. In March 1991, I booked a holiday for May in Tenerife for Bob, my three youngest children, Andrew, Julie and Kevin and me. I thought this would be something different for Bob, as he had never been on a plane. I took him to Newport to get his passport and things seemed to be progressing.

A week before we were due to go, I was getting clothes ready; some had been washed and needed ironing. Bob said he needed to iron a shirt that clearly didn't need ironing and when I pointed this out, he flew into a terrible rage, calling me names and pushing me back against the sink, then picked up the hot iron to throw at me.

I dodged the iron and, terrified of what he was going to do next, grabbed a knife off the kitchen worktop. He seized the knife blade and snapped it off the handle – he seemed to have terrific strength when in a temper. I fled to another room and waited for him to calm down.

'I think you'd better get your things together and go to your flat,' I said. 'This relationship has gone beyond the point of us being able to do anything with it.'

'What about my holiday!' he screamed.

'I can't go away with you with the children not knowing what you're going to do next.'

After a lot of arguing and shouting, he left. I rang Jo and ask her to see if she could get time off work to come away with us, which fortunately she was able to do. The evening before we were due to leave, Bob rang to say sorry and asked if I could take something down to his flat.

'Please stay and have a cup of tea with me,' he said when I arrived. 'I'd like to talk to you.' He made the tea and sat down. 'I don't suppose I can still come on holiday, can I?'

'No, I've changed the ticket so Jo can come.'

Instantly, he was upset, saying how much he had wanted it and how awful his life had been.

I finished my tea. 'Well, I must go now,' I said, 'I've got things to do.'

As I stood up, his face was contorted, his eyes blazing.

'You're not going anywhere. You're never going to leave this flat again – well, not alive anyway.'

He pushed me into an upright chair and had one hand around my throat, the other over my mouth. I struggled and he held me tighter, but took his hand away from my mouth.

'There's no point in screaming, nobody will hear you and even if they did, they wouldn't take any notice.'

'Let go of my throat,' I croaked, 'I can't breathe.'

He slowly loosened his grip and pinned me to the chair by my wrists.

'Let's be sensible about this and talk shall we,' I said quietly. I knew my only chance to get away from him was to try and reason with him.

He started to talk as usual about what his life has been like with the OCD and the times we've had together when things were good; he reminds me about the hypnotherapy and how it had been different for two years before he moved down with me and that he hadn't expected it to come back. He thought he would be able to get a job again and live a normal life.

I was still locked in his grip and if he loosened it and I tried to get away, he instantly tightened it again.

'Don't bother to try. You're not getting away from me.'

'What good do you think you're doing keeping me here?'

'No other man's going to have you. They won't love you like I do.

When you were young and you loved me I stupidly thought I loved my wife. It wasn't until years later when you left me in Bath and went back to Reading that I realised how I felt about you. I knew then that I loved you but because of this illness I didn't think it would ever work ...'

I kept quiet and pretended to listen, quietly waiting for my chance. When he again loosened his grip on me, this time I managed to break free. As it was a small flat I was able to rush through and out of the front door. I ran along the path and jumped into the car and locked the doors. As I drove away, he stood outside, yelling at me.

Once again, my life was in turmoil and I had no idea where it was going.

*****

After the holiday Bob, rang me and managed to talk me into carrying on with the relationship. It was May 1991, and I spent all the spring and summer arranging outings and trips away as they kept Bob's mind more occupied; there was less time for the flare-ups and rages. Some nights were still dreadful though, and I was then too afraid to finish with him because of what he might do. One night he picked up a bronze statuette of a couple embracing – it was virtually unbreakable – and with the strength of his temper smashed it against the breakfast bar and broke both. I was actually relieved though, because he had threatened me with it.

At Christmas, his mother stayed with him in the flat at the top of my house. All my family came and the house was full over the entire holiday. There were one or two difficult moments, as he was jealous of my family and at one point made a huge fuss like a child over something on television.

My eldest daughter Amy had divorced and was getting married again, this time to Mary's son, in April 1992 and had asked Bob if he would give her away as there were problems with her own father doing so. He was very pleased about this and I felt that perhaps it would make him feel more a part of my family. When all the celebrations were over and the

285

family had left, I still had Bob's mother staying and was beginning to wonder when she might be leaving. She was always with Bob wherever he was and he constantly expected me to sit and talk and amuse them.

After an evening meal in January 1992, I was in the kitchen cleaning up and as things had got quite messy over Christmas, I decided to bleach everything down. Bob and his mother were watching TV in the lounge.

'When are you going to come in?' he asked at the door.

'When I've finished in here.'

He returned to the lounge but I could tell his mood wasn't good. I joined them when I had finished, taking a yogurt with me – neither of them wanted one – and sat down, putting the yogurt without its lid on a small table beside me. Bob picked an argument over something trivial as usual, got up from his seat and kicked the small table up in the air, which hit me on the way down, and the yogurt sprayed all over the room. He then grabbed a Yellow Pages, tore it in half and raised his arm in the air ready to hit me. His mother was screaming at him to stop and pulling at his sweater. I ran into the kitchen and, leaning on the door, managed to dial 999 because I was terrified. The police came immediately and asked me what I wanted them to do.

'Please take both of them back to his flat.'

Bob and his mother left with the police without another word.

*****

That night a problem returned that I had had intermittently since Brendan. After they had gone, I went to the kitchen and got a bowl of water and a cloth. I sat on the floor in front of the television and started cleaning off the yogurt, then I started to sob uncontrollably. After crying for some while, I went back to the kitchen to get something to eat – and I just kept on eating. I was back to compulsive eating and the addiction wouldn't go away in spite of diets and counselling.

I realised then that in some ways sex had been an addiction for me, even when I didn't enjoy it, and I had sometimes replaced it with eating. I was also aware that the addiction, in whatever form it took, had resulted from an attempt to satisfy the craving in me that reaches deep back into my life and my psychic history, for the love I wasn't given as a child. Just as I had needed to legitimise the sex through marriage and the church, maybe my self-protective instinct had made me turn to food rather than drink or drugs – I had wanted to fill the empty feeling inside but something had stopped me from the destructive urge of alcohol and narcotics.

The next day the police rang me. 'Will it be OK if we come around with Bob to collect some of his belongings?'

'Yes as long as you don't leave him with me.'

His mother came with him. The policemen went upstairs with Bob to collect the things and his mother came into the kitchen.

'Please will you have him back?' she said. 'I always felt that while he was with you there would be someone to look after him when I'm gone. I want to see him settled.'

'I can't have him back. You saw what he was like last night.'

'Well, wouldn't it be better to be with him as he is rather than be on your own?'

'No, at the moment I really don't think so.'

The police came downstairs with him and left.

'Well, he's not giving me away at my wedding,' Amy said and asked her brother Andrew instead.

Chapter Fifty-Five

Amy's Wedding

Bob had always told me that there was no violence in his marriages. I decided to go and see his second wife in Bath. According to Bob, he left her because she taunted him about the OCD. I couldn't ask her about this, as no one would admit to that, but she seemed pleasant enough. After their divorce, she told me, she sometimes had him around for a meal because she felt sorry for him as he had no friends. As for his temper, she showed me a blouse he had ripped off her one night and a dent in the ceiling where he had kicked something out of her hand.

Although I knew all these things, something in me couldn't let go. When he phoned in March, I agreed to meet him in town. I was not going to his flat again, so we chose a coffee bar. When he touched my hands it sent shivers down my spine. I prided myself on being an intelligent woman, but all sense seemed to leave me where he was concerned.

We met a few times and talked, and he asked about the wedding. I told him what Amy has decided.

'You know how sorry I am about all that. Do you think she'd let me and Mum still come to the wedding?'

'I don't know, I'll ask her. It will just have to be as ordinary guests.'

Amy agreed to it for my sake.

'You look as if you've put on some weight,' Mary said two weeks before the wedding. 'Do you think you should try your suit on?'

I did and of course it was too small. Mary and Amy were hysterical with laughter and I had to buy another outfit. I knew the weight gain was because I had been unable to control my eating since that awful night.

*****

After the wedding, Bob asked if we could talk about our relationship. He said how afraid he was of losing me.

'Well, you will if you keep on going as you are.'

'I'd feel safer if you'd marry me.'

'There's no chance of that unless we can get you sorted out.'

He agreed to try again, this time with a form of hypnotherapy involving regression. For the next three months, I took him to Bournemouth once a week for the therapy and he improved a lot. When the course it was finished, both he and the therapist thought he would be OK, but there was no permanent cure for OCD.

By July 1992, my financial position was becoming desperate, so I decided to do bed and breakfast for the local housing department as a means of paying my mortgage and holding on to my house. Only Kevin was still living at home with me by then and we moved to the ground floor and let out the rooms as bedsits for more permanent income. This made life difficult again as the house was full of people and the change proved to be bad for Bob.

The local authority said that to run a house in multiple occupation, I needed to do work on the house. I applied for a grant and although they eventually agreed to give me the full amount, I realised that the house would have to be emptied during the conversion and I would lose the income. I was already in arrears with my mortgage, the building society were threatening repossession and Bob's OCD started up again as he couldn't take the stress. He decided to go back to Bath and the mental health services help him get a hostel quite quickly.

After he had left, everything else to do with the property I had been involved with seemed to crumble around me. I put my big Victorian house on the market and moved to the three bedroom semi-detached that I had been renting out.

*****

On my own again, I felt very lonely. We had booked as a family to go to Butlins for Christmas 1992 but Bob wouldn't be coming.

When Amy married in April, we invited my old friend David from Reading. He got in touch with me when his father's motor business went into liquidation, leaving him unemployed for the first time ever, and his marriage had ended in divorce. I invited him down for a few days, went to Reading for a weekend with him and as Christmas drew near it seems a good idea to offer the place at Butlins to him. Along with Amy and her husband Mark, we took my two youngest and Amy's two.

The time away was a lot of fun, but David wanted to make a permanent relationship with me, to try and find work, and live with me. I had to say no because he was now in a worse financial position than even I was, and although it was fun for a while, I didn't feel anything for him. I explained to him that the odd couple of nights we spent in bed previously were just sex and there was none of that at Christmas – I made sure we were in separate chalets.

We said goodbye and I later learned that afterwards he met someone through a dating agency; they had married and gone to live in Bournemouth.

Chapter Fifty-Six

Still Crazy After All These Years

In January 1993, there was another bombshell. My daughter Lana, from my second marriage to Roger, phoned to tell me about her wedding plans. These didn't include all the family and certainly not her father, although she had been in touch with him for many years. She had told me that she went to stay with him when she was younger to get away from Brendan but that as she got older, she just found him and his wife Margaret an embarrassment. Even so, I was rather shocked at her attitude, so I decided to visit Roger to see how he felt about the situation. He had been married again for many years and worked for himself as a taxi driver in Chippenham, a short drive from the village he lived in. I drove to Chippenham railway station where I knew he worked on the rank. I didn't want to go to his home to cause trouble because I knew Margaret was very jealous.

He wasn't on the rank when I arrived and one of the drivers said he was at home, so I found a phone box and called him. He was extremely pleased to hear from me and said his wife was out so he would meet me in a pub for a drink. When he arrived, we had one drink and he suggested we go somewhere else, as he was very well known there. We drove out into the country in his big Volvo estate and he parked. We talked about our daughter for a little while and he told me about the problems in his marriage: through it all his wife had stayed with him, but there was no love left and he worked all the hours he could to stay out of the house.

'I have never loved anyone but you,' he suddenly said, 'and I'm very sorry for everything I put you through. Once they diagnosed me as schizophrenic and got me on to my present injections I have been OK. I have to take medication – and another one to counteract the side effects – for life.'

He put his arms around me and kissed me and it was like we were youngsters again. We were all over each other then he put all the seats down in the car and made love on a blanket like we did when we were young.

Afterwards he said, 'Do you have to go back tonight or can I book a room in a Travelodge or hotel?'

'I can stay, but what about your wife?'

'I'll take you back to your car, and then I'll go home and let her know I'm working on the rank for the night and meet you afterwards.'

We arranged where to meet, he went off home and I went to shop for some clean underwear for the next morning. I rang home to make sure there was adequate provision for Kevin, who was 12.

We booked into a small hotel as husband and wife and had sandwiches and coffee brought to our room.

'Let's have a bath together like we always used to,' Roger said.

'OK, I'll run it, but you can have the tap end.'

We sat in the bath and talked about the past, adding more hot water and still sitting until it was nearly cold. Then we went to bed and he made love to me, beautifully like he always had done, and I remembered why I put up with so much.

*****

We had to leave early in the morning to get home. Later in the morning I went to see Mary, the only person I could tell.

'Watch what you're getting into now,' she said.

'It will be OK. This is just going to be a brief affair, for old time's sake.'

Roger phoned me two or three times a day and either came to me and booked a room somewhere for the afternoon or I drove up to see him. Within a few weeks, he wanted to leave his wife and buy somewhere with me. I told him it was all too quick and there were lots of problems.

'If you're worried about my illness,' he said, 'come with me to see my nurse when I go for my next injection and talk to her about the long term.'

I agreed to do so and learned that later in life there could still be problems, and the last thing I wanted was to get involved, yet again, with any more mental illness.

The following week, he phoned me.

'I've left my wife and I've moved into a room in a small hotel in Chippenham. Come up and see me.'

I went there to see him twice and we spent the whole time making love. He told me again how much he loved me and had never stopped loving me and that he had told his wife that he wanted a divorce so we could get married again.

At home, I thought about what was happening and then I got a phone call from Roger's wife.

'Is this true, that he wants to marry you?' she said, 'because he's left it rather late in my life to leave me.'

She was fifty-six, ten years older than Roger, and they had been together for nearly twenty years. I assured her that none of this was my idea, that he had got carried away with what he wanted and that I was shocked when he had left her. Afterwards, I sat down and wrote a letter to Roger explaining that I couldn't do it because my feelings for him weren't the same as his for me and that he should go back to his wife. I knew she would take him back. And I asked him not to phone me any more.

I photocopied the letter and sent a copy to his wife so she knew what I had said to him. I then received a letter from Roger saying how upset he was and that he would always love me. After that, thankfully, there was no more contact.

I was very sad when Lana phoned me five years later to say he had died of a heart attack, and felt worse when she told me that after the short affair with me (although she didn't know about that), he had another breakdown and had been hospitalised again for some time. I felt that this was my fault, because I had got back in touch with him in the first place.

Chapter Fifty-Seven

For Better or For Worse

After these flings with David and Roger, I thought more about Bob again. He had always said that his jealousy was because I wouldn't marry him and he felt insecure and that if we were married things would be better. Somehow I didn't feel I could give up on this relationship until I had tried everything.

In February 1993, I went to Bath to meet him. We met in a coffee shop and the minute he looked at me and touched my hands (he still had beautiful hands), shivers went down my spine and in a mad moment I said to him, 'I'm only going to ask you the next question once. Do you want to marry me? Just a straight yes or no?' I had been married six times by then but this was the first time I had been the one to make the proposal – to which he said yes.

We went to the Register Office, booked a special licence for the following week and planned to keep it just to ourselves until we had arranged for a church blessing and reception at home for all the family and friends. I travelled back to Bath next week, only to find that the information had been incorrect: we couldn't get married until the following day, so it would be a night in the hotel before the wedding. I then started thinking about Amy who was constantly in our lives and decided to ring her.

'What are you doing tomorrow?'

'Nothing particular.'

'Well, if you want to come to Bath, Bob and I are getting married.'

She was speechless at first then said, 'Of course I'll be there.'

I told her not to tell anyone anything about it. It was fortunately arranged so that she could fit in, seeing to her children and Kevin as well before she came.

So on 5 February 1993, I married the man who from the age of fifteen, I had wanted to marry (or so I had thought desperately at different times in my life). I was emotional and could hardly say my vows as I was crying. There were only six of us present: myself and Bob, Bob's mother and Nigel, Bob's one friend (who also had a mental illness), my daughter and son-in-law. We all went for a meal afterwards and then they left to go home. Amy had said she would look after Kevin so we could stay for another couple of days.

Back at the hotel, Bob told me that because of his illness he had been offered a bungalow by Bath Council just a couple of doors away from where he lived before.

'What shall I do about it?' he said.

'I think you should still take it and give notice to the agent on the flat you have rented of mine and we can perhaps divide our time between both places.'

*****

Although I had married Bob to give it one last chance, because he has always said he wouldn't then be afraid I'd leave him, I suppose in my heart I knew it was very unlikely that he would change. But for the first six weeks of our marriage, everything was wonderful. Even my son-in-law said that perhaps it was what Bob had needed.

During this time, no one else was aware of our marriage. We went to see the vicar at our nearest Anglican church and booked a date for a church blessing after talking with him about why we wanted to do it. I'm afraid my story had to be economical with the truth: we said that we're both divorced but that we had married and were older and were sure that it was for ever and we would like his blessing. It was not so much what we told him as what we didn't.

298

We booked the church hall and catering and ordered a wedding cake. This was the way we had planned to tell the rest of the family and the children.

I had also arranged to go back to work with a nursing agency. My business situation was getting worse and the building society was threatening to repossess my house. I managed to sell it to the man next door so he could make it part of his nursing home.

We were still packing, although a lot had been packed for some while as I had thought I had sold it once before. It was a Saturday, just after lunch, and for some reason Bob picked a fight about why I didn't want to tell anyone we were married. Then he told me that he had told the woman who was giving him driving lessons.

'I told her before even giving it a thought,' he said.

'Well, it wouldn't have mattered if it hadn't been someone I've known since I was at school,' I replied.

Then, without any warning, he started screaming abuses at me and punched me, mostly around the head. When he had punched me almost senseless, I grabbed my handbag and ran into the drive. He was right behind me but I managed to get down the drive and into the garage. I crouched down in the corner at the back of the garage while he stood in the doorway, picking things up and throwing them at me. He was screaming at the top of his lungs so that the whole neighbourhood could hear that he was married to me and that I was a fucking whore.

Then suddenly he stopped, walked back up the drive and into the house. I stayed in the corner of the garage for a long while, terrified to move in case he came back out again. Gradually I took my hands away from my head, uncurled my body and stood up. My head really hurt, but I needed to stretch out. I thought about what I should do and decided to go into town, where I bought a magazine and went to sit in a coffee shop.

I was at my wits' end.

Chapter Fifty-Eight

Seven Times Unlucky

When I finally got back home, Bob was waiting for me.

'I've been really worried about you and I'm very sorry about what happened. I don't know what happened to me – it was like voices in my head were telling me to hurt you.'

I knew then that things could only get worse.

We talked about what we were going to do: I didn't know how much longer I could go on. We had spent a lot of time and money on hypnotherapy, which clearly had done very little to improve the situation. We talked about the possibility of his seeing a psychiatrist who could perhaps be able to scan his brain to see if there was another operation available now that things are more advanced. We had already seen a psychiatrist where I lived and thought it might be better if he saw someone back in Bath where they would be able to source all his previous records.

I was about to move from my large house to the three-bedroom semi and Bob once again got it into his head that this could be a new start for us and everything would be different. Moving meant I could pay the mortgage off on my house, but I had many other worries and, for the foreseeable future, I still had to work part time.

Nothing changed, in fact they got worse because Bob hated me working. There were terrible rows: he said he could see through my white uniform and kept on and on about the men I looked after, even though they were in their eighties. Everything was much worse in a small house because the neighbours were bound to hear the rows.

Night times were dreadful: I perched on the end of the bed and waited until he was asleep, then slid out of bed and crept downstairs just to get some peace on my own. This never worked as he would wake up and follow me down. I tried to keep things quiet because of Kevin, but this was of no interest to Bob. He kept on for hours about how I didn't understand what it was like to have his illness and that I was his wife, so I should be in bed with him.

Sex became something I dreaded and dared not refuse because of his temper and violence. I wondered how something that had once been so good could be so awful. Even though he had his own illness, he couldn't understand or help me with my food problem.

All he could do was taunt me about how much weight I was putting on. 'Aren't you ever going to stop eating?'

We saw a psychiatrist in Bath and started going to a clinic for regular appointments. The psychiatrist seemed to treat those sessions more like marriage guidance than trying to do anything about Bob's mental illness, and on one visit, when Bob started shouting at me and threatening to hit me, I said to the psychiatrist, 'Perhaps now you can see what I have to live with,' and I left the meeting. I wrote a letter to someone higher up to say how disappointed I was with the lack of treatment.

Bob finally saw someone who has the notes from the operation he had in the 1960s. After the scans of his head were done, they said that in the original operation they had not really severed all the necessary nerves. We asked if it would be possible to do anything more about it and were told that it might be improved with laser treatment. The risks of other brain damage of course were quite high. There would have to be other tests and then they would decide whether they were prepared to offer the operation. Bob was still staying some of the time in the bungalow in Bath, although most of the time I didn't because I was working.

We were in touch by phone, but I was gradually realising that I had to break from this marriage. I had given it a go as he has begged me to do, but I just couldn't cope any more. It was autumn 1993, and Bob was home with me again and had heard from the hospital that they would do the operation if he wanted them to. We talked about the various possibilities. It could make him better, there may be little or no change, or he could end up completely brain damaged.

'What do you think I should do?' he asked me.

'I can't make this decision for you, you have to do it for yourself.'

'I'll have the operation for you.'

'I don't want you to have it for me, you have to have it for yourself,' I said. 'I have to be honest and tell you that I'm not sure that I can stay with you, even if you have the operation, because I think there's been too much damage in this marriage.'

Chapter Fifty-Nine

Last Gasp

The end came after a day out shopping for clothes for Bob in January 1994. He had made a big thing of how I had money and he had never had any because of his illness. It didn't make any difference how much I told him about all the hardships I had been through or how much money I had given him, and he also seemed unable to grasp that I no longer had the money due to the financial climate.

Back indoors, he hurled abuse at me and I finally lost my temper.

'I think perhaps you only ever wanted my money,' I said.

I could see the rage in his eyes. 'I have never wanted you for your money!'

'Well, you've been only too pleased to spend it. All the places I've taken you, all the clothes I've bought you, to say nothing of the thousands I've spent on the bungalow for carpets, curtains and furniture.'

'You can keep your fucking money!' he screamed, throwing the carrier bags of clothes we had just bought for him at my expense.

'And you can leave on the train in the morning.'

*****

The next morning, he packed all his things (including all the clothes from the previous day) and I drove him to the station. For days he kept phoning me: claiming that everything was my fault and shouting abuses at me. I kept putting the phone down.

One day, a lady phoned me from marriage guidance in Bath, saying that Bob had been to see her a few times and wanted me to see her to try to make our marriage work. I replied that there really isn't any chance of that, but she persuaded me to make an appointment. Once I started talking with her, it was obvious that Bob had told her little of the real problems and had led her to believe that I was impossible to live with. After I had told her as briefly as I could what our lives had been like, she said, 'It seems obvious to me that you have had as much as you can take and it's best left as it is.'

Along with all the new things I had bought for Bob's bungalow, I also took to Bath a few pieces of Mum's antique furniture and a lot of expensive china, because at the time I was determined to make the marriage work, even if we did live in two places.

Bob was very difficult about letting me have these things back, but my son-in-law Mark hired a van and went to Bath to get them. He managed to bring back the furniture and a few pieces of china, but there was also an expensive set of plates that Bob put in a plastic bag and then kicked in a temper. My son-in-law offered to go again and try to get the rest but I told him not to – I didn't want any more trouble.

There were more phone calls, all abusive. One day a friend of mine answered the phone and Bob told her that I picked him up out of the gutter, showed him a different way of life and now I had dropped him back in the gutter again.

The final contact was a blatant piece of emotional blackmail, when he sent through the post a music tape including a couple of songs that were special to us and some labels of things we bought in Bath when we were married.

When I didn't reply to this, the phone calls stopped, thank God. The ending was difficult and in spite of the way it had been, I sat and cried for hours and wondered what I will do with the rest of my life. I spent as much time as I could working so that I wouldn't be on my own, and so that I could try to get my financial situation sorted out.

I don't dislike my own company and although it could be argued that all my marriages so far had been an attempt to escape from myself, I don't necessarily feel this is true. In this case, I didn't want to be on my own because, strange though it may seem after all that has happened, I still have an urge to go to Bob. When I'm at home on my own, I have to force myself not to jump in the car and drive off to Bath to see him.

But one thing I was certain about: I would never marry again.

Chapter Sixty

Never Say Never

During the summer of 1994, I was involved in a collision with a tanker on my way home from work one morning. The car was a write-off, but apart from a few aches and pains, I was able to walk away from it. My daughter wanted me to go to the hospital, but I said I was fine and as we were planning a trip to Reading that day to see some friends, I borrowed a car and went anyway.

Little was I to know how the accident would change my life. I started to be very unwell and between October and December was taken into hospital several times but the doctors couldn't diagnose the problem. I was constantly in pain, sometimes acute, and it was becoming more and more difficult for me to work as I was caring for people often on my own in their homes.

I was eventually unable to work at all and spent a great deal of time in bed, very ill. Eventually, after nearly three years of constant pain, I went to see a rheumatologist who diagnosed an illness called fibromyalgia. It was little known at the time, but in years to come a lot more would come to be known about it; and there's nothing very much that can be done for it except a cocktail of drugs to try to keep you on your feet.

In July 1996, I suffered the great shock of my best friend Mary passing away at the age of forty-nine. This was a tremendous blow to me but also to her husband Ted who had also been my friend for fourteen years.

Ted and I were inevitably a great comfort to each other. I was ill a lot of the time, including the day of Mary's funeral, but managed to drag myself there, as nothing would have kept me away. She had always been there when I needed her.

By September, Ted and I were almost inseparable. He was an absolute saviour for me because he cared about me and did everything that he could for me when I was ill.

Ted had made it clear to me how he felt about me while Brendan was in prison, but he had said that the right person always turned up at the wrong time. He had made one physical advance towards me and I said at that time that I needed and wanted Mary as my friend and I would never want to betray that friendship.

On the day that I married Guy, Ted and I were left at his house on our own waiting for the car to collect us as he was giving me away. He said on that day that he wished we could just drive away somewhere together. I have a snapshot of Ted and me taken that day as he accompanied me up to the steps of the church. We're both looking slightly anxious and apprehensive, and I later realised that that was probably for rather different reasons.

For years after that, I always called Ted 'Dad'. It started as a joke but it stuck and I would send him Father's Day cards and presents.

On the evening of my mother's funeral, most people gathered in my house had had too much to drink and I think Ted had had enough to drink to forget who the company was.

'Well, I've been in love with my 'daughter',' he said, meaning me, 'for years and where does that leave me?'

I tried to cover up this remark as quickly as I could, but I was sure some people must have noticed.

'So what is the position with you and Bob?' he asked me one evening. 'Are you divorced?'

'No, I didn't bother because I'd made up my mind never to marry again.'

'Would you marry me – when the time is right?'

'Are you asking me to marry you?'

'Yes.'

'I would love to marry you, Ted, but do you realise what you might be letting yourself in for. I'm never likely to be fit again unless they find some miraculous cure and it means that I'm unable to do very much for myself as you know – like cleaning, shopping or cooking. I have some good times, but as you know some very bad times.'

'That is what marriage is all about,' he said, 'to look after one another.'

*****

After that evening, I asked my solicitor to get me a divorce. I had been on my own for two years and hadn't bothered to end my marriage legally so I think it came as a surprise to Bob. In spite of what he had always said, he tried to get money from me during the divorce process, but my solicitor made it clear that there was no chance of his getting any. We were finally divorced in May 1997, four years and three months after our marriage.

Ted and I planned to marry in September 1997, exactly one year to the day after he asked me. I had some really bad bouts of illness before the wedding and there was always the worry on my mind whether I would actually make it on the day. The Lord was very kind to me and I was in good health on the day of our wedding, which took place in the small village church we both still attend.

Since then, we have been very happily married for over thirteen years. My only regret was that this wonderful man has had the worst part of my life to deal with. Along with my fibromyalgia and the severe migraines I have suffered all my life, I have developed arthritis in my neck so severe that I now need regular injections to relieve the extreme pain. The severe beating I took on my neck by my second husband Roger caused this.

*****

Like ripples in a pond after a stone sinks into its still waters, the actions of our parents and our parents' parents have deep, powerful and unforeseen consequences.

I am ashamed to say that it didn't occur to me that my actions, my decisions and my life would have such deep and in some cases disastrous consequences on the lives of my children until my life with Bob was over. I had always thought that I had one life to live and I would live it as I chose. It now sometimes seems as though I have lived at least eight lives and with hindsight, of course, I would have done things differently.

There have been repercussions for every one of my children, both for them individually, and in the guilt I felt for what I have done to them. Fortunately, I have had Ted to help me through not only my physical pain but also the mental torture that has sometimes plagued me.

So, although I now, at last, have the wonderful husband and marvellous marriage I had always longed for, the ripples have continued to spread throughout our marriage and probably will for the rest of my life. The repercussions will affect the lives of my children's children and their children after them.